Public Opinion, Legitimacy and Tony Blair's War in Iraq

> Strong's book is excellent, pushing our understanding of the relationship between public opinion and foreign policy in novel directions. The research is rigorous and well-grounded in theory and methods. I highly recommend it, to scholars, students, and any readers interested in democratic politics, British foreign policy, or the legitimacy of international interventions.
>
> Juliet Kaarbo, *Professor, Politics and International Relations, University of Edinburgh, UK*

In the wake of the publication of the Chilcot report, this book reinterprets the relationship between British public opinion and the Blair government's decision-making in the run-up to the 2003 invasion of Iraq. It highlights how the government won the parliamentary vote and got its war, but never won the argument that it was the right thing to do. Understanding how, why and with what consequences Britain wound up in this position means understanding better both this specific case and the wider issue of how democratic publics influence foreign policy processes.

Taking an innovative constructivist approach to understanding how public actors potentially influence foreign policy, Strong frames the debate about Iraq as a contest over legitimacy among active public actors, breaking it down into four constituent elements covering the necessity, legality and morality of war, and the government's authority. The book presents a detailed empirical account of the British public debate before the invasion of Iraq based on the rigorous interrogation of thousands of primary sources, employing both quantitative and qualitative content analysis methods to interpret the shape of debate between January 2002 and March 2003.

Also contributing to the wider foreign policy analysis literature, the book investigates the domestic politics of foreign policy decision-making, and particularly the influence public opinion exerts; considers the domestic structural determinants of foreign policy decision-making; and studies the ethics of foreign policy decision-making, and the legitimate use of force. It will be of great use to students and scholars of foreign policy analysis, as well as those interested in legitimacy in international conflict, British foreign policy, the Iraq War and the role of public opinion in conflict situations.

James Strong is a Fellow in Foreign Policy Analysis and International Relations in the Department of International Relations at the London School of Economics, UK.

Routledge Studies in Foreign Policy Analysis
Series Editors: Christopher Alden
London School of Economics, UK
and
Amnon Aran
City University of London, UK

www.routledge.com/series/RSIHR

The Foreign Policy Analysis (FPA) series covers a broad intellectual canvas, which brings together scholars of International Relations, Area Studies, Politics, and other related fields such as Political Psychology and Administrative Studies. It also engages with a wide range of empirical issues: from the study of the foreign policy of individual countries, to specific aspects of foreign policy such as economic diplomacy or bureaucratic politics, through germane theoretical issues such as rationality and foreign policy. The Series aims to specialize in FPA as well as appeal to the wider community of scholars within International Relations, related fields, and amongst practitioners. As such the range of topics covered by the Series includes, but is not be limited to, foreign policy decision-making; the foreign policy of individual states and non-state actors. In addition it will include analytical aspects of foreign policy, for instance, the role of domestic factors; political parties; elites. Theoretical issue-areas that advance the study of foreign policy analysis, for example, FPA and Gender, Critical FPA, FPA in a new media landscape, Ethics and FPA, are also be welcomed.

Public Opinion, Legitimacy and Tony Blair's War in Iraq
James Strong

Forthcoming:

Colombian Agency and the Making of US Foreign Policy
Intervention by Invitation
Alvaro Mendez

Power, Perception and Foreign Policymaking
US and EU Responses to the Rise of China
Scott Brown

Public Opinion, Legitimacy and Tony Blair's War in Iraq

James Strong

LONDON AND NEW YORK

First published 2017
by Routledge
2 Park Square, Milton Park, Abingdon, Oxon OX14 4RN

and by Routledge
711 Third Avenue, New York, NY 10017

Routledge is an imprint of the Taylor & Francis Group, an informa business

© 2017 James Strong

The right of James Strong to be identified as author of this work has been asserted by him in accordance with sections 77 and 78 of the Copyright, Designs and Patents Act 1988.

All rights reserved. No part of this book may be reprinted or reproduced or utilized in any form or by any electronic, mechanical, or other means, now known or hereafter invented, including photocopying and recording, or in any information storage or retrieval system, without permission in writing from the publishers.

Trademark notice: Product or corporate names may be trademarks or registered trademarks, and are used only for identification and explanation without intent to infringe.

British Library Cataloguing in Publication Data
A catalogue record for this book is available from the British Library

Library of Congress Cataloging in Publication Data
A catalog record for this book has been requested

ISBN: 978-1-138-20071-5 (hbk)
ISBN: 978-1-31551-401-7 (ebk)

Typeset in Times New Roman
by Wearset Ltd, Boldon, Tyne and Wear

Contents

List of illustrations vii
Acknowledgements viii
List of abbreviations ix
Dramatis personae x

1 Introduction: understanding a controversial war 1
Structure 4

PART I
Public opinion 13

2 British public influence over foreign policy 15
Searching for the Loch Ness Monster 16
A constructivist approach 25
Conclusion 28

3 The Iraq debate: an overview 33
Rallying 'round the flag 34
Pockets of support 38
Salience and communication 43
Conclusion 51

PART II
Legitimacy 57

4 Understanding legitimacy 59
Legitimacy as a discursive construct 60
Studying the Blair government's discursive legitimization
  efforts 64
Categorizing the debate 66
Conclusion 68

vi *Contents*

5 Threat and WMD 71
Judgement 72
Nuance 77
Evidence 82
Conclusion 87

6 Legality and the UN 94
Defining the UN's role 96
Procedural ambiguities 99
Clashing timetables 107
Conclusion 110

7 Morality and regime change 119
Understanding Tony Blair 120
Legality and morality 127
Regime change 129
Conclusion 133

8 Politics and authority 140
The 'special relationship' 142
Blaming France 151
Domestic politics 156
Conclusion 163

PART III
Tony Blair's war in Iraq 173

9 Aftermath 175
Reality asserts itself 177
David Kelly 180
The 2005 general election 185
Conclusion 190

10 Implications 195
Selling the Iraq war 196
A holistic approach 200
A two-level debate 204
Conclusions 206

Index 212

Illustrations

Figures

3.1	Aggregate UK opinion poll data on the prospect of British military action in response to the 11 September attacks	35
3.2	Aggregate UK opinion poll data on the prospect of British military action in Iraq, January 2002–March 2003	36
3.3	Distribution of views expressed in newspaper commentary, by publication	40
3.4	Distribution of net average views expressed in parliamentary speeches, by party	42
3.5	Raw average monthly press, parliamentary and poll positions on the prospect of war in Iraq	43
3.6	Average salience of Iraq War across parliament, press and polls	45
3.7	Salience-adjusted average monthly press, parliamentary and poll positions on the prospect of war in Iraq	45
9.1	Opinion poll data showing approval of the decision to invade Iraq, March 2003–January 2005	178

Table

3.1	Salience measures	44

Acknowledgements

This book exists thanks to the kindness and active assistance of numerous family members, colleagues, students and friends, and their patient endurance through eight years of research. Dad and Paul helped pay my way through the PhD. Mum and Steve, Katie and the Old Folk offered moral and practical support. John Kent supervised my thesis, Toby Dodge mentored me through my fellowship, Inez von Weitershausen was a great research assistant and Chris Alden suggested I submit this manuscript to Routledge, where Lydia de Cruz guided me through the process and three reviewers offered helpful feedback. Caro blazed the trail I now follow. Karina made the final stages vastly more worthwhile. My students kept me entertained, and LSE kept me employed, while I wrote. Numerous other kind souls read extracts, offered guidance and advice and simply showed the way. Thank you all. Any errors, omissions and other shortcomings remain very much my own.

Abbreviations

DIS	Defence Intelligence Staff
FCO	Foreign and Commonwealth Office
FPA	Foreign Policy Analysis
IISS	International Institute for Strategic Studies
JIC	Joint Intelligence Committee
MoD	Ministry of Defence
SCR	(UN) Security Council Resolution
SIS	Secret Intelligence Service (MI6)
UNMOVIC	UN Monitoring, Verification and Inspection Commission
UNSCOM	UN Special Commission on Iraqi WMD
WMD	Weapons of Mass Destruction

Dramatis personae

10 Downing Street

Political

Tony Blair	Prime Minister of the United Kingdom
Jonathan Powell	Chief of Staff
Alastair Campbell	Director of Communications
Baroness Morgan	Director of Government Relations
Philip Gould	Labour Party Pollster

Civil service

David Manning	Prime Minister's Foreign Policy Advisor
Matthew Rycroft	Private Secretary (Foreign Affairs) to the Prime Minister

Security and Intelligence Services

John Scarlett	Chairman of the JIC
David Omand	Intelligence and Security Co-Ordinator, Cabinet Office
Richard Dearlove	Chief of SIS (known as "C")
Stephen Lander	Director General, Security Service (MI5)
Eliza Manningham-Buller	Deputy Director General, Security Service (MI5)

Foreign and Commonwealth Office

Jack Straw	Foreign Secretary
Simon McDonald	Principal Private Secretary to the Foreign Secretary
Michael Jay	Permanent Under-Secretary
Peter Ricketts	Policy Director
John Williams	Director of Communications

Michael Wood	Legal Advisor
Elizabeth Wilmshurst	Deputy Legal Advisor
Christopher Meyer	Ambassador to the US
Jeremy Greenstock	Ambassador to the UN
John Holmes	Ambassador to France
John Sawyers	Ambassador to Egypt

Ministry of Defence

Geoff Hoon	Defence Secretary
Simon Webb	Policy Director
Admiral Boyce	Chief of the Defence Staff
Air Vice Marshall French	Chief of Defence Intelligence
Major General Laurie	Director-General, Intelligence Collection
Tom McKane	Director-General, Resources and Planning
Martin Hemming	Legal Advisor
David Kelly	Chemical Weapons Expert

Attorney General's Office

Lord Goldsmith	Attorney General
David Brummell	Legal Secretary to the Law Officers
Cathy Adams	Legal Counsellor, Legal Secretariat to the Law Officers

Cabinet

Clare Short	International Development Secretary
Robin Cook	Leader of the House of Commons, former Foreign Secretary

Parliament

Iain Duncan Smith	Leader of the Conservative Party and Leader of the Opposition
Bernard Jenkin	Conservative Shadow Defence Secretary
Charles Kennedy	Leader of the Liberal Democrats
Menzies Campbell	Liberal Democrat Foreign Affairs Spokesman
Donald Anderson	Chairman of the Foreign Affairs Committee
Tam Dalyell	Labour MP, Father of the House (longest serving MP)
George Galloway	Labour, later Respect Party, MP

Non-UK

Hans Blix	Chairman, UNMOVIC
Jacques Chirac	President of France
Dominique de Villepin	Foreign Minister, France
George W. Bush	President of the United States
Dick Cheney	Vice-President of the United States
Donald Rumsfeld	US Secretary of Defense
Colin Powell	US Secretary of State
Condoleezza Rice	US National Security Advisor
General Richard B. Myers	Chairman of the Joint Chiefs of Staff
William H. Taft IV	State Department Legal Advisor

1 Introduction: understanding a controversial war

Britain has fought controversial wars before, but its involvement in the 2003 invasion of Iraq proved unusually contentious. Negative opinion polls, hostile media commentary, the largest parliamentary rebellion ever and the largest street protests in history failed to stop the Blair government joining the Bush administration in overthrowing Saddam Hussein. From an FPA perspective, this all looks somewhat odd. Democracies are not supposed to fight unpopular wars. Britain did. Rational politicians are not supposed to court career disaster by ignoring what the public wants. Blair government ministers did exactly that. Studying what made this possible offers us the chance to say something more general about democratic foreign policymaking. Does public opinion matter? Does this case prove that determined leaders can ignore even quite concerted domestic opposition as they pursue their chosen foreign policy course? What did the 2003 invasion mean, to ministers, to elites and to the public at large? What does it mean as we look back on it now, in the aftermath of the Chilcot Report?

To answer these questions, this book investigates how the British domestic debate over Iraq played out. It defines public opinion in constructivist terms, as a social fact constituted through elite debate, and highlights its relationship with foreign policy legitimacy. It uses dozens of opinion polls, hundreds of parliamentary speeches and thousands of press comment pieces to reconstruct both the direction and the nature of public attitudes. It draws on contemporary government statements, declassified and leaked government documents and the recent Chilcot Report to chart both the outlines and the narratives of what was a twisting, broad and often angry debate. It is an empirical study, in other words, but one structured by a particular FPA approach.

The book's underlying goal is to understand how it was possible that Britain wound up fighting what many British people considered an illegitimate war in Iraq. In the process, it aims to say something about the domestic legitimacy deficit that still surrounds the prospect of using force abroad. That many people in this country think the Iraq war illegitimate seems obvious. One poll on the invasion's tenth anniversary found just 27 per cent of respondents agreed it had been the right thing to do. Over 50 per cent disagreed (YouGov 2013). A clear-cut victory on the ground might have dispelled pre-invasion doubts (Mueller 2005, 109; Michalski and Gow 2007, 151). Pre-invasion doubts, however, ensured few British people expected a clear-cut victory on the ground. It is in any event difficult to 'win' the sort of messy, 'post-modern' conflict that the Iraq War became. It is doubly so when domestic audiences consider the entire enterprise to be wrong (Finnemore 2003, 18; Reus-Smit 2007, 165).

Even after four major public inquiries, the most recent and most comprehensive of which produced a report two million words long, the Iraq issue still retains an unparalleled capacity to provoke argument. Its legacy casts a pall over how Britain thinks about taking military action abroad (Daddow 2013; Strong 2015b). Parliament now gets involved in major combat deployment decisions. Tony Blair felt forced to grant MPs the chance to veto his invasion. His successor David Cameron followed suit to prove how much more open and consultative he was compared to Blair. Together they set new precedents and forged a new political convention, a "parliamentary prerogative" that grants the House of Commons a say over the use of force as a foreign policy tool (Strong 2015a). This development made a direct difference in August 2013, when MPs voted against intervention in the Syrian Civil War. Iraq made the Syria veto possible, by putting pressure on Blair to concede power to MPs. It also made it thinkable, by giving MPs a language in which to justify saying no. Before 2013, no government had lost a House of Commons vote on a matter of military action since 1782, when Lord North's administration collapsed over its failure to rein in the rebellious North American colonies. Against the backdrop of Iraq, a repeat suddenly became practically possible and conceptually conceivable. Newly empowered as self-appointed guardians against dangerous military overreach, MPs saw too many shadows of Blair's conduct ten years before in the Cameron government's approach to Syria. They felt the "spectre of the debate on Iraq" behind them. They saw "the ghost of Tony Blair" looming overhead. They did not trust their leaders to tell the truth about the need for force. One Conservative backbencher told Cameron she could "not sit here and be duped again" (Hansard 2013, cols. 1473, 1545 and 1510). Four years after British troops withdrew from Basra, MPs saw the prospect of further military intervention through the prism of Iraq.

Two related factors drove this phenomenon. To begin with, the Iraq War obviously went wrong. It lasted far longer, cost more in treasure and in lives (mainly Iraqi, though also British) and delivered less peace and stability than most opponents, let alone supporters, anticipated. Even Blair, who otherwise still defends the approach he took, accepted partial responsibility for the rise of Da'esh in a 2015 interview (Blair 2015). More pernicious still was the sense, widely shared, that the entire enterprise was wrong from the start, however it turned out. This stemmed above all from the widespread belief that the Blair government did not tell the truth during the build-up to war (Heffernan 2006, 592; Kennedy-Pipe and Vickers 2007, 206; Hill 2007, 276; Dunne 2008, 340). Internal Labour Party polling, conducted after the 2005 general election and later leaked, found 60 per cent of voters thought "the people and the Parliament were lied to about the reasons for going to war" (Penn, Schoen and Berland 2005). This was an incredible figure. It marked a dramatic turnaround for Tony Blair's once unimpeachable public image. It underscored the crisis of legitimacy he faced. And it made sense. British ministers claimed that Iraq's continued development of banned WMD posed a threat, both directly to national security and indirectly to the international order. But Iraq was not actually developing WMD. They said the war was legal even without explicit UN Security Council approval. That turned out to be an aggressive and eminently contestable interpretation of international law. Most legal experts disagreed with the Attorney General's arguments, finally leaked shortly before the 2005 election, while Chilcot dismissed the claim that ignoring the Security Council was the only way to uphold the Council's own wishes. Blair repeatedly asserted his personal authority to direct Britain's armed forces in the name of its citizens. But many insisted he did not speak for them, accusing him instead of being President Bush's 'poodle', an impression he struggled to dispel. Blair argued that changing the Iraqi regime was the morally proper thing to do. But Iraq, after Saddam, deteriorated into a drawn-out sectarian conflict from which it is yet to emerge. Doubts about how the government made the case for war reinforced concerns stoked by casualties and battlefield setbacks. Every death, and every disaster, made ministers' pre-invasion claims look that much worse. As Blair himself admitted, every time something went wrong on the ground it reminded people that they doubted that British forces should be in Iraq at all (Blair 2010, 374).

Understanding how all this was possible from a FPA perspective offers us the opportunity to say something more general about Britain's recent doubts about military action. Even more active in military terms than Blair, after coming to office in 2010 David Cameron repeatedly asked MPs to approve the use of force. Every time he felt compelled to refer to Iraq. Asking approval for a no-fly zone over Libya in March 2011, he promised "this is not another Iraq" (Cameron 2011, col. 709). Looking to respond to the use of chemical weapons on civilians in Syria in August 2013, he insisted "this situation is not like Iraq" (Cameron 2013, col. 1427). Proposing to fight Da'esh in Iraq in September 2014, he maintained "this is different to the decision the House made in 2003" (Cameron 2014, col. 1263). Calling for further action to fight Da'esh in Syria in December 2015, he concluded by observing "this is not 2003" (Cameron 2015, col. 339). Jeremy Corbyn won the Labour Party leadership thanks in part to his concerted opposition to Tony Blair's wars. Corbyn was chairman of the Stop the War coalition, an anti-war pressure group founded to campaign against Western states using force in the aftermath of the 11 September attacks. He was one of only 13 MPs who voted against intervention in Libya. True to form, Corbyn warned MPs considering action against Da'esh in Syria to acknowledge the "spectre of Iraq, Afghanistan and Libya" haunting them (Corbyn 2015, col. 347). A strong sense remains amongst political elites, the media and the wider public that the invasion of Iraq was fundamentally wrong. It fuels a wider scepticism about the use of force abroad. This, in turn, raises significant questions about Britain's role as a great power, as an ally and a permanent member of the UN Security Council. It leaves the integrity of the office of the Prime Minister, of the intelligence services and the government's legal advisors in doubt. Understanding Iraq is, consequently, still vitally important if we are to get to grips with contemporary Britain's attitudes to the use of force.

Others have written books about Iraq. This study builds on published participant accounts in the form of memoirs (Cook 2003; Blair 2010), wider theoretical reflections (Powell 2010) and edited diaries (Campbell and Stott 2007). It is further enriched by evidence produced in a series of public inquiries, from Lord Hutton's account of the untimely death of British chemical weapons expert Dr David Kelly, through Lord Butler's dissection of the government's 'dossier' on WMD to Sir John Chilcot's comprehensive investigation of every aspect of the war.

This book adds two things. First, it adds an FPA perspective on how Britain wound up fighting in Iraq, and what the consequences were. It adopts a constructivist theoretical approach, aimed at "understanding" the meaning of the debate from the perspective of insiders rather than "explaining" it from outside (Hollis and Smith 1990). Constructivists prefer "how possible" to "why" questions, looking at how particular interactions among participants make certain outcomes thinkable and others not (Doty 1993, 298). The book consequently explores how the way the Iraq debate played out made both the decision to go to war and the legitimacy deficit that subsequently surrounded it possible. It will, in the process, contribute to a wider constructivist literature on the discursive construction of legitimacy in international conflict. With the Cold War over, the question of what makes a Western state's engagement in international conflict legitimate has become more complex. There is no longer a single clear overarching narrative of international politics within which such decisions are subsumed (Cole 1996, 105; Clark 2005, 158; Voeten 2005, 546). Most contemporary conflicts involve intervention in other states' internal affairs rather than the more traditional form of inter-state war (Finnemore 2003, 2). That makes the sort of debate chronicled here all the more important.

Second, this book adds a detailed empirical focus on the pre-war period, something the current literature does not really address despite its importance (Robinson *et al.* 2010). It presents an in-depth, original analysis driven by contemporary primary sources, including 2,115 newspaper comment pieces and 333 parliamentary speeches alongside dozens of official documents and participant accounts. In the process, it aims both to debunk some of the later myths about the pre-war debate, and to present a well-evidenced 'first cut' historical account.

Structure

This book proceeds in three related parts. Part I looks at public opinion. Chapter 2 makes the case for adopting a constructivist approach to understanding the relationship between British public opinion and foreign policy. It sets out ontological, epistemological and methodological foundations for the empirical investigations reported through the remainder of the book. It highlights how 'public opinion' exists to the extent a society, or a group within a society such as a political elite, thinks that it exists. Public opinion, from this perspective, is best described as a "social fact" constituted through public debate (Kratochwil and Ruggie 1986, 765; Onuf 1989, 94; Wendt 1992, 406; Searle 1995, 27). This chapter consequently suggests a 'holistic' empirical approach combining survey results with quantitative and qualitative analysis of press commentary, parliamentary debate and street protests to build up an interpretive picture of public attitudes, while using contemporary documents and public statements alongside later reflections to triangulate policymakers' views. In the case of Britain's involvement in the invasion of Iraq, it also shows how the range of material produced by repeated public inquiries and continued public and media interest can support academic research.

Chapter 3 presents a predominately quantitative overview of the UK public debate prior to the invasion of Iraq, derived from a large-scale content analysis exercise showing the pattern of public attitudes across the different sources comprising the holistic approach. It highlights three factors that help us understand how it was possible that concerted public opposition failed to stop Britain joining the Iraq war. To begin with, although opinion polls, press commentary and parliamentary speeches showed consistent opposition to the prospect of war throughout the pre-invasion period, the Blair government accurately predicted a 'rally 'round the flag' effect once battle commenced. Second, ministers enjoyed significant pockets of support in public debate, including politically pivotal forces such as Rupert Murdoch's media empire and the opposition, the Conservative Party. Both supported military action against Saddam Hussein more vociferously even than Tony Blair himself. Finally, official communication efforts largely worked, at least in the short term. While they may not have changed many minds, the government's contributions to public debate successfully lowered the salience of Iraq as an issue. In effect, they reduced the intensity without changing the direction of public opposition, and that proved sufficient. Through setting out these points, this chapter further highlights key 'moments' in the debate that prove significant in Part II.

Part II moves on to talk about legitimacy. Chapter 4 outlines a discursive understanding of what legitimacy is and where it comes from. It argues for treating legitimacy as a product of public debate, and introduces two distinct "Foucauldian" and "Habermasian" normative approaches to understanding how this works and what it means in practice (Reus-Smit 2002, 487). For Foucauldians, government communications can generate consensus, but not legitimacy in any normative sense. Whatever support ministers achieve reflects their power over domestic audiences, nothing more. For Habermasians, by contrast, a properly conducted public deliberation can produce the sort of agreement among democratic actors that legitimacy derives from. To secure this normative status, leaders must be honest, open to public debate and flexible in the face of opposition. Understanding the legitimacy deficit surrounding Iraq therefore means looking both at the substance of the arguments the Blair government made, and the form in which it made them.

The following discussion breaks down the pre-invasion debate along lines of reasoning that the Blair government and its critics actually used. In the process, it sacrifices the conceptual insight that bringing in an outside framework, such as Just War Theory, might offer. This seems a reasonable step to take in pursuit of greater empirical detail. We wind up talking about four distinct dimensions of the official case for war; the need to address the Iraqi threat, the legality of using force and the role of the UN, the morality of military intervention and the politics involved. These dimensions emerge from an inductive reading of the debate. They also accord with criteria used in existing legitimacy research.

Chapter 5 recounts the Blair government's attempt to frame military action in Iraq as a necessary response to the threat posed by Iraq's alleged development of banned WMD. The claim that Iraq represented a security threat to Britain should have strengthened the invasion's legitimacy while also raising both public interest in and public approval of the prospect of military action (Finnemore 2003, 2; Hansen 2006, 34–35). That it did not do so reflected three major shortcomings in the way the government made its case. First, officials and ministers misjudged the danger Iraq actually posed, a point underlined after the invasion by the absence of WMD. SIS placed too much weight on sources that were later proven unreliable. The JIC drew inferences from Iraq's past record that went beyond what the available evidence could support. Ministers believed Iraq posed an even greater threat than did the JIC, and then exaggerated the strength of their beliefs when speaking publicly. At each stage, what was in fact an uncertain picture grew apparently more concrete, exacerbating the damage done when it was, in practice, proved wrong. Second, this exaggeration damaged the government's credibility. The now-notorious 'dossier' published in September 2002 failed to disclose how much the case for confronting Iraq depended on a changed "calculus of threat" in the aftermath of the 11 September attacks, rather than new evidence (Butler 2004, 34). It did not reflect the uncertainty underpinning JIC judgments, and placed too much weight on too little knowledge. It was, as a result, "deceptive" (Herring and Robinson 2014). Finally, the government exploited the information advantage it enjoyed over other participants in public debate in order to push its preferred policy line. At the same time it claimed it sought a well-informed public debate, and presented political judgments as neutral facts. This was problematic in terms of its normative claim to legitimacy.

Chapter 6 looks at the debate over the legality of war with Iraq in the absence of explicit UN Security Council approval. It does three things. To begin with, it highlights the range of different views within British public debate of what the UN was properly supposed to do. Some saw it as a legal arbiter, some as a moral authority and some as a forum for political deal-making. Unambiguous Council approval might have satisfied everyone. But after the high-point marked by the passage of Security Council Resolution (SCR) 1441 in November 2002, the shaky consensus among the great powers soon fell apart. Second, Chapter 6 talks about the procedural ambiguities that surrounded Britain's engagement with the UN over Iraq. SCR 1441 deliberately left unclear the question of whether the Council itself or its individual member states possessed the authority to resort to force in the event of apparent Iraqi non-compliance. Ministers failed to frame UNMOVIC, the UN weapons inspection body, as an auditor rather than a detective agency. That led to questions about the need for 'smoking guns'. Finally, there was a fundamental clash between the US military timetable and the UN inspection programme. It might have been possible to exhaust inspections in time for the preferred US start date for war, but only in the event of clear Iraqi obstructionism. Equally, unambiguous Iraqi co-operation might have made war politically impossible. Iraq, however, co-operated moderately but not as well as UNMOVIC wanted. This created still more ambiguity, and left the Blair government struggling to find arguments to allow it to bridge the gap between the US drive to war and its own stated commitment to upholding international law. The resulting process, as Chilcot put it, was "far from satisfactory" (Chilcot 2016, 62).

Chapter 7 considers questions of morality and 'regime change'. To begin with, it highlights Blair's personal belief that the 'international community' had a responsibility to spread freedom and justice, faith in the utility of force as a tool for good and conviction of his own superior moral judgment. This both provided him with cognitive insulation in the face of public criticism and made him inflexible when presented with reasonable counter-arguments. Next, it talks about the underlying clash between Blair's cosmopolitan vision of international morality and the pluralist principles underpinning international law. Ministers never confronted, let alone resolved, the fact it was logically impossible to pursue regime change on moral grounds legally. Finally, it considers in some detail how in practice this clash manifested through difficult debates about whether regime change was a legitimate policy goal, a legitimate consequence of legitimate policy goals or a US obsession with little relevance to the UK. It was not until early 2003 that the moral arguments for war really achieved any prominence in public debate, and by that point the government already lacked credibility. Ministers' refusal to admit their commitment to regime change contributed to the political difficulties they faced.

Chapter 8 investigates the political dynamics surrounding the Blair government's case for war. It considers first the challenge ministers faced as they sought to balance their international-level commitment to supporting the Bush administration against the domestic-level imperative to demonstrate independence from the US line. Britain faced a classic "two-level game" problem, in FPA terms (Putnam 1988, Gourevitch 1978, Walt 1985, Fearon 1994). In the end, the government gambled on being able to reconcile the competing pressures it faced, and lost. As Chapter 8 discusses second, one way it tried to resolve its difficulties was by blaming France for its own failure to reach consensus at the Security Council. This was a rare example of a questionable pre-invasion claim that did not later damage the Blair government's political support. France was not in fact responsible for the lack of agreement. But with the British press primed to look favourably on narratives based on French perfidy, the argument succeeded. Finally, the chapter considers the longer-term parliamentary politics of Iraq, including the impact of MPs' new veto powers. Conservative support helped protect the Blair government from defeat in the 18 March House of Commons vote. From an FPA perspective, the role of opposition politicians directly affects both how effective public attitudes are in influencing decision-makers, and how far decision-makers can possibly face electoral punishment for their stance (Key 1961, 556). The fact Blair implied he would resign if defeated made a difference, too. He dared his MPs to decide between overthrowing their most successful leader ever, and overthrowing Saddam Hussein. Most chose to overthrow Saddam. It was a classic political disciplining measure, well known in the literature on legislative politics (Huber 1996, 269; Diermeir and Feddersen 1998, 611). And it worked.

Part III considers the broader implications of what we can reasonably call 'Tony Blair's war' in Iraq. Chapter 9 looks at the consequences of the invasion, highlighting how the basis of support built up by March 2003 crumbled over the following years of grinding, directionless war. It talks about the "elasticity of reality" (Baum and Groeling 2010), the way brute material facts can assert themselves over public debates previously shaped by rhetoric that did not reflect the position on the ground. In Iraq, the missing WMD and the coalition's failure to stabilize the country together served to undermine the Blair government's arguments. Chapter 9 also considers a key moment in the growth of the legitimacy deficit surrounding Iraq, the death of British chemical weapons expert Dr David Kelly in the summer of 2003. Kelly told a BBC reporter named Andrew Gilligan of doubts within the intelligence community about some elements in the government's WMD 'dossier'. Gilligan publicly claimed that Downing Street knowingly 'sexed up' its claims about the Iraqi threat, causing a public furore. Lord Hutton's inquiry, the first of three major independent investigations into Britain's war, followed (Hutton 2004). It did not end the clamour for more information and more investigations, though perhaps the Chilcot Report will do that. Finally, Chapter 9 considers the 2005 general election campaign. Though foreign policy rarely affects how democratic electorates behave, in this case the distrust built up by Iraq did impact on the vote, though not enough to deny the Blair government power. During the election campaign, someone gave the *Guardian* the 'full' version of the Attorney-General's legal advice, previously only published in summary form. The full version differed markedly from the summary, not necessarily in substance – it still concluded the war was legal – but definitely in tone (Goldsmith 2003). The effect was to place questions about trust in government at the heart of the election campaign. Interestingly, by 2005 most Conservative voters opposed the war while most Labour voters supported it, reversing the position at the time of the invasion (Penn *et al.* 2005). Either the government lost votes because of the war (which it did to some extent) or, more likely, Labour voters came to support the war because they supported the Labour government, an interesting if incidental demonstration of a foreign policy heuristic in effect (Mueller 1973).

Chapter 10 draws out the book's key empirical and theoretical implications. A number of points stand out. First, the Blair government was, to a large extent, the author of its own failures over Iraq. It pursued a communicative approach to foreign policy legitimization without meeting the normative standards required for such an approach to work. At the same time, it made unconvincing and at times incoherent or contradictory arguments that reduced its persuasiveness. Ministers faced a difficult battle in 2002 and 2003. Public attitudes do not shift easily, and they are not particularly susceptible to official pressure, especially when the best official arguments depend on information the government feels unable to share (Hurrell 2005). But it played the cards it held badly. Second, treating public opinion as a sociological phenomenon and linking it to the intersubjective construction of foreign policy legitimacy works. This study offers a number of insights about how and why the pre-invasion British public debate over Iraq played out the way it did, and what it meant for the policy in the long term. These insights go beyond what most informed observers report. For example, they show that the common perception that Tony Blair dragged the British people reluctantly to war is only partially true, but that Blair's partial approach to truthfulness ultimately did more political harm than good. Third, the way a government talks about a foreign policy decision affects the kinds of decisions it can make. This is an important point in FPA terms, as it points to how efforts at opinion management can generate feedback into the policymaking process. Several of the difficulties the Blair government faced resulted from making commitments at one stage of the pre-invasion debate it later struggled to honour, such as the commitment to work through a UN process. This points towards a constructivist version of the 'two-level game' model.

References

Baum, Matthew, and Tim Groeling. 'Reality asserts itself: public opinion on Iraq and the elasticity of reality.' *International Organization* 64, no. 4 (2010): 443–479.
Blair, Tony. *A Journey*. London: Hutchinson, 2010.
Blair, Tony. Interview by Fareed Zakaria. *CNN: Fareed Zakaria GPS* (26 October 2015).
Butler, Lord. *The Butler Report*. London: HMSO, 2004.
Cameron, David. *Hansard House of Commons Debates*. 6th Ser. Vol. 525, 21 March 2011.
Cameron, David. *Hansard House of Commons Debates*. 6th Ser. Vol. 566, 29 August 2013.
Cameron, David. *Hansard House of Commons Debates*. 6th Ser. Vol. 585, 26 September 2014.
Cameron, David. *Hansard House of Commons Debates*. 6th Ser. Vol. 603, 2 December 2015.
Campbell, Alastair, and Richard Stott. *The Blair Years: Extracts from the Alastair Campbell Diaries*. London: Arrow Books, 2007.
Chilcot, John. *Report of the Iraq Inquiry: Executive Summary*. London: HMSO, 2016.
Clark, Ian. *Legitimacy in International Society*. Oxford: Oxford University Press, 2005.
Cole, Timothy. 'When intentions go awry: the Bush administration's foreign policy rhetoric.' *Political Communication* 13, no. 1 (1996): 93–113.
Cook, Robin. *The Point of Departure*. London: Simon & Schuster, 2003.
Corbyn, Jeremy. *Hansard House of Commons Debates*. 6th Ser. Vol. 603, 2 December 2015.
Daddow, Oliver. 'The use of force in British foreign policy: from New Labour to the coalition.' *The Political Quarterly* 84, no. 1 (2013): 110–118.
Diermeir, Daniel, and Timothy Feddersen. 'Cohesion in legislatures and the vote of confidence procedure.' *American Political Science Review* 92, no. 3 (1998): 611–621.

Doty, Roxanne. 'Foreign policy as social construction: a post-positivist analysis of US counterinsurgency policy in the Philippines.' *International Studies Quarterly* 37, no. 3 (1993): 297–320.

Dunne, Tim. 'Britain and the gathering storm over Iraq.' In *Foreign Policy: Theories, Actors, Cases*, by Steve Smith, Amelia Hadfield and Tim Dunne, 339–358. Oxford: Oxford University Press, 2008.

Fearon, James. 'Domestic political audiences and the escalation of international disputes.' *American Political Science Review* 88, no. 3 (1994): 577–592.

Finnemore, Martha. *The Purpose of Intervention: Changing Beliefs About the Use of Force*. Ithaca, NY: Cornell University Press, 2003.

Goldsmith, Lord. 'Iraq: legal advice: memo to Tony Blair.' 7 March 2003. http://image.guardian.co.uk/sys-files/Guardian/documents/2005/04/28/legal.pdf (accessed 20 August 2015).

Gourevitch, Peter. 'The second image reversed: the international sources of domestic politics.' *International Organization* 38, no. 4 (1978): 881–912.

Hansard. *House of Commons Debates*. 6th Ser. Vol. 566, 29 August 2013.

Hansen, Lene. *Security as Practice: Discourse Analysis and the Bosnian War*. Abingdon: Routledge, 2006.

Heffernan, Richard. 'The Prime Minister and the news media: political communication as a leadership resource.' *Parliamentary Affairs* 59, no. 4 (2006): 582–598.

Herring, Eric, and Piers Robinson. 'Report X marks the spot: the British Government's deceptive dossier on Iraq and WMD.' *Political Science Quarterly* 129, no. 4 (2014): 551–584.

Hill, Christopher. 'Bringing war home: foreign policy making in multicultural societies.' *International Relations* 21, no. 3 (2007): 259–283.

Hollis, Martin, and Steve Smith. *Explaining and Understanding International Relations*. Oxford: Oxford University Press, 1990.

Huber, John. 'The vote of confidence in parliamentary democracies.' *American Political Science Review* 90, no. 2 (1996): 269–282.

Hurrell, Andrew. 'Legitimacy and the use of force: can the circle be squared?' *Review of International Studies* 31, no. 1 (2005): 15–32.

Hutton, Lord. *The Hutton Report*. London: HMSO, 2004.

Kennedy-Pipe, Caroline, and Rhiannon Vickers. 'Blowback for Britain?: Blair, Bush, and the war in Iraq.' *Review of International Studies* 33, no. 2 (2007): 205–221.

Key, Vladimer. *Public Opinion and American Democracy*. New York: Knopf, 1961.

Kratochwil, Friedrich, and John Ruggie. 'International organization: a state of the art on an art of the state.' *International Organization* 40, no. 4 (1986): 753–775.

Michalski, Milena, and James Gow. *War, Image and Legitimacy: Viewing Contemporary Conflict*. Abingdon: Routledge, 2007.

Mueller, John. *War, Presidents and Public Opinion*. New York: Wiley, 1973.

Mueller, John. 'Force, legitimacy, success, and Iraq.' *Review of International Studies* 31, no. 1 (2005): 109–125.

Onuf, Nicholas. *World of Our Making: Rules and Rule in Social Theory and International Relations*. Columbia, SC: University of South Carolina Press, 1989.

Penn, Schoen & Berland Associates, Inc. 'Survey of likely voters and strategy discussion.' 8 June 2005. http://s.telegraph.co.uk/graphics/viewer.html?doc=202568-doc2 (accessed 19 July 2016).

Powell, Jonathan. *The New Machiavelli: How to Wield Power in the Modern World*. London: The Bodley Head, 2010.

Putnam, Robert. 'Diplomacy and domestic politics: the logic of two-level games.' *International Organization* 42, no. 3 (1988): 427–460.

Reus-Smit, Christian. 'Imagining society: constructivism and the English School.' *British Journal of Politics and International Relations* 4, no. 3 (2002): 487–509.

Reus-Smit, Christian. 'International crises of legitimacy.' *International Politics* 44, no. 2 (2007): 157–174.

Robinson, Piers, Peter Goddard, Katy Parry, Craig Murray, and Philip Taylor. *Pockets of Resistance: British News Media, War and Theory in the 2003 Invasion of Iraq.* Manchester: Manchester University Press, 2010.

Searle, John. *The Construction of Social Reality.* New York, NY: The Free Press, 1995.

Strong, James. 'Why parliament now decides on war: tracing the growth of the parliamentary prerogative through Syria, Libya and Iraq.' *British Journal of Politics and International Relations* 17, no. 4 (2015a): 604–622.

Strong, James. 'Interpreting the Syria vote: parliament and British foreign policy.' *International Affairs* 91, no. 5 (2015b): 1123–1139.

Voeten, Erik. 'The political origins of the UN Security Council's ability to legitimize the use of force.' *International Organization* 59, no. 4 (2005): 527–557.

Walt, Stephen. 'Alliance formation and the balance of world power.' *International Security* 9, no. 4 (1985): 3–43.

Wendt, Alexander. 'Anarchy is what states make of it: the social construction of power politics.' *International Organization* 46, no. 2 (1992): 391–425.

YouGov. 'Iraq trends.' 11 March 2013. http://cdn.yougov.com/cumulus_uploads/document/raghpsamv0/YG-Archives-Pol-Trackers-Iraq-130313.pdf (accessed 11 August 2015).

Part I
Public opinion

2 British public influence over foreign policy

This chapter lays conceptual foundations for the empirical analysis of British public attitudes towards the invasion of Iraq that follows. Drawing on specialist public opinion scholarship and relevant FPA literature, it proposes a constructivist approach to understanding the relationship between what the public thinks and what decision-makers do. It makes the case for treating public opinion as a social fact constituted through press and parliamentary debate, rather than as a material force that exists independently of how elites talk about it. Though ordinary people can have a say, as potential voters and poll respondents, they do not set the policy agenda independently in this formulation. That role remains reserved to active participants in public life, especially media commentators, elected representatives and prominent citizens.

Treating public attitudes this way allows us to consider public influence in a manner more consistent with the goals of an FPA study and to prefigure the discussion of legitimacy that begins in Chapter 4. Public opinion and legitimacy are related concepts. Foreign policy decisions look legitimate to the extent that they enjoy public support, and attract public support to the extent that they look legitimate. Unpicking this relationship is hard. It is co-constitutive rather than causal, and iterative rather than fixed. Sometimes public attitudes matter more than legitimacy, sometimes legitimacy matters more than public attitudes. Both are defined, shaped and constituted through a constant process of elite debate. This chapter takes a necessary first conceptual step, but will not uncover the entire picture yet.

Though the constructivist mindset advocated here is unusual in the public opinion literature, it is not entirely new. Most specialist studies assume there is such a thing as 'the' public, and that 'the' public has opinions. All the scholars who are interested in public attitudes need to do is observe and quantify their distribution, typically using survey methods known as 'opinion polls'. More critical analysts maintain, however, that these assumptions depend on unstable theoretical foundations. They question whether it makes sense to treat the disaggregated mass of non-governmental actors in a society as a coherent, thinking whole. They point out that the mainstream approach fails to consider where public attitudes come from, and the central role polling plays in sustaining the idea that public opinion exists. Specialist studies set aside serious epistemological shortcomings that, this chapter argues, reduce the validity of the survey-based approach. Survey methods struggle to capture variations between individual interest in, knowledge about and influence over foreign affairs. They cannot tell us whether poll respondents reveal hidden preferences or simply give off-the-cuff answers.

Adopting a constructivist approach means siding with the critical tradition within the specialist literature, and defining public opinion as a social rather than a material fact. Constructivists take seriously the role played in political life by social facts, things that exist because a critical mass of us believe they do. Material facts, by contrast, exist whether we accept them or not. Treating public opinion as a social fact means treating it as something defined by social interaction, something that influences policymaking because elites believe in it rather than because it acts independently. It enables us to study public attitudes in their proper context, through a holistic empirical approach that combines poll results with both quantitative and qualitative analyses of press commentary and parliamentary debate, and considers both what the public said and how the government responded.

This chapter begins by discussing the downsides of opinion polls, defining what we mean by 'public' and 'public opinion', highlighting the epistemological implications our definitions raise and then talking about how, in theory, public attitudes affect foreign policy decisions. It then makes the case for a constructivist, holistic research design. The holistic mindset serves as an antidote to the shortcomings of survey methods. It better reflects what policymakers actually do and it keeps our focus, as good foreign policy analysts, not on what the British public thought about the prospect of war with Iraq, but on how the particular constellation of opinions circulating in the public sphere made it possible for the Blair government to proceed despite concerted opposition. Our ultimate goal, after all, is not to understand the public, but to understand the policy.

Searching for the Loch Ness Monster

This first section describes how the FPA literature understands the relationship between public opinion and policymaking, defines public opinion in constructivist terms and discusses the problems raised by opinion polls. Christopher Hill warned in an early survey of research in this field that "a search for public opinion and its influence over British foreign policy" was "of the same order as the search for the Loch Ness Monster – intriguing, but fanciful" (Hill 1981, 60). In the process, Hill echoed the prevailing twentieth-century understanding of the public's foreign policy role. Writing in the aftermath of the First World War, the American journalist Walter Lippmann concluded that ordinary people did not care about international affairs, "so long as nobody has to fight and nobody has to pay" (Lippmann 1922, 241). Gabriel Almond, a political scientist, concurred. He observed that "the characteristic [public] response to questions of foreign policy is indifference" (Almond 1950, 53). James Rosenau, a founding father of FPA, similarly characterized the public as a "mob" and public opinion as "impulsive, unstable, unreasoning, unpredictable, capable of suddenly shifting direction or of going in several contradictory directions at the same time" (Rosenau 1961, 36). It was a pessimistic picture.

FPA began in the early 1990s to challenge what Ole Holsti labelled the "Almond–Lippmann consensus" (Holsti 1992). Detailed empirical research confirmed that most ordinary people know relatively little about foreign policy (Converse 1964, 245; Holsti 1996, 215). But it also underlined a crucial point: ignorance does not necessarily prevent people forming opinions. Individual citizens are quite good at using heuristics to judge how best to respond to political questions asked of them (Sobel 2001, 21; Isernia *et al.* 2002; Klarevas 2002; Jacobsen 2008, 351). They consider how successful a policy appears to be, the benefits it promises to bring or the costs it seeks to avoid in judging its worth (Gelpi *et al.* 2005; Eichenberg 2005, 163; Klarevas 2006, 193; Gelpi *et al.* 2007, 158). Individuals hold irrational views, but the public, as a whole, looks more rational and coherent, as individual irrationalities cancel each other out across the population and over time (Page and Shapiro 1992, 14; Nincic 1992, 31, 42, 45). Hill's scepticism is still to some extent warranted. If we ask random British citizens what they think about foreign policy, the only honest answer most of them can offer is that they do not know. What more recent work suggests, however, is that most ordinary people know enough to choose between a few different options, with reasonably coherent overall results.

Studying public opinion as an influence on policymaking is therefore not the potentially frivolous activity that Hill implied. There remain, however, two aspects of how FPA understands the public's role that are worth addressing before we proceed to analyse our case. First, we need to pin down what exactly we mean when we talk about 'public opinion'. V.O. Key, for example, distinguished between "latent" and "activated" public views. Latent attitudes exist in the minds of citizens, but they crystallize and shape behaviour only in response to external stimuli. Activated opinions, by contrast, emerge visibly in the public sphere. Both affect policymakers, but what matters above all is the question of how latent attitudes become activated (Key 1961, 245). One of the major problems with survey methods, which is discussed in greater depth below, is that their artificial activation of latent opinions fails to reflect actual socio-political processes (Herbst 1993, 41).

Second, we need also to consider the causal mechanisms linking public attitudes to policymaking behaviour. We can begin by noting that rational politicians rarely take decisions they know will harm their re-election prospects. Foreign policy generally does not influence voter choice too directly. What it does do, though, is shape the broader way electorates think about policymakers. Those who appear unsuccessful tend to suffer electoral costs (Verba *et al.* 1967, 317; Hagan 1990, 4; Nincic 1992, 91–92; Bueno de Mesquita and Siverson 1995, 853; Partell 1997, 508–509). Individual leaders differ, however, over how important they consider public approval to be. Some think public support is necessary for successful policymaking. Others think it is desirable but not required (Foyle 1997, 145). Crucially, from an FPA perspective, we need to pay

18 *Public opinion*

particular attention, not to what public opinion *says*, but to how leaders *interpret it*. Ultimately any influence the British public had over the decision to go to war in Iraq was filtered through decision-makers. Our account assumes, in line with David Patrick Houghton's (2007) work on the relationship between constructivist theory and the cognitive school of FPA research, that public influence takes place through a two-step process. In the first step, elite participants in public debate collectively construct a sense of what 'the public' wants. In the second step, that sense gets filtered through the prism of how decision-makers see the world. Only then, and only in this slightly roundabout fashion, do public attitudes count.

What is public opinion?

It is deceptively difficult to define what we mean by 'public opinion'. Our difficulties begin at the most basic definitional level. Does the 'public' in 'public opinion' describe *who* holds certain views, or *where* those views arise? Is it an adjective or a noun? Is public opinion the opinion *of* the public or an opinion expressed *in* public? How we answer these questions shapes how we go about trying to understand what public opinion is and the influence it exerts.

Most studies looking at public opinion treat 'public' as a noun and define public opinion as the opinion of the public. Even these accounts, however, recognize the difficulties involved in treating the more or less differentiated cacophony of individual and institutional actors operating in a society as a single coherent unit. They note, as Roger Hilsman put it, that "there is not one public, but many" (Hilsman 1987, 243). Some members of 'the' public act collectively, through political parties, interest and pressure groups or media organizations. Others are more individual, perhaps leveraging socio-economic power to amplify their views. Each follows a unique script. Often, they disagree profoundly with each other. Their only indisputably shared characteristic is that they are not part of the government. Historically, this has not been a bar to studying public opinion. As Key concluded, it is "unnecessary to assume that 'the public' exists in any particular sort of loosely structured association or other ghostly sociological entity" (Key 1961, 15). There are public actors. We can study them. That is enough.

Accepting that 'the' public is actually a collection of publics does require us to come up with a framework for differentiating between them. Most FPA accounts adopt a hierarchical approach, distinguishing between 'mass', 'attentive' and 'elite' groups on the basis of their interest in, knowledge about and influence over foreign policy (Almond 1950, 138; Rosenau 1961, 33–34; Hilsman 1987, 284; Risse-Kappen 1991, 482; Sobel 2001, 12). For our purposes, we might identify the mass public with the hypothetical '(wo)man on the Clapham omnibus': the attentive with readers of elite newspapers like the *Financial Times* and the elite with opinion leaders in the media, business, political and academic worlds. At a theoretical level, this way of thinking about 'the' public seems sensible enough (Hurwitz and Peffley 1987). There *should* be a link between how important an actor thinks foreign policy is, how much they know about it and how influential they are over it. Equally, it makes good sense for actors who feel no great personal interest in international affairs not to bother learning much about it, however heretical that may seem to a foreign policy analyst (Page and Shapiro 1992, 14; Nincic 1992, 31).

At a practical level, however, the hierarchical approach has weaknesses. It is surprisingly difficult to distinguish between mass, attentive and elite publics using the sort of survey methods that most public opinion research employs (more on this below). Elites do not necessarily hold substantially different views from the mass, not least because they often influence what mass public actors think (Verba *et al.* 1967, 331–332). One of the main heuristics that inattentive actors use in responding to questions about foreign policy is the positions of trusted elites (Berinsky 2007). It is hard to pick out attentive actors from the mass, using survey methods alone. By seeking to activate a latent attitude, the act of asking a survey question prompts previously inattentive respondents to think about an issue. Every poll respondent consequently looks at least somewhat attentive. Often the only way to use surveys to study elite, attentive and mass attitudes is to decide in advance which actors belong to which category. It is possible to do this reliably, especially with panel studies that approach the same individuals on consecutive occasions. But it risks imposing inappropriate criteria on a group of actors before their views can possibly be known.

A minority of FPA accounts adopt a more behavioural approach to differentiating between groups of public actors. John Mueller, for example, identified four distinct ways that US public actors responded to government foreign policy initiatives. His "followers" went along with whatever the president proposed, regardless of their party-political preferences or the substance of a given policy choice. His "partisans" sided with a president from their own preferred political party, whether Republican or Democrat, and against a president from the opposite side of the spectrum, regardless of the issue under consideration. Mueller's "believers" held a set of independent ideological beliefs that guided their engagement with foreign policy issues, while the "self-interested" asked only how a particular choice might affect them personally (Mueller 1973, 71, 116, 140). Slavko Splichal, similarly, wrote about

> a "voting public" (i.e. the body of actual voters), an "attentive public" (characterised by the interest in politics and at least occasional participation in debates on political issues), an "active public" (representing the elite of the attentive public), and "sectoral" or "special publics".
>
> (Splichal 1999, 16)

Both Mueller and Splichal, crucially, proposed approaches that worked without assuming in advance that different groups must hold particular views. This allowed the actors under observation to categorize themselves through their behaviour rather than forcing the observer to do the categorization for them. Just as hierarchical stratification works better in theory than it does in practice, however, so too functional differentiation works better in practice than in theory. If what distinguishes one actor from another is something they do rather than something they are, there is no guarantee that individuals will remain in the same category across issue areas or time periods. Neither approach always works.

At this point it makes sense to revisit the idea that the 'public' in 'public opinion' might be an adjective rather than a noun, and that the term 'public opinion' refers to opinions expressed *in* rather than *by the* public. Before survey methods came along, this was the only viable approach. Key's latent attitudes lay beyond what interested elites could observe (Noelle-Neumann 1979, 152). Public opinion was "'usually equated with riots, strikes, demonstrations, and boycotts' and more generally with the opinions of those individuals who choose to enter the public sphere to express themselves" (Hopkins and King 2007, 1; Tilly 1983, 462). There was still a public sphere before opinion polls. There were still individual citizens interested in influencing the government through the public sphere. Building on the functional differentiation approach, we can distinguish between 'active' and 'passive' individuals on the basis of whether or not they contribute to public debate: active citizens do, passive citizens do not. Doing so gets around the theoretical issues the functional approach usually involves because only one behavioural distinction matters. We are not trying to put our actors into a range of different categories; just determining whether they act publicly or not, a distinction they choose for themselves. Only those who participate in public debate really count as 'public' actors. Only they hold truly 'public' opinions.

The problems of opinion polls

Defining public opinion in these terms immediately brings our approach into conflict with the thinking underpinning the conduct of opinion polls. This is deliberate. Survey methods are not designed to gauge the attitudes of individuals who already contribute to public debate (Berinsky 1999, 1209). They are designed specifically to activate Key's latent opinions. Their greatest strength is their ability to ensure, as Verba and Converse put it, that "the wind of opinion" does not always blow "from the better parts of town" (Verba 1996, 6; Converse 1987, 14). That was Hill's fear as he warned against "the tendency to confuse a part with the whole" (Hill 1981, 57). It would indeed be an error to treat active public debate as a fair representation of the wider set of latent attitudes passive actors hold. But that is not the point. The point is to recognize that latent attitudes do not influence policymaking. They only matter once they are activated. Polling can play a democratizing role by activating the views of individuals who might not otherwise contribute. That is not, however, how it usually works. Pierre Bourdieu argued in a highly critical essay on the polling industry that "public opinion does not exist". Using survey methods to gauge the public's political views meant accepting three "implied postulates" he thought were insurmountably problematic (Bourdieu 1979, 124). Our approach to understanding public opinion builds on Bourdieu's three-part critique. It argues that polls are better understood as artefacts of active public debate rather than as objective guides to truth (Solomon 2009, 269).

To begin with, Bourdieu observed that the practice of surveying a sample of citizens to gauge the attitudes of the population as a whole works on the assumption that every individual already possesses an opinion on every possible topic. This makes sense when studying voting intentions, for example, because every citizen holds the right to vote, and individual respondents' views can be weighted in line with how likely they are in practice to exercise that right. It is more problematic when it comes to studying foreign policy. As Mueller observed, "many people simply do not *have* opinions on a number of questions" about international affairs (Mueller 1973, 2). Poll respondents instead react "on the fly" to questions placed in front of them, raising real questions about how rational poll results can possibly be. Respondents draw on reasonably coherent underlying beliefs to select among the options placed before them (Zaller and Feldman 1992, 579–580; Althaus 2004, 278). But they often hold many incommensurable beliefs, especially when the more remote issues raised by foreign policy questions are concerned (Gaubatz 1995). How an individual responds to a question depends on which of several potentially contradictory beliefs is activated at the moment of a poll. Which belief gets activated in a given context depends, for example, on how the question(s) posed prime those interviewed to respond (Achen 1975), or what the respondent happened to read in the newspaper on the morning of the poll.

Herbert Blumer's celebrated early attack on the nascent polling industry underlined the point. Polls do not *measure opinions*, instead they *aggregate responses*, and that is not the same thing (Blumer 1948, 542). Polls create many of the attitudes they ostensibly reveal, attitudes that were not just latent but nonexistent before being stimulated by the survey instrument (Peer 1992, 231). Recognizing this in turn raises questions about how politically meaningful poll results on policy matters actually are (Zaller 2003, 311). The extent to which a poll predicts voting behaviour, or estimates reactions to an issue that is likely to affect voting behaviour can still be quite important. But foreign policy rarely decides elections, and most ordinary people hardly think about it at all. There is little point estimating how the population as a whole would respond to a foreign policy question that most people would not otherwise think about. Not, that is, unless the question will actually be put to the population as a whole, for example through a referendum.

Second, Bourdieu complained that polling treats each respondent as if their views matter equally. This is, again, clearly untrue. Different individuals hold different social, political or economic roles, roles that permit them more or less influence over decision-makers, and each other. Herbert Blumer also highlighted this point. Speaking as a sociologist, Blumer argued that it made no sense to equate 'public opinion' with aggregated individual opinions. Societies do not work that way. The public sphere is a social arena where individuals interact constantly with others. They refine, develop, adopt and discard ideas through interactions with the media, co-workers, family, friends and strangers. Some join organizations, like Trade Unions or pressure groups, that promote overt political objectives. Others avoid politics entirely. Some go out and canvas. Some donate. Some keep their activism on Facebook. These individuals are not equal participants in public life. But polling treats them as if they are. In the process, it downplays the substantive importance of more influential respondents' views and elevates those who ordinarily would not participate in politics at all (Blumer 1948, 545). As Cohen put it, one of the big problems with using polls is that they reveal "most about the foreign policy opinions of the people who, overall, are least likely to participate in foreign policy discussions and activities" (Cohen 1973, 4). All poll responses may be equal, but poll respondents themselves are not.

Bourdieu argued, finally, that the polling industry fails to appreciate how its own activities create the phenomenon it claims to observe. Here the fault lies with the unthinking extension of survey methods, from predicting voting behaviour, their original purpose, to the much more ambitious objective of observing latent attitudes on a wide range of policy areas. When surveying likely voters, it is possible to align the range of choices respondents face with those they will encounter on election day. The list of parties is both fixed and known well in advance. Foreign policy does not look this way. A state's foreign policy agenda can encompass a huge range of issues, geographical locations and events. It will have several possible options open to it in each case, and more sophisticated policymakers will appreciate how choices they make in one arena can impact on others. In order to impose order on both the foreign policy field itself and the way individual citizens consider it, pollsters artificially determine what issues to ask about and limit the options available to respondents.

We have seen already how the way polling offers stimuli and collates the results misidentifies responses as opinions. Bourdieu's third complaint is more political. Polling gets presented as a neutral guide to public attitudes. In reality, it imposes elite concerns on the passive mass. Elites possess the resources required to commission survey research, and so it is elites who set the agenda for opinion polls. Most poll results accordingly reflect the concerns of politicians seeking re-election or journalists seeking headlines (Beniger 1992, 216; Herbst 1992, 223). They therefore tell us less about what 'the public' thinks and more about elite concerns. This is true even for well-designed survey methods that successfully minimize question bias. It becomes even more concerning when we consider "the ability of the poll question writer to manipulate" (Mueller 1973, 121). How a survey question frames a foreign policy issue can and will affect the responses it generates. Crucially, this means elites can ask poll questions designed to produce the results they want (Gamson and Modigliani 1989; Page and Shapiro 1992, 4–5; Cohen 1995, 53–54; Powlick and Katz 1998, 33). As an example of what this looks like in practice we can look at how British journalists commissioned and reported polls during the Iraq debate. The *Guardian* published an editorial on 11 October 2001 arguing against extending the nascent 'war on terrorism' to Baghdad, and presenting an opinion poll it paid for that showed respondents largely agreed (*Guardian* 2001). No one else was talking seriously about Iraq at this point, even within Downing Street. US and UK forces were only days into their long campaign to oust the Taliban from Afghanistan. It was not the mass public that pushed for a stand against war with Iraq in October 2001, it was the *Guardian* itself, or more specifically its editorial board, which then used an opinion poll as a signalling device to justify its stance. This is not evidence of public opposition as FPA traditionally thinks about it. It is an example of elite debate at work.

Both Blumer and Bourdieu face criticism from scholars determined to defend opinion polls. We have acknowledged already that polling has a democratizing purpose, that it ensures at least some ordinary people's attitudes are heard. It is also true that the ontological and epistemological issues raised here matter less for high-salience foreign policy issues, like wars. Much of the response to the critical approach, however, remains disappointing. Philip Converse, for example, offered an equally celebrated riposte to Blumer. But rather than engaging Blumer's critique, he instead simply argued that public opinion scholars should set aside ontological and epistemological questions and focus instead on methodological refinement. Polls measured public opinion, and public opinion was best defined as whatever polls revealed. Response bias could and should be eliminated. But there was no need to delve deeper or to address Blumer's sociological concerns (Converse 1987, 14). Much of the mainstream public opinion literature similarly answered Bourdieu by insisting public opinion must exist, since if it did not "the activity of all those who claim to explore, measure and interpret it would be a little odd" (Osborne and Rose 1999). These arguments are tautological (Splichal 1999, 90). The criticism levelled at polling is that it creates the attitudes it claims to observe, by prompting responses, setting agendas and framing issues. Pointing out that polling produces results does not prove those results reflect unobserved phenomena that actually exist.

Public opinion specialists would do well to take Blumer and Bourdieu's criticisms more seriously. They are not, however, our primary concern. As foreign policy analysts, we need to recognize that the use of opinion polls involves a number of problematic assumptions, chief among them the definition of 'public opinion' as 'the' opinion of 'the' public. We need to acknowledge that polling can potentially play a democratizing role while also questioning its capacity to do so in every circumstance. Polling can still be useful, and the following analysis makes use of opinion polls. But to use polls effectively we will need to remember what they actually do. Polls do not measure public attitudes, they construct them in line with elite debate. Polls do not observe public opinion, they contribute to the discursive exchanges among elites that constitute it. Looking at polls in isolation will not serve. We need to embed the results they produce in a wider analysis of public debate.

Understanding public influence

Of course, our ultimate goal as foreign policy analysts is not to understand what public opinion *is* but rather to consider what it *does*. Specifically, we are interested in understanding how British public opinion might have influenced the

Blair government as it prepared for war in Iraq. The FPA literature offers us a range of guidance on how the relationship between the public and policymakers operates in practice. At a basic level, a number of studies show substantive policy changes echoing corresponding shifts in poll results (Page and Shapiro 1992, 2; Shapiro and Jacobs 2000, 225; Everts and Isernia 2001, 17; Aldrich et al. 2006, 478). These results may reflect governments paying attention to public preferences, public attitudes following policy orthodoxy, or both. In Britain, for example, the Cameron government's decision to intervene against Da'esh in Iraq followed a significant drop in opposition amongst survey respondents. Da'esh publicly murdered a series of Western hostages during the summer of 2014. Poll support grew for a British response from 37 per cent in July to 57 per cent in September while opposition dropped from 36 per cent to 24 per cent (YouGov 2014). Parliament then approved British military operations. The House of Commons debate before the vote makes it clear that the shift in poll results helped win over some MPs. But parliament still restricted British action to Iraq and ruled out intervention in Syria despite the fact that the polls supported striking Da'esh in both. The government was in any event keen to do something, not least to assuage some of the embarrassment it faced when parliament vetoed intervention against the Assad regime the year before. There would probably have been a vote regardless of the polls, with the outcome dependent more on party politics than public preferences (Strong 2015).

Public attention can meanwhile raise the salience of particular issues or events for democratic governments (Hilsman 1987, 233). The more interested public actors are in a given policy area, the more likely the government is to take their concerns on board, a point that is underlined in Chapter 3 (Schuster and Maier 2006, 228; Knecht and Weatherford 2006, 705). One major reason why FPA downplayed the public's role for so long was the recognition that foreign policy is generally a low salience issue for most people. Two implications flow from this observation. First, if a majority takes no interest in a policy area, dedicated minorities can gain considerable traction, especially in multi-cultural societies like Britain (Hill 2007, 2013). Their views may or may not reflect what the population as a whole thinks, or would think if it took the issue seriously (Key 1961, 17–18, 92; Risse-Kappen 1991, 510; Everts 2000, 187). Second, and relatedly, if the public as a whole pays little attention to an issue, the government can more easily ignore even vociferous opposition (Key 1961, 21; Graham 1994, 195–196). Protests in London following the collapse of the Tamil resistance movement in Sri Lanka reflected both implications in practice. Most British people knew little or nothing about Sri Lanka's long civil war. But for the sizeable British Tamil community, the military's advance into rebel-held territory and the consequent civilian casualties raised huge concerns. Though they failed, in the end, to alter the government's policy of non-intervention, they did succeed in attracting wider attention for their cause. This sort of minority-driven public opinion can help highlight issues that should attract wider concern, though without majority support it may struggle to influence policy. At the same time, it also limits how coherent 'public opinion' is overall.

Public influence depends, in turn, on the access routes available to actors hoping to shape decision-making (Cohen 1973, 43, 1995, 53). Britain has a relatively open domestic political system and a free media. British ministers are also Members of Parliament, directly elected by and accountable to relatively manageable groups of constituents. They knew what people in the country thought about Iraq (Chan and Safran 2006, 145). FPA accounts identify a range of sources that decision-makers draw upon in gauging what the public wants. They listen to opinion polls, of course. But they pay attention also to legislators, journalists, academics, business leaders, pressure groups and personal contacts (Cohen 1973, 78, 107, 125; Herbst 1992, 228; Powlick 1995, 433–435; Entman 2004, 21). They aim to interpret the "climate of opinion", often relying on their own individual instincts, rather than expecting any one data source to do the job (Noelle-Neumann 1979, 148). Their adoption of impressionistic, discursive and intersubjective attitudes to gauging public opinion points us toward a constructivist approach.

A constructivist approach

This book puts forward a constructivist approach, both to reflect the way the Blair government actually thought about public opinion and to address some of the conceptual concerns raised in this chapter. Treating public opinion as a social construct allows us to draw on a range of different sources, echoing what policymakers do while embedding more established research practices, like opinion polling, in their proper political context. We need not assume that there is any inherent benefit to activating latent public attitudes, as survey methods do, or to relying on those already actively expressed in the public arena. This, in turn, allows us to set aside the question of whether public opinion objectively exists, and instead focus on defining the public opinion that influences policymaking as an emergent characteristic of a particular type of policy debate (Campbell 1992, 4; Hansen 2006, 10; Althaus 2004, 297). Defining public opinion as a social fact forces us to recognize the contingent circumstances under which it emerges (Adler 1997, 327). It also allows us to take account of how elites invoke public support to legitimize their own views (Brookes *et al.* 2004, 63; Solomon 2009, 269), and of the feedback loop that links polling, policymaking and public attitudes. After all, if individuals draw on a range of stimuli in responding to survey questions, it seems reasonable to assume at least some will be aware of the results of previous polls (Herbst 1993). We will accordingly highlight the role played by public debate in pre-invasion Britain both in shaping the idea of public opinion itself and in affecting how policymakers behaved. This will lead us, in Part II, to consider how both the form and the content of the debate undermined the invasion's legitimacy.

In practice adopting a constructivist approach means approaching the study of the relationship between British public opinion and the Blair government's decision to take the country to war in Iraq in terms of "how possible" rather than "why" questions, which is part of what makes this a 'constructivist' FPA approach (Doty 1993, 298). Specifically, we will consider how it was possible that Britain went to war in the face of apparently concerted public opposition, and how the balance of views expressed by different groups of public actors permitted the government to use force. Having defined public opinion itself as a social construction and emphasized the importance from an FPA perspective of viewing the domestic influences on foreign policy decisions through decision-makers' eyes, we will adopt a discursive epistemology and an "interpretivist" mindset (Bevir *et al.* 2013). Our goal will be to "understand" how the British public debate made some outcomes possible, rather than trying to "explain" the causal relationships at work (Hollis and Smith 1990). This means siding slightly more with the 'post-modernist' and critical traditions within constructivism (Campbell 1992, 4; Hansen 2006, 10) and less with the more positivist 'modernist' approach (Jepperson *et al.* 1996, 67; Finnemore and Sikkink 1998, 892; Wendt 1999, 41). We will, however, use positivist methods where appropriate, for example when answering quantifiable questions about the balance between pro-war and anti-war views. Positive observations do influence policymakers, after all – just not exclusively.

Sources

The following analysis draws on multiple empirical sources to reconstruct the pre-invasion British public debate. It thus presents what might be termed a 'holistic' approach to understanding the discourse surrounding the prospective war. Initially, in Chapter 3, it focuses on the simple question of how far the Blair government's domestic audiences approved of or rejected its approach to war with Iraq. Part II then builds on this analysis by breaking down the debate along four distinct dimensions, introduced in Chapter 4, associated with the broader question of whether removing Saddam Hussein from power was the right thing to do. Crucially, Part II highlights the feedback loop linking the discursive construction of public opinion with questions about legitimacy. It both builds on and moves beyond the discussion in Part I.

Our first set of source materials comprises public statements made by ministers and officials, especially by Prime Minister Tony Blair, from 11 September 2001 until the invasion of Iraq in March 2003, with a focus on January 2002 onwards. Unlike subsequent interviews or memoirs, contemporary statements cannot be revised with the benefit of hindsight (Laver and Garry 2000; Laver *et al.* 2003). Ministers said what they said, and we can check. At the same time, thanks partly to the Chilcot Inquiry, we can triangulate claims made publicly in 2001–2003 by drawing on contemporary government documents and later participant reflections. These additional sources allow us to see how the actors involved interpreted their engagement in public debate, as well as highlighting discrepancies between what they thought in private and what they claimed in public. As Sir John Chilcot put it when presenting his report, "the evidence is there for all to see" (Chilcot 2016). Both the report itself, and the materials published to accompany it, represent a considerable scholarly resource. Indeed, as

Glen Rangwala put it, the Chilcot Report can be understood as "the longest work of academic history ever" (Rangwala 2016).

We will discuss hundreds of newspaper comment pieces published during the Iraq debate in the leading UK newspapers of the day, namely the *Daily Mail, Daily Telegraph, Guardian, Independent, Mirror, Times, Sun* and their respective Sunday sister papers. Not only does this list cover the most-read morning daily and Sunday publications in the UK's crowded newspaper market according to the Audit Bureau of Circulations, it also encompasses the full spectrum of mainstream political views, with publications drawn from the left, right and centre ground. Given the greater space available in print compared to broadcast formats, newspaper commentary is employed here as a proxy for media debate as a whole, on the basis that it is unlikely that any arguments are featured prominently on television or radio without also appearing in print, while the converse seems more plausible (Gamson *et al.* 1992; Norris 2000, 25; Robinson 2008, 141). The digital media arena was still in its infancy during this period; although most major news organizations operated websites, there was not yet such a thing as 'social' media. Facebook, YouTube or Twitter were still years away, and blogging remained a niche pursuit. A study looking at contemporary events would have to take the digital arena far more seriously, and consider it far more centrally, than this study does. For us, traditional media should suffice.

Alongside these articles, we will look at a series of published opinion polls, as well as 333 parliamentary speeches. Opinion poll data comes from three commercial polling companies that were active in Britain during our period: ICM, YouGov and Ipsos MORI. Owing to the slightly different approach each company adopted, and in particular the different questions they asked, the data they generated was not always comparable. Where that was the case, data from each is presented separately. Helpfully, ICM asked respondents: "Would you approve or disapprove of Britain backing American military action against Iraq?" at regular intervals from the Summer of 2002 until the start of the war in early 2003 (see, for example, Travis 2003). Though this is not a neutral question – it primes those with particularly positive or negative views on US power to respond accordingly, and it downplays Britain's ability to decide its stance independently – it does at least enable us to track changes over time. Parliamentary speeches, meanwhile, are preserved in *Hansard*, the official report of debates in the House of Commons. This study focused on oral rather than written statements, on the grounds that these are more likely to reflect the actual views of the speaker rather than advisors. It also excluded statements by government ministers (though these do appear in the qualitative discussion) in order to focus solely on arguments made by MPs who were free to challenge the official line.

Method

A Lexis Nexis search covering the period from 1 January 2002 to 20 March 2003 and using the keywords "Iraq" and "Blair" (to keep the focus on policy-oriented coverage) produced an initial corpus of 4,449 potentially relevant newspaper pieces. An initial review stage identified 2,115 pieces that fit a definition of 'commentary' looking at whether the author wrote in the first person, whether they expressed a normative judgement on the necessity or desirability of war and whether the article appeared under a heading that explicitly identified it as a comment piece. A search for parliamentary debates on Iraq using Hansard's internal indexing identified 30 relevant parliamentary occasions and a total of 333 individual speeches for consideration.

Two coders analysed the resulting corpus to produce the data presented in Chapter 3. A primary coder assigned each text a value depending on the position its author took towards the prospect of Britain using force against Iraq, with pro-war texts coded "1", anti-war texts coded "–1" and neutral texts coded "0". This made generating summary statistics for different sources relatively easy, since it was possible simply to average the responses across a class of texts. A secondary coder then tested the reliability of the coding frame that was adopted by using it to code a randomly-selected sample of documents drawn from the same corpus. The coders agreed 92 per cent of the time on whether the texts analysed expressed pro-war, anti-war or neutral views. A test of inter-coder reliability using Krippendorff's widely-used 'alpha' measure (Krippendorff 2004) produced an α-score of 0.893. A content analysis frame is generally considered very highly reliable at α-score levels of 0.90 and above, highly reliable at levels of 0.80 and above and acceptable at levels of 0.66 and above (Bauer 2000, 144). These results suggest the coding framework that was used was highly (bordering on very highly) reliable.

Conclusion

Studying public opinion as a potential influence on democratic foreign policy can be complicated. The commonplace reliance on survey methods to 'measure' public attitudes raises epistemological difficulties, given the way polling actually works. Furthermore, policymakers often treat survey results as just one information source among many, listening at least as much to active contributors to public debate. Given our interest as foreign policy analysts in understanding how public views shape decision-making, it makes sense to adopt an empirical approach that echoes how decision-makers behave. That means reconstructing the broad 'climate of opinion' surrounding them at different moments, while also looking at what they said both publicly and in private to try and triangulate their views. In seeking to understand the British public debate over Iraq, we will adopt a 'holistic' approach using multiple information sources in a deliberate echo of how the Blair government worked. Initially, that will involve considering the simple balance between pro-war and anti-war arguments. In Part II we will take a more expansive approach, looking at the construction of policy legitimacy in discursive terms, and linking that back to the balance between public attitudes and policymaking. Underpinning everything will be a constructivist mindset in which social interaction and social context matter. None of this is straightforward, but it is logically coherent, consistent with the FPA literature and useful for understanding our particular case in turn.

References

Achen, Christopher. 'Mass political attitudes and the survey response.' *American Political Science Review* 69, no. 4 (1975): 1218–1231.

Adler, Emanuel. 'Seizing the middle ground: constructivism in world politics.' *European Journal of International Relations* 3, no. 3 (1997): 319–363.

Aldrich, John, Christopher Gelpi, Peter Feaver, Jason Reifler and Kristin Thomson Sharp. 'Foreign policy and the electoral connection.' *Annual Review of Political Science* 9 (2006): 477–502.

Almond, Gabriel. *The American People and Foreign Policy*. New York: Harcourt, 1950.

Althaus, Scott. *Collective Preferences in Democratic Politics: Opinion Surveys and the Will of the People*. Cambridge: Cambridge University Press, 2004.

Bauer, Martin. 'Classical content analysis.' In *Qualitative Researching with Text, Image and Sound*, by Martin Bauer and George Gaskell, 131–151. London: Sage, 2000.

Beniger, James. 'The impact of polling on public opinion: recalling Foucault, Habermas, and Bourdieu.' *International Journal of Public Opinion Research* 4, no. 3 (1992): 204–219.

Berinsky, Adam. 'The two faces of public opinion.' *American Journal of Political Science* 43, no. 4 (1999): 1209–1230.

Berinsky, Adam. 'Assuming the costs of war: events, elites and American public support for military conflict.' *Journal of Politics* 69, no. 4 (2007): 975–997.

Bevir, Mark, Oliver Daddow and Ian Hall. 'Introduction: interpreting British foreign policy.' *British Journal of Politics and International Relations* 15, no. 2 (2013): 163–174.

Blumer, Herbert. 'Public opinion and public opinion polling.' *American Sociological Review* 13, no. 5 (1948): 542–549.

Bourdieu, Pierre. 'Public opinion does not exist.' In *Communication and Class Struggle: 1. Capitalism, Imperialism*, by Armand Mattelart and Set Siegelaub, 124–130. New York: I.G. Editions, Inc, 1979.

Brookes, Rod, Justin Lewis and Karin Wahl-Jorgensen. 'The media representation of public opinion: British television news coverage of the 2001 General Election.' *Media, Culture and Society*, 2004: 63–80.

Bueno de Mesquita, Bruce, and Randolph Siverson. 'War and the survival of political leaders: a comparative study of regime types and political accountability.' *American Political Science Review* 89, no. 4 (1995): 841–855.

Campbell, David. *Writing Security: United States Foreign Policy and the Politics of Identity*. Manchester: Manchester University Press, 1992.

Chan, Steve, and William Safran. 'Public opinion as a constraint against war: democracies' responses to Operation Iraqi Freedom.' *Foreign Policy Analysis* 2, no. 2 (2006): 137–156.

Chilcot, John. 'Statement by Sir John Chilcot.' 6 July 2016. www.iraqinquiry.org.uk/media/247010/2016-09-06-sir-john-chilcots-public-statement.pdf (accessed 15 July 2016).

Cohen, Bernard. *The Public's Impact on Foreign Policy*. Boston: Little, Brown and Co., 1973.

Cohen, Bernard. *Democracies and Foreign Policy: Public Participation in the United States and the Netherlands*. Madison, WI: University of Wisconsin Press, 1995.

Converse, Philip. 'The nature of belief systems in mass publics.' In *Ideology and Discontent*, by David Apter, 206–261. New York: Free Press, 1964.

Converse, Philip. 'Changing conceptions of public opinion in the political process.' *Public Opinion Quarterly* 51, no. 2 (1987): 12–24.

Doty, Roxanne. 'Foreign policy as social construction: a post-positivist analysis of US counterinsurgency policy in the Philippines.' *International Studies Quarterly* 37, no. 3 (1993): 297–320.

Eichenberg, Richard. 'Victory has many friends: US public opinion and the use of military force 1981–2005.' *International Security* 30, no. 1 (2005): 140–177.

Entman, Robert. *Projections of Power: Framing News, Public Opinion, and US Foreign Policy*. Chicago: University of Chicago Press, 2004.

Everts, Philip. 'Public opinion after the Cold War: a paradigm shift.' In *Decision Making in a Glass House: Mass Media, Public Opinion, and American and European Foreign Policy in the 21st Century*, by Brigitte Nacos, Robert Shapiro and Pierangelo Isernia, 177–194. Lanham, Maryland: Rowman & Littlefield, 2000.

Everts, Philip, and Pierangelo Isernia. *Public Opinion and the International Use of Force*. New York: Routledge, 2001.

Finnemore, Martha, and Kathryn Sikkink. 'International norm dynamics and political change.' *International Organization* 52, no. 4 (1998): 887–917.

Foyle, Douglas. 'Public opinion and foreign policy: elite beliefs as a mediating variable.' *International Studies Quarterly* 41, no. 1 (1997): 141–169.

Gamson, William, and Andre Modigliani. 'Media discourse and public opinion on nuclear power: a constructionist approach.' *The American Journal of Sociology* 95, no. 1 (1989): 1–37.

Gamson, William, David Croteau, William Hoynes and Theodore Sasson. 'Media images and the social construction of reality.' *Annual Review of Sociology* 18 (1992): 373–393.

Gaubatz, Kurt. 'Intervention and intransitivity: public opinion, social choice, and the use of military force abroad.' *World Politics* 47, no. 4 (1995): 534–554.

Gelpi, Christopher, 'Iraq the vote: retrospective and prospective judgements on candidate choice and casualty tolerance.' *Political Behaviour* 29 (2007): 151–174.

Gelpi, Christopher, Peter Feaver and Jason Reifler. 'Success matters: casualty sensitivity and the war in Iraq.' *International Security* 30, no. 3 (2005): 7–46.

Graham, Thomas. 'Public opinion and US foreign policy decision making.' In *The New Politics of American Foreign Policy*, by David Deese, 190–215. New York: St Martin's Press, 1994.

Guardian. 'Leading article', 10 October 2001.

Hagan, J. *Political Opposition and Foreign Policy in Comparative Perspective*. London: Rienner, 1990.

Hansen, Lene. *Security as Practice: Discourse Analysis and the Bosnian War*. Abingdon: Routledge, 2006.

Herbst, Susan. 'Surveys in the public sphere: applying Bourdieu's critique of opinion polls.' *International Journal of Public Opinion Research* 4, no. 3 (1992): 220–229.

Herbst, Susan. *Numbered Voices: How Opinion Polling Has Shaped American Politics*. Chicago, IL: University of Chicago Press, 1993.

Hill, Christopher. 'Public opinion and British foreign policy since 1945: research in progress?' *Millennium: Journal of International Studies* 10, no. 1 (1981): 53–62.

Hill, Christopher. 'Bringing war home: foreign policy making in multicultural societies.' *International Relations* 21, no. 3 (2007): 259–283.

Hill, Christopher. *The National Interest in Question: Foreign Policy in Multicultural Societies*. Oxford: Oxford University Press, 2013.

Hilsman, Roger. *The Politics of Policymaking in Defense and Foreign Affairs: Conceptual Models and Bureaucratic Politics*. Englewood Cliffs: Prentice-Hall, 1987.

Hollis, Martin, and Steve Smith. *Explaining and Understanding International Relations.* Oxford: Oxford University Press, 1990.

Holsti, Ole. 'Public opinion and foreign policy: challenges to the Almond-Lippmann Consensus.' *International Studies Quarterly* 36, no. 4 (1992): 439–466.

Holsti, Ole. *Public Opinion and American Foreign Policy.* Ann Arbor: University of Michigan Press, 1996.

Hopkins, Daniel, and Gary King. 'Extracting systematic social science meaning from a text.' *Unpublished Manuscript*, 2007.

Houghton, David Patrick. 'Reinvigorating the study of foreign policy decision making: toward a constructivist approach.' *Foreign Policy Analysis* 3, no. 1 (2007): 24–45.

Hurwitz, Jon, and Mark Peffley. 'How are foreign policy attitudes structured? A hierarchical model.' *American Political Science Review* 81, no. 4 (1987): 1099–1120.

Isernia, Pierangelo, Zoltan Juhasz and Hans Rattinger. 'Foreign policy and the rational public in comparative perspective.' *The Journal of Conflict Resolution* 46, no. 2 (2002): 201–224.

Jacobsen, John. 'Why do states bother to deceive? Managing trust at home and abroad.' *Review of International Studies* 34 (2008): 337–361.

Jepperson, Ronald, Alexander Wendt and Peter Katzenstein. 'Norms, identity, and culture in national security.' In *The Culture of National Security: Norms and Identity in World Politics*, by Peter Katzenstein, 33–75. New York, NY: Columbia University Press, 1996.

Key, Vladimer. *Public Opinion and American Democracy.* New York: Knopf, 1961.

Klarevas, Louis. 'The "essential domino" of military operations: American public opinion and the use of force.' *International Studies Perspectives* 3 (2002): 417–437.

Klarevas, Louis. 'Correspondence: casualties, polls, and the Iraq War.' *International Security* 31, no. 2 (2006): 186–198.

Knecht, Thomas, and Stephen Weatherford. 'Public opinion and foreign policy: the stages of presidential decision making.' *International Studies Quarterly* 50 (2006): 705–727.

Krippendorff, Klaus. 'Reliability in content analysis: some common misconceptions and recommendations.' *Human Communication Research* 30, no. 3 (2004): 411–433.

Laver, Michael, and John Garry. 'Estimating policy positions from political texts.' *American Journal of Political Science* 44, no. 3 (2000): 619–634.

Laver, Michael, Kenneth Benoit and John Garry. 'Extracting policy positions from political texts using words as data.' *American Political Science Review* 97, no. 2 (2003): 311–331.

Lippmann, Walter. *Public Opinion.* New York: Harcourt, Brace and Co., 1922.

Mueller, John. *War, Presidents and Public Opinion.* New York: Wiley, 1973.

Nincic, Miroslav. *Democracy and Foreign Policy: The Fallacy of Political Realism.* New York: Columbia University Press, 1992.

Noelle-Neumann, Elizabeth. 'Public opinion and the classical tradition: a re-evaluation.' *Public Opinion Quarterly* 43, no. 2 (1979): 143–156.

Norris, Pippa. *A Virtuous Circle: Political Communications in Postindustrial Societies.* Cambridge: Cambridge University Press, 2000.

Osborne, Thomas, and Nikolas Rose. 'Do the social sciences create phenomena? The example of public opinion research.' *British Journal of Sociology* 50, no. 3 (1999): 367–396.

Page, Benjamin, and Robert Shapiro. *The Rational Public: Fifty Years of Trends in Americans' Policy Preferences.* Chicago: University of Chicago Press, 1992.

Partell, Peter. 'Executive constraints and success in international crises.' *Political Research Quarterly* 50, no. 3 (1997): 503–528.

Peer, Limor. 'The practice of opinion polling as a disciplinary mechanism: a Foucauldian perspective.' *International Journal of Public Opinion Research* 4, no. 3 (1992): 230–242.

Powlick, Philip. 'The sources of public opinion for American foreign policy officials.' *International Studies Quarterly* 39, no. 4 (1995): 427–451.

Powlick, Philip, and Andrew Katz. 'Defining the American public opinion/foreign policy nexus.' *Mershon International Studies Review* 42, no. 1 (1998): 29–61.

Rangwala, Glen. 'An epic treatise on the folly of war.' *Times Higher Education*, 21 July 2016.

Risse-Kappen, Thomas. 'Public opinion, domestic structure, and foreign policy in Liberal democracies.' *World Politics* 43, no. 4 (1991): 479–512.

Robinson, Piers. 'The role of media and public opinion.' In *Foreign Policy: Theories, Actors, Cases*, by Steve Smith, Amelia Hadfield and Tim Dunne, 137–154 Oxford: Oxford University Press, 2008.

Rosenau, James. *Public Opinion and Foreign Policy: An Operational Formulation.* New York: Random House, 1961.

Schuster, Jurgen, and Herbert Maier. 'The rift: explaining Europe's divergent Iraq policies in the run-up of the American-led war on Iraq.' *Foreign Policy Analysis* 2, no. 3 (2006): 223–244.

Shapiro, Robert, and Lawrence Jacobs. 'Who leads and who follows? US presidents, public opinion, and foreign policy.' In *Decision Making in a Glass House: Mass Media, Public Opinion, and American and European Foreign Policy in the 21st Century*, by Brigitte Nacos, Robert Shapiro and Pierangelo Isernia, 223–245. Lanham. Maryland: Rowman & Littlefield, 2000.

Sobel, Richard. *The Impact of Public Opinion on US Foreign Policy Since Vietnam: Constraining the Colossus.* New York: Oxford University Press, 2001.

Solomon, Ty. 'Social logics and normalisation in the War on Terror.' *Millennium: Journal of International Studies* 38, no. 2 (2009): 269–294.

Splichal, Slavko. *Public Opinion: Developments and Controversies in the Twentieth Century.* Oxford: Rowman & Littlefield, 1999.

Strong, James. 'Interpreting the Syria vote: Parliament and British foreign policy.' *International Affairs* 91, no. 5 (2015): 1123–1139.

Tilly, Charles. 'Speaking your mind without elections, surveys or social movements.' *Public Opinion Quarterly* 47, no. 4 (1983): 461–478.

Verba, Sidney. 'The citizen as respondent: sample surveys and American democracy.' *American Political Science Review* 90, no. 1 (1996): 1–7.

Verba, Sidney, Richard Brody, Edwin Parker, Norman Nle, Nelson Polsby, Paul Ekman and Gordon Black. 'Public opinion and the war in Vietnam.' *American Political Science Review* 61, no. 2 (1967): 317–333.

Wendt, Alexander. *Social Theory of International Politics.* Cambridge: Cambridge University Press, 1999.

YouGov. 'ISIS: how a majority came to favour air strikes.' *YouGov.* 26 September 2014. https://yougov.co.uk/news/2014/09/26/isis-how-majority-came-favour-air-strikes/ (accessed 15 December 2015).

Zaller, John. 'Coming to grips with V.O. Key's concept of latent opinion.' In *Electoral Democracy*, by Michael MacKuen and George Rabinowitz, 311–336. Ann Arbor, MI: University of Michigan Press, 2003.

Zaller, John, and Stanley Feldman. 'A simple theory of the survey response: answering questions versus revealing preferences.' *American Journal of Political Science* 36, no. 3 (1992): 579–616.

3   The Iraq debate: an overview

Even deep, angry public opposition failed to keep Britain from war in Iraq. This chapter discusses how the way that the pre-invasion debate played out made this outcome possible. Employing the holistic methods introduced in Chapter 2, it sets poll results alongside a quantitative content analysis of press and parliamentary debate to chart the rise and fall of pro-war and anti-war views. At the same time, it considers how the ebbs and flows of public debate, the balance of power amongst MPs and in the media, and the Blair government's attitude to public criticism facilitated what followed.

Three key points stand out. First, though the British public consistently opposed the use of force against Iraq, the polls, the press and parliament all rallied round the flag once the invasion became inevitable. Ministers justified ignoring public opposition by predicting exactly this result. It fit New Labour's broader philosophy, and it worked. Second, within a predominately hostile public sphere lurked pivotal pockets of support. Chief among them were Rupert Murdoch's powerful media empire and the Conservative opposition. Retaining the backing of the *Sun* newspaper made a big difference. Not only was it Britain's top-selling daily newspaper, and widely considered an influential factor in bringing the Blair government to power, it was also an aggressive participant in active public debate. With a potential Conservative challenge neutralized, meanwhile, ministers enjoyed a cushion against Labour Party rebellions in the House of Commons and protection against electoral backlash – though as Chapter 9 discusses, that protection was imperfect. Third, the government's strategy of responding to spikes in public opposition by stepping up its communications largely proved effective. Tony Blair's public statements during his visit to President Bush in April 2002, the release of the WMD 'dossier' in September and the 'moral turn' and 'masochism strategy' of early 2003 changed few minds. They did, however, allow the government to influence the agenda of public debate. Crucially, well-timed official interventions lowered Iraq's salience as a political issue, at least during 2002. That did not change the direction of public beliefs, but it did reduce their intensity, buying time for policymaking to go on. To satisfy media critics, in particular, ministers often only had to say something, anything, reportable. Substituting official comment for speculation cooled tempers and left opponents less to argue about. This observation helps us understand how it was still possible for

Britain to wind up fighting in Iraq despite extensive public antipathy. It also points towards how public debate shaped the invasion's legitimacy, which is considered in Part II.

Rallying 'round the flag

The Blair government took public opinion seriously. Tony Blair repeatedly referred to hostile poll results in his private missives to President Bush (Chilcot 2016d, 290, 559). Downing Street commissioned regular surveys and a focus group from Labour Party polling guru Philip Gould, who briefed the Prime Minister and his inner circle personally (Campbell and Stott 2007, 610). In line with the conceptual points set out in Chapter 2, however, key figures remained sceptical about linking poll results to policy too directly. Chief of Staff Jonathan Powell believed that "a wise leader should use quantitative polling as a tool but not as a substitute for his own political instincts" (Powell 2010, 136–137). Blair himself thought polls were useful, but also limited. He wrote that they could offer "an instant snapshot of public opinion (i.e. real, but superficial and therefore potentially transient)", or that they could "indicate a trend (i.e. potentially of lasting significance)". The problem was "you never know which it is" (Blair 2010, 298). Downing Street listened to polls. But Blair and his advisors reserved the right to decide how best to respond. That was significant. John Zaller pointed out that "when a politician believes that he knows better than the public what means will lead to desired ends, he will ignore the polls and follow his own beliefs" (Zaller 2003, 313). Elisabeth Noelle-Neumann agreed, noting that the "strong and successful politician is characterised by the conviction that whenever he encounters an opposing public opinion he will be able to overcome the trend" (Noelle-Neumann 1979, 155). In Douglas Foyle's terms, Blair was an "executor"; he considered public support for military action in Iraq desirable, but not necessary (Foyle 1997, 145). He was willing to work to win people over, noting to Powell in early 2002 that "the persuasion job on this seems very tough" (Blair 2002b). He believed he would win the argument, telling Cabinet on 13 February 2003 that the polls would "shift before we got to the point of military action", and President Bush on 19 February that public opinion could still be persuaded that using force was the right thing to do (Chilcot 2016d, 239, 290). Ultimately, though, he told journalists that regardless of contemporary attitudes, "history would be his judge" (Ashley 2003). He expressed similar reviews in responding to the Chilcot Report (Blair 2016).

Waging war on terrorism

Blair had some grounds for this faith. Britain is not a pacifist country. Public opinion strongly supported the first stage of the 'war on terrorism' in late 2001. Blair pledged to stand "shoulder to shoulder with our American friends" in the immediate aftermath of the 11 September attacks (Blair 2001a). Survey results showed that most respondents approved. Figure 3.1 shows strong opinion poll

The Iraq debate: an overview 35

support for British involvement in military action against the terrorist threat. On average, 67.9 per cent of those questioned backed the use of force in Afghanistan from the first completed polls on 14 September until the fall of Kabul in late November. Just 20.5 per cent, on average, opposed Britain playing a part.

Even at this stage, however, there were signs of trouble to come. The brief dip visible in Figure 3.1 reflects an ICM poll that was completed on 16 September, which made no direct reference to terrorism when asking about support for military action in Afghanistan. Changing the stimulus changed the response, as the conceptual points made in Chapter 2 predicted. Specifically, this finding suggests that around 10 per cent of respondents supported the use of force on the basis that it was directed against the perpetrators of the 11 September attacks. Since no one in Britain believed (and no one in the Blair government claimed) that Iraq was behind 11 September, that suggested winning support for an attack on Baghdad would be more problematic.

More critically, there is no sign in Figure 3.1 of a "rally round the flag" effect around the commencement of military action on the night of 7 October. In theory, public support for a given use of force should spike upwards once troops actually go into combat (Mueller 1970; Baker and Oneal 2001). This apparently did not happen in Britain at the start of the Afghan conflict. In fact, the first poll of British attitudes conducted after airstrikes commenced on the night of 7 October (an Ipsos MORI survey) and published two days later on 9 October,

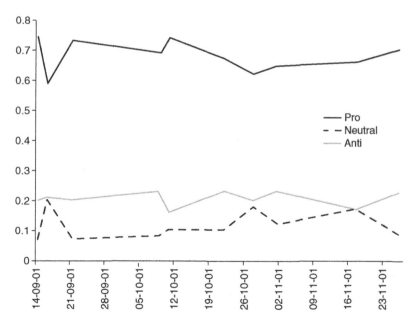

Figure 3.1 Aggregate UK opinion poll data on the prospect of British military action in response to the 11 September attacks.

Source: ICM/Ipsos MORI.

36 *Public opinion*

reported a small drop in public support compared to the position in late September, though this was reversed by 11 October. As Matt Baum rightly points out, we are far less likely to see a rally effect at the start of conflicts that are already popular. There will always be some share of an electorate unwilling to contemplate military action under any circumstances. If public support is high before the fighting starts, it has nowhere to go (Baum 2002). So, the relative absence of a rally at the start of the Afghan conflict might simply reflect the fact that most of the country supported the decision before the fighting began.

There appears to be more to this missing rally effect, however. As Figure 3.2 shows, there was a sizeable rally at the start of the war in Iraq. Between 16 and 23 March ICM found public support for the invasion jumped from 38 per cent to 54 per cent. This was a qualitatively significant shift, giving the pro-war camp a majority for the first time in the pre-war period, and at a pivotal juncture to boot. In line with Baum's expectation, the relatively low levels of public support before the fighting started left plenty of room for poll results to spike in the government's favour. Yet the absolute numbers involved are clearly much less favourable than what Figure 3.1 shows at the start of the Afghan conflict. Even after their March 2003 rally, poll results showed support for war in Iraq 20 percentage points lower than they did for action in Afghanistan in October 2001. On the one hand, the Blair government was somewhat vindicated in its faith that the public would eventually support the use of force against Saddam Hussein.

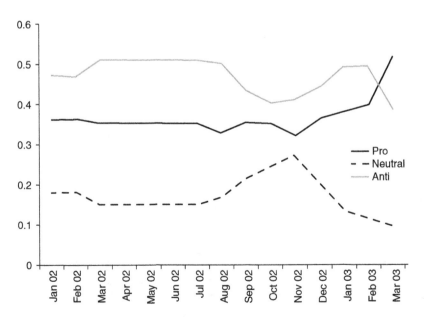

Figure 3.2 Aggregate UK opinion poll data on the prospect of British military action in Iraq, January 2002–March 2003.

Source: ICM/YouGov.

By the morning of the 18 March parliamentary debate it was able to point to polls moving in its favour. On the other, this support was far from wholehearted, or robust.

Historically, British opinion polls have shown the most significant rally effects (as well as higher support overall) at the start of conflicts most respondents considered necessary acts of self-defence (Lai and Reiter 2005, 268). Contrasting Figure 3.1 and Figure 3.2 allows us to suggest that the British people regarded the invasion of Afghanistan as a direct response to a threat and the invasion of Iraq as a discretionary act. Blair himself unwittingly pointed out the difference. In a speech to the Trades Union Congress just before the anniversary of the 11 September attacks, Blair pointed out that public support for war in Afghanistan would have been close to zero on 10 September 2001, whereas a week later it was over 70 per cent (Blair 2002g). There was, in other words, a substantial rally effect at the start of the earlier conflict. It was just that most people thought the Afghan war started on 11 September rather than 7 October 2001, which in turn implied it was a war of self-defence. Several commentators noted at the time of the Afghan invasion that the government benefitted from these beliefs. Ben MacIntyre, for example, acknowledged in *The Times* on 9 October that the "war [in Afghanistan] began on 11 September" (MacIntyre 2001). Stephen Glover of the *Daily Mail* opposed action in Afghanistan, but nevertheless conceded that "the allies have right on their side after the atrocities of September 11" (Glover 2001). Very few people in Britain felt that way about Iraq.

Hostile poll results failed to change the Blair government's course, in sum, because ministers believed the public would rally when the fighting actually started, and because this belief proved correct. Challenges remained, from an FPA perspective. Chief among them was the difference between what British polls showed and what surveys conducted in the United States suggested, differences that made it hard for the two allies to work effectively together. The Blair government was well aware of the issue. Britain's embassy in Washington regularly updated London on the situation across the Atlantic, as the Chilcot Report recounts. A poll for the *Washington Post* in November 2001 found 78 per cent of respondents favoured invading Iraq. By March 2002 that figure was up to 88 per cent, though support dropped when the question posed referred directly to US ground troops. In October, US public approval of military action hovered around 60 per cent, with wide variations between polls depending on whether the questions asked envisaged the US securing UN and allied support. These figures held steady into early 2003 (Chilcot 2016b, 350, 481, 2016c, 253, 2016d, 196). Differences between US and UK poll results continued to cause problems after the invasion. One study found that "15–30 percent of the [US] public thought during the period from May 2003 to April 2004 that Iraqi weapons of mass destruction had actually been found" (Everts and Isernia 2005, 266). No one believed that in Britain. Given it proved impossible for the British government to insulate domestic public debate from statements made by the Bush administration, this made its task all the more difficult (Strong 2017).

Phase Two

Britain's Iraq debate began on 11 October 2001 with the *Guardian*'s publication of poll results showing just 36 per cent of respondents agreed that the 'war on terrorism' should be extended to Baghdad. The survey, conducted by ICM, found that 47 per cent disagreed with the idea that the conflict needed a 'phase two' (*Guardian* 2001a). To an extent, the government was simply not ready to answer questions about Iraq yet. In early December, Blair wrote to President Bush about the prospects for "regime change" in Iraq, noting "we just don't need it debated too freely in public until we know what exactly we want to do" (Blair 2001b). He knew the public would not support removing Saddam Hussein as readily as they backed action against the Taliban. One editorial in an otherwise fairly pro-war newspaper warned Blair that "a return to that theatre of war would divide his party, his country and his allies abroad ... it would be the biggest decision that any British prime minister had been called upon to make in living memory" (*The Times* 2001a). Given what the poll results reported in Figure 3.2 showed, this was a reasonable assessment. Though there were moments when elite participants in public debate suggested the mood might be changing, in reality, the polls remained stubbornly consistent.

President Bush's decision in September 2002 to act through the United Nations seemed to help. As one television report put it, "diplomacy" was "being given one more chance" (ITV News 2002). This was not just important to ensuring the invasion's legitimacy, it was also useful politically. Releasing the WMD 'dossier' also appeared to make a difference. On 17 September, the *Guardian* reported that public opposition was falling. It described the shift as "a vindication of the prime minister's belief that the gap in the polls would close once the public began to focus on the debate over Iraq's capability to wage nuclear and chemical warfare" (Travis and White 2002). We can indeed see a drop in opposition at this time in the data reported in Figure 3.2. Crucially, however, this decline did not translate into an increase in support, and a plurality of respondents remained opposed to war. In early 2003 *The Times* reported that most poll respondents believed military action might be necessary, but also that the alternatives were not yet exhausted (*The Times* 2003a). That was essentially why the initial support the government enjoyed at the time of the invasion did not ultimately hold up.

Pockets of support

It was clear already during the Afghan debate that British public opinion would divide into pro-war and anti-war camps if given the chance. Several critics complained that the positive poll results reported in Figure 3.1 failed to capture underlying scepticism (*Mirror* 2001a; Dalyell 2001, col. 632). Some sought to shift the goalposts; it was true, for example, that ministers lacked a "full consensus" domestically for their policy (O'Hagan 2001), though that is the case for pretty much everything that any government does. Anti-war columnists attacked the "conservative press" (primarily meaning the *Sun*) for the "irresponsible distortion of public opinion" because it suggested that the British people supported removing the Taliban (*Independent* 2001). These complaints ignored the fact that this is exactly what the polls showed. Indeed, commentators on both sides of the argument sought to discredit poll results that did not fit their preconceived views about public opinion (*The Times* 2001b). Seeking 'better' estimates, they focused on personal contacts (Osborne 2001, col. 874, *Daily Telegraph* 2001b) or response methods such as the letters written to editorial pages (*Daily Telegraph* 2001a). Similar arguments arose repeatedly during the Iraq debate. It was no accident that pro-war publications commissioned opinion polls far less often than their anti-war counterparts. Poll results rarely reinforced the arguments they sought to make.

A wide coalition of journalists and parliamentarians supported the invasion of Afghanistan. Conservative Party spokesmen complained only that the nascent 'war on terrorism' did not go far enough (Duncan Smith 2001, col. 815). Liberal Democrat MPs broadly agreed with the strategy, though they did raise questions about its implementation (Kennedy 2001, col. 817). At this stage, the most vocal opponents of the use of force, Labour backbench MPs George Galloway and Tam Dalyell, were dismissed as "the usual suspects" (Riddell 2001). Robin Cook, then still in the Cabinet, observed that many of those "who would normally have reservations about military action are also those who are most respectful of international cooperation". Given the breadth of the coalition assembled in the aftermath of 11 September, "they found it impossible flatly to resist military action" (Cook 2003, 45–46).

Press commentary

The government benefitted from this unity. It benefitted, furthermore, from the way its supporters took upon themselves the task of policing public debate. Several powerful media voices backed a forceful response to 11 September. Indeed, Alastair Campbell told the Chilcot Inquiry that at one stage, late in the Iraq debate, Rupert Murdoch personally lobbied Tony Blair to hold firm in his support for war (Chilcot 2016d, 446). Murdoch's chief UK newspaper, the *Sun*, proved especially vocal in its treatment of those who dared speak out against war. During late 2001 it attacked the "Anti-American, anti-Tony Blair press", describing critics of the use of force as "traitors", "fools", "wobblers" and appeasers. The *Observer, Independent, Mirror*, and prominent *Mirror* columnist John Pilger received special recognition. At one stage the *Sun* even included Conservative defence spokesman, Bernard Jenkin on a list of "wobblers", apparently because he suggested trying to minimize civilian casualties (*Sun* 2001). This was not just a tabloid phenomenon, nor one specific to NewsCorp. The *Daily Telegraph* complained in similar terms about

> inveterate anti-Americans, pacifists, alarmists who think we are all about to be killed by Anthrax, Muslim fundamentalists, anti-Semites, Continental

European adventurers, and broadcasters, like the BBC, whose sense of self-worth comes chiefly from lacerating the society which pays their wages.

(*Daily Telegraph* 2001c)

The anti-war *Mirror* tried to hit back, calling the *Sun* "an offensive, racist, sexist, misogynistic, tawdry, lying little rag" and "a *Pravda*-like government propaganda sheet" (*Mirror* 2001b). But there had already been a chilling effect (Robinson et al. 2009, 537). Few people wanted to be labelled "traitors" in a newspaper read by more British people than any other (*Sun* 2002).

Despite this pressure, the Iraq War still produced a range of views. Stark variations emerged in the positions adopted by different publications and political parties.

As Figure 3.3 shows, the print media were divided along broadly partisan lines, with the more right-leaning publications supporting the use of force and the more left-leaning speaking out against it. Two top-selling tabloids dominate the extremes of the distribution, with the right-wing *Sun* backing military action and the left-wing *Mirror* opposing it. Alongside the *Sun* at the pro-war end of the spectrum lie *The Times*, its broadsheet sister, as well as the traditionally conservative and pro-military *Telegraph*. At the other end of the spectrum we find the left-wing *Guardian* and *Independent* but also the more right-wing *Daily Mail*, which adopted an isolationist stance. Although its editorial board ultimately supported the war, the *Observer* published more anti-war than pro-war commentary, hence its position on the left-hand side of this chart. Crucially,

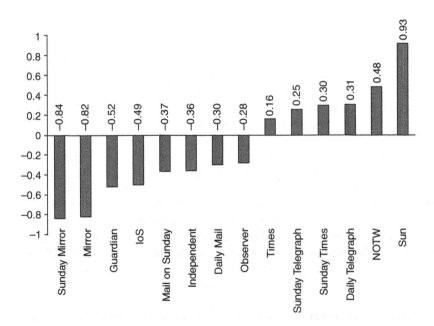

Figure 3.3 Distribution of views expressed in newspaper commentary, by publication.

these publications were not equally powerful. On a typical day during this period the *Sun* sold 15 times as many copies as the *Independent*, nine times as many as the *Guardian* and 1.7 times as many as the *Mirror*. Publications identified as predominantly pro-war during this period sold an average of 1.88 million copies of each edition, compared to anti-war publications which managed an average of 1.24 million copies. Our discussion of summary statistics below takes account of this fact by weighting each publication's contribution to the overall balance between pro-war and anti-war views to reflect their relative share of the newspaper market in any given month. Though a clear majority of newspapers *published* more anti-war than pro-war commentary, the picture looks more finely balanced once we consider the views *circulated*. Governments lacking majority approval can still prosper provided they retain pivotal backing of this sort.

Parliamentary debate

Conservative Party support also helped insulate the government against punishment for its Iraq stance. The interaction between domestic political structures and foreign policy views serves as an important intervening variable limiting how far public opposition influences decision-makers' behaviour (Risse-Kappen 1991, 479–480, 1994, 238; Shapiro and Jacobs 2000, 228; Schuster and Maier 2006, 223). As Key pointed out, "the ultimate weapon of public opinion is the minority party" (Key 1961, 556). Voters who disagree profoundly with a government's approach to foreign policy can elect its rivals instead. In competitive political systems, rational opposition leaders should seek to capitalize on any evidence of public dissatisfaction (Ramsay 2004, 460). There should be alternative electoral options for disgruntled citizens. Conversely, however, where opposition actors are too weak to put up a credible challenge, or where they agree with the government's stance, policymakers find themselves insulated from opposition (Sobel 2001, 23–24; Kreps 2010, 199). The Iraq debate took place at a time when Labour dominated British politics, holding nearly two thirds of the House of Commons' 659 seats. This protected the Party from any Iraq-related electoral backlash.

Figure 3.4 shows the distribution of views between MPs of different political parties during the course of parliamentary debates on Iraq. The fact that Conservative MPs supported the Iraq War more wholeheartedly than even the government's own backbenchers offered ministers additional protection, even if it raised questions about internal party management. Slightly over half of the 152 speeches by Labour MPs coded in the course of this project expressed anti-war views. The remainder split fairly evenly between support for the invasion and neutrality. Only the Liberal Democrats consistently refused to back the use of force. None of the 51 Liberal Democrat speeches studied offered the government support. To an extent this is to be expected. Some Labour MPs adopted what the *Guardian* columnist Polly Toynbee described as the "hard liberal", pro-intervention position (Toynbee 2001). Ann Clywd, a long-time campaigner on behalf of the Iraqi Kurds, was a prominent example. Some simply sided with their leader, either trusting his judgment or seeking to further their own careers.

42 *Public opinion*

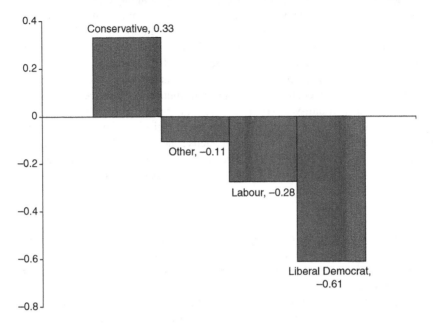

Figure 3.4 Distribution of net average views expressed in parliamentary speeches, by party.

It was easier for the Liberal Democrats, none of whom would find themselves accused of disloyalty for opposing war.

Overview

Figure 3.5, finally, highlights how press, parliament and polls all predominantly showed that Britain opposed the prospect of war in Iraq. There were moments where support outweighed opposition, especially in the press, which saw spikes of support in February, July and November 2002 in addition to joining the March 2003 rally effect discussed above. Most of those who participated in public debate, however, spoke against the use of force. Blair's accurate prediction that the public would rally to support the war when the time came helped his government overcome the opposition ranged against it. The fact these headline figures disguise critical pockets of support, including the powerful Murdoch press and the Conservative Party, helped even more.

The rest of this chapter underlines a further point. The salience of the Iraq issue rose and fell at different stages of the debate. Often a surge in public interest coincided with a spike in anti-war views, while the apparently pro-war periods visible in Figure 3.5 occurred during lulls in public debate. The government responded to these anti-war surges with a series of communications initiatives, and these largely worked. Though they changed few minds, they answered calls for information,

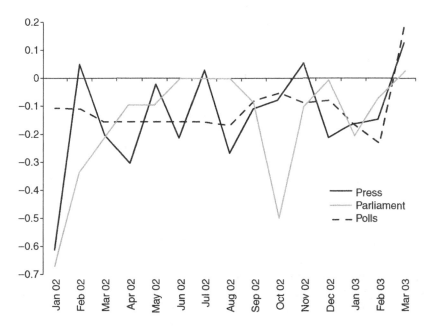

Figure 3.5 Raw average monthly press, parliamentary and poll positions on the prospect of war in Iraq (1 = entirely pro-war, −1 = entirely anti-war).

calmed speculation and quieted critics for several months. Ultimately this bought time for ministers to make key decisions away from the public glare. By the time public opinion really mattered, the decision was made and the rally effect begun.

Salience and communication

The holistic approach allows us to consider how the salience of an issue varies over time. This is possible with polls alone, but it is also problematic given that foreign policy usually does not matter to most people and the act of asking about it likely raises its significance for respondents. Salience matters for two reasons. It matters first because it indicates how likely an issue is to affect voter behaviour in subsequent elections. Since the assumption in the FPA literature is that leaders will listen to public opposition to the degree they think it likely to affect their re-election prospects, there is a qualitative difference between what the public thinks about a low-salience issue compared to what it thinks about a high-salience issue. As Key put it, "a government sensitive to public attitudes confronts a different problem when 90 percent of the people are for and 10 percent against a proposition than when the division is 50:50", or indeed where "15 percent are pro, 10 percent are anti, and 75 percent are unaware of the question" (Key 1961, 21). Salience matters second because it indicates how loudly public actors expressed their views during different phases of the debate. Bernard Cohen for example found some

44 Public opinion

evidence that public protests exert more influence on policymakers the larger they are (Cohen 1995, 62–63). In our case, it helps us highlight how widely the volume of the Iraq debate varied at different times.

Table 3.1 presents data showing the relative salience of the prospect of military action in Iraq across press, parliamentary and poll sources during the 15 months leading up to the invasion of Iraq. The press and parliamentary data reflect the actual number of sources identified during this project's source selection phase. The poll data comes from Ipsos MORI's monthly political issue polls, and reflects the proportion of respondents who identified defence, foreign affairs or international terrorism as the most important issue facing the country.

Figure 3.6 meanwhile presents summary statistics showing the combined average monthly share of total press, parliamentary and poll interest in Iraq across the pre-war period. The figures of 0.05 for March and April 2002, for example, indicates that on average 5 per cent of the total poll, press and parliamentary interest in Iraq identified by this study arose in each of those two months. Figure 3.6 reveals three distinct salience spikes between January 2002 and March 2003. Each related to a significant moment in the developing public debate. When we interact these salience measures with the data on the public positions adopted by different actors presented in the previous section, we can see more clearly what these spikes meant. Figure 3.7 reproduces the data

Table 3.1 Salience measures

Month	Press n[†]	Propn.	Parliament n[†]	Propn.	Polls n[‡]	Propn.	Average
Jan-02	11	0.01	3	0.01	6	0.02	0.01
Feb-02	34	0.02	6	0.02	3	0.01	0.01
Mar-02	136	0.06	23	0.07	7	0.02	0.05
Apr-02	90	0.04	31	0.09	8	0.03	0.05
May-02	31	0.01	0	–	4	0.01	0.01
June-02	14	0.01	2	0.01	5	0.02	0.01
July-02	72	0.03	2	0.01	5	0.02	0.02
Aug-02	107	0.05	0	–	5*	0.02	0.02
Sep-02	302	0.14	54	0.16	23	0.08	0.13
Oct-02	97	0.05	16	0.05	23	0.08	0.06
Nov-02	49	0.02	29	0.09	23*	0.08	0.06
Dec-02	61	0.03	2	0.01	20	0.07	0.03
Jan-03	200	0.09	44	0.13	48	0.17	0.13
Feb-03	444	0.21	40	0.12	55	0.19	0.17
Mar-03	467	0.22	81	0.24	54	0.19	0.22
Total	2,115		333				

Notes
[†] Actual number of texts identified by source selection process.
[‡] Proportion of respondents to Ipsos MORI political issue polls identifying "Defence/Foreign Affairs/International Terrorism" as the most important issue facing the country.
* No data. Extrapolated from previous month.

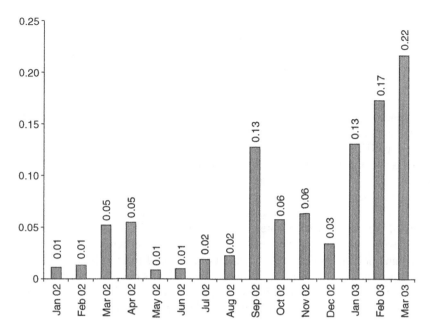

Figure 3.6 Average salience of Iraq War across parliament, press and polls.

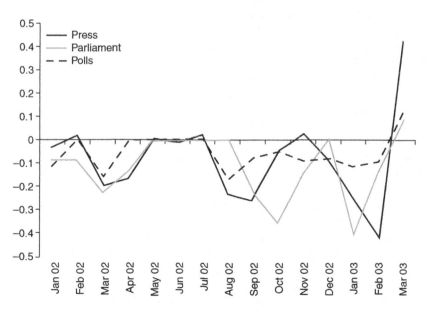

Figure 3.7 Salience-adjusted average monthly press, parliamentary and poll positions on the prospect of war in Iraq (1 = entirely pro-war, −1 = entirely anti-war).

presented in Figure 3.5, but with the results for each month scaled to match the proportions reported in Figure 3.6. It consequently shows figures reflecting the combined direction *and* intensity of attitudes.

Figure 3.7 shows how closely our three measures of public attitudes echoed each other. Simple covariance measures show a strong association ($R = 0.87$) between poll results and press commentary. Given the press commissioned most of the publicly available polls conducted during this period, this relationship makes sense. There was also, however, a reasonably strong association ($R = 0.60$) between press and parliamentary attitudes. Indeed, this might have been stronger still were parliament free to discuss Iraq whenever MPs wanted to do so. Journalists discussed Iraq prominently during August and September 2002. With the exception of a special debate to mark the publication of the government's WMD dossier on 24 September, MPs had to wait until they returned from their summer recess in October to respond. Figure 3.7 also underlines how anti-war views dominated the pre-invasion debate. The first two spikes in public attentiveness, visible around March and September–October 2002, reflected press, parliamentary and poll opposition to the prospect of the use of force in Iraq. The third spike, from January 2003 onwards, involved an initial surge in opposition followed by a rally effect that took in journalists and MPs as well as poll respondents. The following discussion analyses each of these moments in turn.

March 2002: the Crawford meeting

The first surge in opposition, visible primarily in March 2002, preceded Tony Blair's visit to President Bush's ranch in Crawford, Texas at the start of April. It followed Bush's first State of the Union address at the end of January, in which he named Iraq as part of an "axis of evil" linking rogue states "and their terrorist allies" (Bush 2002). This did not go down well in Britain. Commentators warned darkly that "rhetoric on occasion does change reality. And the axis of evil is for real" (Cornwell 2002). Over 100 Labour MPs signed an Early Day Motion published on 4 March condemning the US for plotting to invade Iraq (House of Commons 2002). Several criticized the British government in a special Westminster Hall debate on 6 March organized by veteran anti-war MP Tam Dalyell. By the time Vice-President Cheney visited London on 11 March, a visit that coincided with the announcement that Blair would go to Crawford, a number of commentators on both sides of the debate expected an imminent invasion. Those who opposed the use of force struck first, warning "it would be lunacy to attack Iraq at the moment, madness for Britain to back an American assault, and complete insanity to make any large-scale commitment of our troops" (*Mirror* 2002). Pro-war writers retaliated, insisting that Cheney was in London to "listen and not lecture" (*The Times* 2002a). This was, they claimed, a genuine opportunity for Anglo-American co-operation. A joint press conference between Vice President and Prime Minister passed off well. Both insisted that the proliferation of WMD posed a potential threat, while maintaining that no decisions had been made over what to do about Iraq's alleged weapons development. Cheney, however, caused some concern by echoing the 'Axis of Evil' speech, warning of a "potential marriage" between al-Qaeda and Iraq (Blair 2002a). Cheney's words comforted pro-war commentators, themselves convinced that "rogue groups" were working closely with "rogue states" (*The Times* 2002b). Critics fulminated that there was no evidence of any such link (Freedland 2002). As Chapter 5 discusses, they were right.

Despite this wave of press and parliamentary hostility, opinion polls identified little change in respondents' attitudes to questions about Iraq. ICM data published in March 2002 showed a 1 percentage point drop in support for military action and a four-point increase in opposition compared to previous studies conducted in late 2001. Neither shift was statistically significant. But Blair still warned his Downing Street aides that public opinion was "fragile" (Blair 2002b). He was probably responding to the wave of press interest at this time, as well as relying on his own individual instincts. He may equally have been affected by growing signs of discord in the Labour Party. Jack Straw cautioned shortly before the Crawford trip that Blair could not rely on his colleagues' support should he choose to act against Iraq (Straw 2002). Colin Powell similarly briefed President Bush ahead of the Crawford meeting that the Prime Minister would face domestic political difficulties if it came to war (Powell 2002). As the ICM data suggests, however, this apparent wave of opposition said more about the state of active public debate than it did about mass attitudes.

As Figure 3.7 makes clear, the wave of complaints that peaked in late March subsided by early May. Blair made two public appearances in Texas, a joint press conference on 6 April and a speech at the George H.W. Bush Presidential Library the following day. He also made a statement to the House of Commons upon his return to London. Though these interventions left many questions unanswered, Blair's repeated insistence that "no decisions have been taken" on Iraq (Blair 2002a, 2002c) seemed to calm nerves. By admitting that the US was indeed concerned about Iraq, while downplaying the prospect of imminent military action, Blair shut down speculation while simultaneously reasurring potential critics. Ministers consequently enjoyed a period of relative calm that lasted until the start of the summer parliamentary recess. Amongst MPs, only Donald Anderson and Tam Dalyell regularly asked about Iraq. Press commentators similarly lost interest, though a handful continued to attack Blair as a "moral crusader … eager for action" (Young 2002), condemning "his slavish stance towards the Americans" (Rowson 2002), describing him (generally only in the *Mirror*) for the same reason as a "poodle" (Reade 2002), and denouncing his planned "Western crusader invasion" of Iraq (Galloway 2002). Overall, Blair's statements in Crawford delivered the desired effect.

A broader communications campaign followed, one designed to increase the government's influence over both the press agenda and the framing of its policies in public debate. It had three components. First, ministers granted an increased number of media interviews. Blair submitted to a three-part grilling by *BBC Newsnight* presenter Jeremy Paxman in mid-May, with the second part focusing almost entirely on Iraq. These appearances gave the press something solid to report on, reducing the space available for speculation about Iraq. Second, Blair began to hold regular open press conferences covering whatever topics journalists wished to discuss, starting on 20 June. Over the following months these occasions played an important part in the developing Iraq debate, both allowing the government to set the press agenda and reminding Blair of the hostility he faced among elites. Third, on 16 July Blair appeared before the House of Commons Liaison Committee, a super-committee comprised of MPs who chaired other committees. This also became a regular fixture, supplementing the weekly 'question time' sessions in the main debating chamber.

It was not unusual for British ministers to speak to the media (Blair 2012, 2), but the idea of a formal press conference was new, as was the Liaison Committee appearance. Both attracted positive comment, as well as some pointed criticism. Journalists praised the Liaison Committee discussion, arguing it was "astonishing ... that this was not done before", and criticised the "inane" Prime Minister's Questions while contrasting its "partisan knockabout" with the "sensible public conversation" managed by the Committee (Jenkins 2002). Several praised the committee chairs for their "polite, non-partisan" approach "designed to elicit real answers" (*The Times* 2002c; Ashley 2002), though the *Mirror* labelled them "poodles" on account of their polite, non-partisan approach (Hardy 2002). Blair also faced continued criticism that he was not doing enough to inform public debate. He complained at the first press conference that it seemed "a bit unfair" for journalists to make such claims given "I have got you all here in the room" (Blair 2002d). Critics found this a difficult argument to refute. Given, as Robin Cook pointed out, much of the public opposition the government faced on its Iraq position in early 2002 reflected speculation "generated by the newspapers themselves" (Cook 2003, 113), government efforts to communicate more regularly worked even if the statements it made changed few minds. At this stage, quieting speculation was enough.

September 2002: the WMD dossier

The second surge in opposition to the prospect of war in Iraq arose in August and September 2002. Westminster traditionally empties in the summer, when parliament does not sit. Even the Prime Minister goes on holiday. During August 2002, however, the Iraq debate on the US side of the Atlantic stepped up a gear. British journalists, starved of information as ministers closed-up shop in late July, lapped up belligerent quotes from Bush administration officials, members of Congress, former policymakers and others who were determined to argue over how President Bush should confront Saddam Hussein. They grew convinced a war was imminent. Tam Dalyell tried to get MPs recalled to debate Iraq just days after their recess started, despite Blair still insisting "we are not at the point of decision yet" (Blair 2002e). Dalyell failed. But such was the scale of critical media speculation during August that the prevailing mood shifted by September. Alastair Campbell wrote in his diary on 1 September that "it was clear that public opinion had moved against us during August" (Campbell and Stott 2007,

632–633). Blair told his monthly press conference on 3 September "it is clear that the debate has moved on" (Blair 2002f). Again, however, it was the media debate that had moved on. Few ordinary people were involved.

Labour MP Graham Allen found a more receptive audience when he took up Dalyell's call for a special debate on Iraq in the aftermath of Blair's press conference, at which the Prime Minister announced his intention to publish the WMD 'dossier'. When the government initially refused, significant numbers of MPs agreed to attend an 'unofficial' sitting of the House of Commons at Church House in Westminster. Former House of Commons Speaker Lord Weatherill agreed to chair the session, the BBC offered to broadcast it live and several major newspapers declared their support (*Guardian* 2002; *Independent* 2002; *Daily Mail* 2002). Facing considerable embarrassment, the government caved and agreed a formal debate to coincide with the dossier's release in late September. Again the government responded to pressure from elites as if it reflected wider popular views. Again, poll figures showed no significant changes in mass attitudes from earlier surveys. It was not the mass public, represented by poll results, that moved. It was the press, and parliamentary opinion itself influenced by press commentary.

Whereas the government's communications efforts largely succeeded in dampening down both speculation and opposition amongst elite commentators in early 2002, by September attitudes were hardening. Parliament's disquiet lasted beyond the special debate on 24 September and carried on well into October, as Figure 3.7 shows. Releasing the WMD dossier helped calm critics down. But it also underlined how serious the government's intention to confront Iraq was. President Bush's speech to the UN General Assembly on 12 September, in which he announced he planned to challenge Iraq through the Security Council, had a similar effect. On the one hand, the fact Bush decided to work through the UN at all, discussed in Chapter 6, reassured some critics. But the determination he showed to do something about Iraq regardless of how the UN process played out underlined concerns. Ultimately the dossier exercise, as Chapter 5 makes clear, changed few minds. Ipsos MORI found 68 per cent of poll respondents reported it made no difference in their views, while 16 per cent swung in favour of military action and 12 per cent against after its release, a net effect of just 4 percentage points barely visible in Figure 3.2 (Ipsos MORI 2002).

February–March 2003: resentment and resignation

By early 2003 most observers recognized that the US was going to war in Iraq, probably with Britain in tow. At first, this caused resentment, and public opposition spiked for a third time. On 15 February the largest public protests in British history shook London and several other major cities. Around one million people marched against the prospective invasion in the capital alone. Media coverage emphasized that most of those marching were not the "usual suspects" who protested against any use of force abroad (*Daily Mail* 2003; Cook 2003, 293). They were "middle-class, middle-aged, politely-mannered and jolly angry" (Ellam 2003). Journalists and MPs both participated in and responded to the protests, while within Downing Street Alastair Campbell noted most officials had family members who joined the march (Campbell 2010, 54). Blair, in Campbell's words, "knew he was in a tight spot" (Campbell and Stott 2007, 667). Though the polls looked similar, the burst of public opposition represented by the protests and replicated in press commentary and parliamentary debate made clear to the government that the British public did not want to go to war in Iraq. Once again, however, ministers responded with communication rather than substance.

The 15 February march deliberately targeted Blair's speech at the Labour Party's Spring Conference. He used the opportunity to push back against the marchers' claims, declaring that "the moral case against war has a moral answer" (Blair 2003). Having believed since early in the Iraq debate that removing Saddam Hussein from power was simply the right thing to do (Blair 2002b), he began for the first time to make the point in public. This 'moral turn', discussed in detail in Chapter 7, salved consciences amongst those whose loyalty to Blair drove their support for war. Philip Gould's focus groups suggested the public possessed "an instinctive understanding that no Prime Minister would do anything as difficult or unpopular as this for the hell of it" (Campbell and Stott 2007, 669). Media commentators acknowledged that Blair was not simply following President Bush's orders, undermining the argument that the Prime Minister was acting like a 'poodle'. Andrew Rawnsley wrote that "never again will it be possible to portray this Prime Minister as a politician who would not put on a tie without first consulting a focus group" (Rawnsley 2003). Deborah Orr described the "mesmerising" spectacle of watching "such awesome blind integrity in action" (Orr 2003). An *Observer* editorial concluded "even [Blair's] critics should acknowledge the remarkable leadership he is exhibiting" (*Observer* 2003). Standing firm worked, at least to a point.

Government efforts to blame France for the failure of the UN process, discussed in Chapter 8, also made a difference. Britain's right-wing newspapers regularly fall prey to outright xenophobia, especially where continental Europe is concerned. They rallied to the notion that President Chirac's conduct risked letting Saddam Hussein off the hook (*Sun* 2003; *The Times* 2003b). Several anti-war MPs wavered in their convictions when faced with having to side against News Corporation and alongside France (Grice 2003). Poll results shifted too. An ICM poll published on 16 March showed 51 per cent of respondents thought President Chirac "has poisoned the diplomatic process" while 61 per cent said "France has put its own interests above the rest of the world by opposing war" (*News of the World* 2003; Smith and Speed 2003). In both cases, the way the questions were worded tells us something about the lines those who commissioned this survey sought to push. Pro-war elites finally possessed poll results worth talking about. At the same time, several critics resigned themselves to the inevitable. Journalists concluded that "the time has passed when war could be averted, so any vote against war cannot be effective or persuasive" (*Daily Telegraph* 2003). Several MPs acknowledged the same argument. Such attitudes help explain the rally effect visible in Figure 3.7.

Conclusion

Public opinion typically exerts only indirect influence over policymaking in representative democracies (Foyle 1997, 141, 148; Shannon and Keller 2007, 82; Keller and Yang 2008, 687). To have an impact, the public's attitudes have to be loudly and consistently articulated in public debate, and supported by opinion polls. Opponents of the government's chosen course must be able to point to credible political rivals who share their stance, and so who might use it to win support at the next election. Ministers must believe that listening to the public is important, either to guard against electoral punishment or to implement their decisions successfully. None of these criteria applied to the British public debate before the invasion of Iraq. Though it was quite clear that most people opposed the use of force, the intensity of their opposition varied widely. Much of it was driven by speculation rather than fact, and often all it took to calm critics down was for ministers to release more information about their developing policy stance, even if nothing substantive changed. The Blair government enjoyed a sizeable protective cushion from electoral penalties given the scale of its 2001 landslide victory. It could also rely on Conservative support in parliament, which helped it fend off internal Labour Party rebels while guarding against a future voter backlash. Members of the Downing Street inner circle largely shared the Prime Minister's view that while public opinion mattered, the job of governments was to lead as much as follow their constituents' attitudes.

Each of these factors helped make it possible for the Blair government to take Britain to war in the face of public opposition. What really made the difference, though, was the way ministers responded to criticism with additional arguments rather than substantive policy changes. In April and September 2002 that was all they needed to do. It was true, as the Chilcot Report subsequently found (and as Chapter 8 discusses in more detail) that the Prime Minister made commitments to President Bush long before he admitted to the British people that they might wind up fighting in Iraq. Nevertheless, much of the early opposition Blair faced stemmed from speculation rather than evidence. Very few people, even in Cabinet, knew what he wrote privately to Bush until after the Chilcot Report came out. It did not really matter what the government said during these periods, only that it said something. Changing minds was not the point. What mattered was shutting down the speculation. Most people remained opposed to the idea of war. But so long as they were not too vocal in their opposition, they would not influence others and could safely be ignored. Admitting in April 2002 that the US and UK planned to confront Saddam Hussein ended speculation about an imminent invasion. Releasing the WMD dossier and recalling parliament in September answered critics' demands for some sort of visible concession and gave journalists something to report. Satisfied, they moved on to other topics for a while, though MPs grumbled for a few weeks more. During February and March 2003 successful government efforts to blame France for wrecking the UN process and claim a share of the moral high ground salved consciences among earlier opponents who then resigned themselves to the inevitability of war.

In Part II we will look to build on this discussion by analysing the pre-invasion debate in detail. To understand how Britain wound up fighting an illegitimate war in Iraq, we need to look beyond the simple dichotomy between pro-war and anti-war attitudes set out in this chapter to see the constellation of beliefs underpinning each stance. We will tell the story, furthermore, of how the way the Blair government tried to win support through engaging in public debate actually undermined the invasion's legitimacy, in both political and normative terms. Public opinion is a social construct. More specifically, it is an emergent property of elite public debate. So is legitimacy. Indeed, the two concepts are closely related. Policies perceived as possessing public support appear more legitimate for it, while those considered illegitimate struggle to attract public support. We will see, over the following chapters, how ministers' success in winning sufficient public support to take Britain into Iraq failed to secure public backing for the decision, and indeed contributed to its questionable legitimacy over the longer term.

References

Ashley, Jackie. 'No question: scrap PMQs.' *Guardian*, 18 July 2002.

Ashley, Jackie. 'No moving a prime minister whose mind is made up: interview with Tony Blair.' *Guardian*, 1 March 2003.

Baker, William, and John Oneal. 'Patriotism or opinion leadership? The nature and origins of the "rally 'round the flag" effect.' *Journal of Conflict Resolution* 45, no. 5 (2001): 661–687.

Baum, Matthew. 'The constituent foundations of the rally-round-the-flag phenomenon.' *International Studies Quarterly* 46 (2002): 263–298.

Blair, Tony. 'Statement on the terrorist attacks in the United States.' 11 September 2001a. http://news.bbc.co.uk/1/hi/uk_politics/1538551.stm (accessed 12 May 2016).

Blair, Tony. 'Letter to President Bush.' 11 October 2001b. www.iraqinquiry.org.uk/media/243721/2001-10-11-letter-blair-to-bush-untitled.pdf (accessed 15 July 2016).

Blair, Tony. 'Press conference with Vice-President Cheney.' 11 March 2002a. http://webarchive.nationalarchives.gov.uk/20020926165953/www.pm.gov.uk:80/textonly/Page4598.asp (accessed 15 February 2016).

Blair, Tony. 'Memo to Jonathan Powell.' 17 March 2002b. www.iraqinquiry.org.uk/media/75831/2002-03-17-Minute-Blair-to-Powell-Iraq.pdf (accessed 17 August 2016).

Blair, Tony. 'Speech at the George H.W. Bush Presidential Library.' 7 April 2002c. www.theguardian.com/politics/2002/apr/08/foreignpolicy.iraq (accessed 22 September 2015).

Blair, Tony. 'Prime Minister's monthly press conference.' 20 June 2002d. http://webarchive.nationalarchives.gov.uk/20061101012618/http://number10.gov.uk/page2999 (accessed 16 May 2016).

Blair, Tony. 'Prime Minister's monthly press conference.' 25 July 2002e. http://webarchive.nationalarchives.gov.uk/20061004051823/http://number10.gov.uk/page3000 (accessed 22 September 2015).

Blair, Tony. 'Prime Minister's monthly press conference.' 3 September 2002f. http://webarchive.nationalarchives.gov.uk/20061004051823/http://number10.gov.uk/page3001 (accessed 22 September 2015).

The Iraq debate: an overview 53

Blair, Tony. 'Speech to the TUC.' 10 September 2002g. http://webarchive.national archives.gov.uk/+/www.number10.gov.uk/Page1725 (accessed 19 May 2016).

Blair, Tony. 'Speech to the Labour Party Spring Conference.' 15 February 2003. http://news.bbc.co.uk/1/hi/uk_politics/2765763.stm (accessed 15 February 2016).

Blair, Tony. *A Journey*. London: Hutchinson, 2010.

Blair, Tony. 'Evidence to the Leveson Inquiry.' 28 May 2012. http://webarchive.national archives.gov.uk/20140122145147/www.levesoninquiry.org.uk/wp-content/uploads/2012/05/Transcript-of-Morning-Hearing-28-May-2012.pdf (accessed 16 May 2016).

Blair, Tony. 'Statement on the Chilcot Report.' 6 July 2016. www.tonyblairoffice.org/news/entry/statement-from-tony-blair-on-chilcot-report/ (accessed 19 July 2016).

Bush, George W. 'The state of the union.' 29 January 2002. http://georgewbush-whitehouse.archives.gov/news/releases/2002/01/20020129-11.html (accessed 15 February 2016).

Campbell, Alastair. 'Evidence to the Chilcot Inquiry, afternoon session.' 12 January 2010. www.iraqinquiry.org.uk/media/95146/2010-01-12-Transcript-Campbell-S1-pm.pdf (accessed 17 August 2016).

Campbell, Alastair, and Richard Stott. *The Blair Years: Extracts from the Alastair Campbell Diaries*. London: Arrow Books, 2007.

Chilcot, John. *Report of the Iraq Inquiry: Executive Summary*. London: HMSO, 2016a.

Chilcot, John. *Report of the Iraq Inquiry: Volume 1*. London: HMSO, 2016b.

Chilcot, John. *Report of the Iraq Inquiry: Volume 2*. London: HMSO, 2016c.

Chilcot, John. *Report of the Iraq Inquiry: Volume 3*. London: HMSO, 2016d.

Cohen, Bernard. *Democracies and Foreign Policy: Public Participation in the United States and the Netherlands*. Madison, WI: University of Wisconsin Press, 1995.

Cook, Robin. *The Point of Departure*. London: Simon & Schuster, 2003.

Cornwell, Rupert. 'Saddam is next in the firing line. It's just a matter of when.' *Independent on Sunday*, 17 February 2002.

Daily Mail. 'Leading article', 6 September 2002.

Daily Mail. 'Leading article', 15 February 2003.

Daily Telegraph. 'Leading article', 22 September 2001a.

Daily Telegraph. 'Leading article', 11 October 2001b.

Daily Telegraph. 'Leading article', 16 October 2001c.

Daily Telegraph. 'Leading article', 18 March 2003.

Dalyell, Tam. *Hansard House of Commons Debates*, vol. 372, 14 September 2001.

Duncan Smith, Iain. *Hansard House of Commons Debates*, vol. 372, 8 October 2001.

Ellam, Dennis. 'Protest virgins.' *Sunday Mirror*, 16 February 2003.

Everts, Philip, and Pierangelo Isernia. 'The polls – trends: the war in Iraq.' *Public Opinion Quarterly* 69, no. 2 (2005): 264–323.

Foyle, Douglas. 'Public opinion and foreign policy: elite beliefs as a mediating variable.' *International Studies Quarterly* 41, no. 1 (1997): 141–169.

Freedland, Jonathan. 'Saddam and al-Qaeda? There's more chance of Will marrying Vanessa.' *Mirror*, 14 March 2002.

Galloway, George. 'Jubilee year is not the time to plan a divorce.' *Mail on Sunday*, 5 May 2002.

Glover, Stephen. 'When in doubt, just shoot the messenger.' *Daily Mail*, 30 October 2001.

Grice, Andrew. 'The week in politics.' *Independent*, 15 March 2003.

Guardian. 'Leading article', 10 October 2001.

Guardian. 'Leading article', 6 September 2002.

Hardy, James. 'You poodles! Soft MPs let Blair off the hook at historic grilling.' *Mirror*, 17 July 2002.

House of Commons. 'Early day motion no. 927.' 4 March 2002. www.parliament.uk/edm/2001-02/927 (accessed 15 February 2016).
Independent. 'Leading article', 21 September 2001.
Independent. 'Leading article', 6 September 2002.
Ipsos MORI. 'Possible war with Iraq: the public's views.' 26 September 2002. www.ipsos-mori.com/researchpublications/researcharchive/1029/Possible-War-With-Iraq-the-Publics-View.aspx (accessed 16 May 2016).
ITV News. *ITV News*, 12 September 2002.
Jenkins, Simon. 'A brand new Blair, and the same old story.' *The Times*, 17 July 2002.
Keller, Jonathan, and Yi Edward Yang. 'Leadership style, decision context, and the poli-heuristic theory of decision making: an experimental analysis.' *Journal of Conflict Resolution* 52, no. 5 (2008): 687–712.
Kennedy, Charles. *Hansard House of Commons Debates*, vol. 372, 8 October 2001.
Key, Vladimer. *Public Opinion and American Democracy*. New York: Knopf, 1961.
Kreps, Sarah. 'Elite consensus as a determinant of alliance cohesion: why public opinion hardly matters for NATO-led operations in Afghanistan.' *Foreign Policy Analysis* 6 (2010): 191–215.
Lai, Brian, and Dan Reiter. 'Rally 'round the Union Jack? Public opinion and the use of force in the United Kingdom, 1948–2001.' *International Studies Quarterly* 49, no. 2 (2005): 255–272.
MacIntyre, Ben. 'Word bombs.' *The Times*, 9 October 2001.
Mirror. 'Leading Article', 19 October 2001a.
Mirror. 'Leading Article', 15 November 2001b.
Mirror. 'Leading Article', 11 March 2002.
Mueller, John. 'Presidential popularity from Truman to Johnson.' *American Political Science Review* 64, no. 1 (1970): 18–33.
News of the World. 'Poll results: Iraq.' *News of the World*, 16 March 2003.
Noelle-Neumann, Elizabeth. 'Public opinion and the classical tradition: a re-evaluation.' *Public Opinion Quarterly* 43, no. 2 (1979): 143–156.
Observer. 'Leading article', 16 March 2003.
O'Hagan, Simon. 'Who says that we should not go to war?' *Independent on Sunday*, 23 September 2001.
Orr, Deborah. 'He has so few followers, yet Blair has never been a more believable leader.' *Independent*, 14 March 2003.
Osborne, George. *Hansard House of Commons Debates*, vol. 372, 4 October 2001.
Powell, Colin. 'Your meeting with UK Prime Minister Tony Blair: Memo to President Bush.' 28 March 2002. https://foia.state.gov/searchapp/DOCUMENTS/April2014/F-2012-33239/DOC_0C05446915/C05446915.pdf (accessed 10 June 2016).
Powell, Jonathan. *The new Machiavelli: How to wield power in the modern world*. London: The Bodley Head, 2010.
Ramsay, Kristopher. 'Politics at the water's edge: crisis bargaining and electoral competition.' *Journal of Conflict Resolution* 48, no. 4 (2004): 459–486.
Rawnsley, Andrew. 'Journey into the unknown.' *Observer*, 2 March 2003.
Reade, Brian. 'The poodle bites back.' *Mirror*, 1 May 2002.
Riddell, Peter. 'Blair can count on support – for the time being.' *The Times*, 18 October 2001.
Risse-Kappen, Thomas. 'Public opinion, domestic structure, and foreign policy in Liberal democracies.' *World Politics* 43, no. 4 (1991): 479–512.
Risse-Kappen, Thomas. 'Masses and leaders: public opinion, domestic structures, and foreign policy.' In *The New Politics of American Foreign Policy*, by David Deese, 238–261. New York: St Martin's Press, 1994.

Robinson, Piers, Peter Goddard, Katy Parry, and Craig Murray. 'Testing models of media performance in wartime: UK TV news and the 2003 invasion of Iraq.' *Journal of Communication* 59 (2009): 534–563.

Rowson, Martin. '1997–2002: good times, bad times.' *Independent*, 1 May 2002.

Schuster, Jurgen, and Herbert Maier. 'The rift: explaining Europe's divergent Iraq policies in the run-up of the American-led war on Iraq.' *Foreign Policy Analysis* 2, no. 3 (2006): 223–244.

Shannon, Vaughn, and Jonathan Keller. 'Leadership style and international norm violation: the case of the Iraq War.' *Foreign Policy Analysis* 3, no. 1 (2007): 79–104.

Shapiro, Robert, and Lawrence Jacobs. 'Who leads and who follows? US presidents, public opinion, and foreign policy.' In *Decision Making in a Glass House: Mass Media, Public Opinion, and American and European Foreign Policy in the 21st Century*, by Brigitte Nacos, Robert Shapiro and Pierangelo Isernia, 223–245. Lanham, Maryland: Rowman & Littlefield, 2000.

Smith, David, and Nick Speed. 'French stance tilts voters towards war.' *Sunday Times*, 16 March 2003.

Sobel, Richard. *The Impact of Public Opinion on US Foreign Policy Since Vietnam: Constraining the Colossus.* New York: Oxford University Press, 2001.

Straw, Jack. 'Crawford/Iraq: memo to Tony Blair.' 25 March 2002. www.iraqinquiry.org.uk/media/195509/2002-03-25-minute-straw-to-prime-minister-crawford-iraq.pdf#search=straw (accessed 29 July 2016).

Strong, James. 'Two-level games beyond the United States: international indexing in Britain during the wars in Afghanistan, Iraq and Libya.' *Global Society*, forthcoming 2017.

Sun. 'The Sun says', 14 November 2001.

Sun. 'The Sun says', 15 February 2002.

Sun. 'The Sun says', 6 March 2003.

The Times. 'Leading article', 25 October 2001a.

The Times. 'Leading Article', 31 October 2001b.

The Times. 'Leading Article', 11 March 2002a.

The Times. 'Leading Article', 12 March 2002b.

The Times. 'Leading Article', 17 July 2002c.

The Times. 'Leading article', 11 February 2003a.

The Times. 'Leading Article', 6 March 2003b.

Toynbee, Polly. 'Limp liberals fail to protect their most profound values.' *Guardian*, 10 October 2001.

Travis, Alan, and Michael White. 'Poll shows big shift in public mood on military action: Saddam caves in on inspections.' *Guardian*, 17 September 2002.

Young, Hugo. 'The terrifying naivety of Blair the great intervener: the prime minister risks turning Britain into the Pentagon's useful idiot.' *Guardian*, 30 April 2002.

Zaller, John. 'Coming to grips with V.O. Key's concept of latent opinion.' In *Electoral Democracy*, by Michael MacKuen and George Rabinowitz, 311–336. Ann Arbor, MI: University of Michigan Press, 2003.

Part II
Legitimacy

4 Understanding legitimacy

Part I shows how it was possible that the Blair government took Britain to war in Iraq despite concerted public opposition. Part II builds on this analysis by presenting a detailed qualitative account of how the pre-invasion public debate played out. Over the course of the following chapters we will try to understand the legitimacy deficit surrounding the decision to go to war by tracing its basis in how ministers and officials solicited domestic support. Part II argues that the way the Blair government made its case backfired, with statements intended to boost the war's legitimacy actually undermining it. This was true even before March 2003. Once the fighting revealed that Iraq lacked WMD, and the effort to impose 'regime change' went sour, unfounded, exaggerated and optimistic predictions made in the heat of a contentious public debate became the criteria the public used to reassess the decision to use force. Its conclusions were deeply critical.

This short chapter prefigures the empirical analysis presented in the rest of Part II. It defines foreign policy legitimacy, very much like public opinion, as a product of domestic public debate – indeed, the two concepts are inextricably linked. The chapter begins by discussing the conceptual foundations underpinning this approach, reaching back into the rich literature on legitimacy for guidance. The first section distinguishes between two ways of defining legitimacy, first as a contingent political attribute, defined by public perceptions in particular circumstances and subject to constant revision, and second as an abstract normative principle, unchanging between cases and consistent over time. Next, it introduces the communicative approach to understanding legitimization, and presents contrasting 'Habermasian' and 'Foucauldian' models of the relationship between rhetoric, deliberation and legitimacy. Next, the second section presents a conceptual framework for assessing the Blair government's approach from a normative perspective. The approach that is employed draws heavily on Habermasian ideas, but tempers their more unrealistic elements with a healthy dose of Foucauldian scepticism. Finally, the third section explains how the pre-invasion debate breaks down into manageable thematic chapters. It makes the case for an inductive approach, setting aside alternative categorizations derived from Just War Theory and from Tony Blair's own 'doctrine of international community'.

Legitimacy as a discursive construct

Legitimacy is a difficult concept to work with. At a basic level, it is a characteristic of the exercise of power. We say power is legitimate to the extent its subjects have a normative obligation to obey. Powerful actors can coerce weaker counterparts into doing what they say. But they cannot claim the *right* to obedience without legitimacy. At a domestic level, the concept of sovereignty implies that ordinary citizens have a normative duty to obey their governments. At an international level, the picture grows more complicated. In short, individuals are under no normative obligation to obey the governments of other states, unless they are residents within them. As a result, understanding how legitimacy attaches to foreign policy is less about specific interactions between those who wield power and those subject to it, and more about the broader relationship within a state between government and governed. Though governments do not direct foreign policy towards their domestic constituents, we can only logically understand its legitimacy at a domestic level. Foreign policy is legitimate to the extent the citizens of a state are under a normative obligation to support it, at least implicitly. That obligation derives from and feeds back into the broader duty that citizens of sovereign states must obey their governments.

Political and normative approaches

Complicating this picture still further is the distinction between rival political and normative understandings of what legitimacy actually is. According to the "Weberian" tradition of scholarship, the exercise of power is legitimate "when its subjects believe it to be so" (Clark 2003, 79). Legitimacy is, in other words, a social construction (Clark 2005, 18; Reus-Smit 2007, 160). Like legality (Onuf 1989, 77), sovereignty (Reus-Smit 2001, 527), national interest (Weldes 1996, 276, 303; Finnemore 1996, 2; Katzenstein 1996, 2; Adler 1997, 337) or even history (Reus-Smit 2008, 404), legitimacy from this perspective exists to the extent members of a society believe in it (Franck 1988, 706; Hurd 1999, 381; Finnemore 2009, 61). It is a political attribute, defined by politics itself, albeit in constructivist terms. Normative accounts rightly complain that this reading "distorts the essential meaning" of legitimacy by denying that legitimacy *has* an 'essential' meaning (Grafstein 1981, 456). Social facts do not exist outside of their social context. That – rather than any particular external normative standard – defines their essence. The problem these contrasting definitions raise is quite clear. It is possible for those who are subject to a given exercise of power to consider it legitimate, and to act as if they are obliged to obey, even if the rigorous application of external normative standards determines they are not. Equally, governments that struggle to assert their legitimacy in the eyes of those they govern can expect little comfort from formal philosophical criteria. There is a logical distinction between whether an action *is* legitimate in theory and whether, in practice, those obliged to yield to it accept that obligation, and concede. Defining legitimacy as a political attribute means privileging subjects' perceptions. Defining it as a normative principle means emphasizing external criteria over what members of a society actually believe.

Clearly there is merit on both sides of the political/normative divide. If a society agrees that a particular exercise of power is legitimate the political consequences will be the same whether or not external normative criteria are met. For studies seeking to elucidate fundamental theoretical principles, the distinction still matters. But this study is more interested in understanding a particular foreign policy case than it is in generating general theories. Similarly, however, if we embrace a political definition too firmly, we risk doing work that only makes sense in very specific, contingent circumstances. Our ability to generalize will suffer. Foreign policy analysis, with its focus on empirical research and case studies, treats generalization as less of a central concern than do other branches of International Relations. It still matters, nonetheless. We need, in other words, to strike a careful balance in the following analysis between understanding how, in what ways and with what consequences the British people considered the legitimacy of the Blair government's decision to go to war in Iraq in March 2003, and assessing that understanding against more general criteria.

Habermas and Foucault

This is where the communicative approach comes in. There has been a "communicative turn" in legitimacy research in recent years (Stephen 2015, 769). Work in this tradition defines legitimacy not just as a social fact, but specifically as a discursive construct, derived from and dependent on the contours of public debate (Steffek 2003; Hurrell 2005; Krebs and Jackson 2007). Adopting such an approach makes empirical sense given how the Blair government sought public backing for its decision to go to war. Ministers, officials and the Prime Minister, in particular, intervened repeatedly in an effort to shape public debate. It would, as one contemporary biographer observed, be "impossible, even for the toughest-minded historian, to ignore entirely what Tony Blair has said" during the pre-invasion period, not least because "on many days he [did] virtually nothing else but speak" (Stothard 2003, 173). Blair made set-piece speeches, held press conferences and published information 'dossiers'. He took questions from MPs and from television studio audiences. He led five major House of Commons debates in addition to his weekly 'question time' grilling. Legitimacy, for the Blair government, was not an unchanging, abstract quality. It was shaped and guided by rhetoric.

Adherents of a discursive approach see public debate as a factor in determining both the political and the normative dimensions of legitimacy (Finnemore and Sikkink 1998, 892; Milliken 1999, 237; Kornprobst 2009). They disagree, however, over the relative importance of the two. Most fall into one of two rival theoretical schools of thought that Christian Reus-Smit labelled "Habermasian" and "Foucauldian" (Reus-Smit 2002, 487). Both Habermasians and Foucauldians agree that public debate plays an important role in generating social consensus, and that a social consensus around the notion that a given exercise of power is normatively right grants it the political attribute of legitimacy (Franck 1988, 706; Hurd 1999, 381; Finnemore 2009, 61). They agree, furthermore, that it is possible for a government to benefit from this sort of consensus despite failing to meet external normative criteria. Crucially, they distinguish between the "first order" question of what legitimacy *is* and the more contentious "second order" question of *where it comes from* (Bjola 2009, 2; Franck 1988, 706; Kratochwil 1989, 11).

Habermasians believe that legitimacy derives not just from social consensus, but from social consensus achieved in the right way, through the right kind of public debate (Risse 2000; Steffek 2003; Muller 2004; Mitzen 2005; Kornprobst 2014). In the process, they seek to bridge the gap between political and normative approaches. Adopting a Weberian mindset, Habermasians acknowledge that it makes little sense from an empirical perspective to adopt a definition of legitimacy that disregards the question of whether the subjects of power consider it legitimate. At the same time, echoing normative concerns, they consider an entirely contingent definition theoretically unsatisfying, given its lack of grounding in general principles. Their remedy emerges from the distinction in Jürgen Habermas' social theory between "communicative action", the collective exercise of reason among free actors seeking a mutually acceptable consensus, and "strategic" persuasion, in which individuals use rhetoric to advance their own particular points of view (Habermas 1981, 295). Habermasians recognize that the subjects of a given exercise of power might believe they are under a normative obligation to obey whether or not that is in fact the case. They acknowledge that the political consequences of such a consensus will be the same either way. At the same time, they argue that it does matter whether the relevant consensus derives from communicative action proper or mere strategic persuasion. Whatever they may believe, in the Habermasian account citizens are only *actually* under a normative obligation to obey power legitimized through open, reasoned deliberation. Equally, Habermasians recognize that without consensus there is, as a political point of fact, no legitimacy.

Foucauldians accept the Habermasian model to some extent, at least as abstract theory. They disagree over how useful it is for understanding actual policymaking. They emphasize that Habermas himself regarded 'communicative action' as a conceptual ideal type rather than a realistic model for behaviour. In practice, they argue, the sort of "evidence-based argument" that lies at the heart of the Habermasian model matters much less than the social, political and economic power that different participants in public debate hold. It is power, for the Foucauldians, that determines when citizens feel obliged to yield to arguments made by stronger actors. What matters is not reason but "rhetorical force" (Bially Mattern 2005, 586). Even within Habermas' own work, the Foucauldians argue that "the real heavy lifting ... is done by persuasion", itself underpinned by power, and not by reason at all (Checkel 2004, 240). While they accept that policymakers engage in public debate in the hope of generating consensus around actions they propose to take, they question whether this process ever meets Habermasian criteria. Habermasians believe that a given exercise of power can possess both political and the normative legitimacy, provided the consensus surrounding it emerged through a fair and open process of public debate. Foucauldians do not believe it is possible, let alone likely, that policymakers engage in public debate in a truly fair and open way. They believe governments only ever employ strategic persuasion. Communicative action, for the Foucauldians, makes sense only in theory. When a consensus emerges from public debate, they believe it reflects power relations, nothing more (Krebs and Jackson 2007, 42).

At a conceptual level the Habermasian and Foucauldian approaches offer incommensurate accounts of how public debate operates. When Thomas Risse first introduced Habermasian thinking to the study of international conflict, he emphasized the rigid ontological distinction between three logics of consequences, appropriateness and communicative action (Risse 2000, 4). For Risse, the fact that communicative action prioritizes reaching a consensus over achieving any particular policy outcome distinguishes it absolutely from most political behaviour. This is probably true, at least in theory. Harald Muller, however, proposed a possible compromise. Muller pointed out that persuasion possesses a normative character of its own. It is defined by a set of unwritten rules just as powerful as those that shape communicative action. The rules are simply different. Muller argued that the Foucauldian and Habermasian models can coexist provided we subsume them under an over-arching logic of appropriateness. Though they do indeed do different things, Muller believed that persuasion and communicative action differed in degree more than in kind (Muller 2004, 413). Markus Kornprobst similarly concluded that the conceptual distinction between the two approaches collapses when we observe the relationship between public communication and social consensus in practice. Kornprobst rightly pointed out that meeting Habermasian criteria makes an argument more persuasive, while visibly trying to avoid an open, reason-based public deliberation leaves leaders struggling to persuade (Kornprobst 2014, 201). This latter point, in particular, proves apposite when studying the Blair government's shortcomings over Iraq.

Part II defines legitimacy, then, in Habermasian terms, as the product of a certain type of public debate. At the same time, it accepts the Foucauldian critique that the Habermasian approach employs criteria no real-world politician is ever likely to meet. The following chapters will consider both how closely the Blair government's conduct approximated communicative action, and to what extent it was persuasive. Rather than setting unrealistic absolute standards for ministers to meet, we will instead consider their degree of compliance, and the broader political circumstances and personal beliefs driving their behaviour. We will make use along the way of Kornprobst's insight, that pursuing a communicative approach can make a government's arguments more persuasive. Sometimes the converse was clearly true for the Blair government, with its efforts to avoid proper deliberation alienating audiences. Sometimes it said things that undermined its claim to legitimacy in a Habermasian sense, but nevertheless proved persuasive.

Studying the Blair government's discursive legitimization efforts

Tony Blair repeatedly claimed he wanted a proper, open, evidence-based public deliberation to shape how Britain dealt with Iraq. During a press conference with Vice President Cheney in early 2002 he promised the country would "reflect and consider and deliberate" before any use of force (Blair 2002a). He played up the contrast between the government's reliance on reason and that terrorists resort to violence (Blair 2002b). He promised to "consider all the options" (Blair 2002c) and to engage in "deliberation and consultation" with public critics (Blair 2002e, col. 11). He maintained that "the fullest possible debate will take place" ahead of any military action (Blair 2002f), and launched what he considered to be "unprecedented" efforts to inform the citizenry (British Government 2002). Even in early 2003, as the prospect of war grew increasingly certain, he still claimed "it is worth having ... a constant dialogue with people" (Blair 2003a). Under intense political pressure the day before the invasion he welcomed MPs' "legitimate" demands for a full House of Commons debate (Blair 2003c, col. 773). So far, so Habermasian.

At the same time, however, the way Blair, his ministers and officials behaved in practice deviated from what we might expect of a government truly committed to open public deliberation. There are three key criteria for distinguishing between communicative action and strategic persuasion in a foreign policy setting, criteria captured most clearly in Corneliu Bjola's model of "deliberative legitimacy" (Bjola 2005, 2008, 2009). As the Foucauldians argue, it seems unlikely any real-world policymaker will consistently meet all three. Having accepted that, however, we can still employ a Habermasian framework to guide our analysis, looking at the degree of divergence between the normative standards the literature sets and how the Blair government behaved, and using that to say something about both the political and the normative dimensions of its unsuccessful push for consensus behind the decision to go to war.

Three criteria

The first criterion, rendered here as 'truthfulness', derives from the basis of communicative action in what Habermas called "truth claims" – implicit commitments embedded in the arguments speakers make about their capacity to provide evidence to support their statements if required (Habermas 1981, 276–279). This criterion builds upon the theory of "speech acts", a set of ideas about the relationship between verbal communication and political consequences ultimately derived from Wittgenstein (Onuf 1989, 82; Kratochwil 1993, 76; Searle 1995, 34). It holds, in short, that actors seeking to legitimize a particular policy approach through public debate must offer a "truthful", "accurate" and "complete" account of the reasoning underpinning their beliefs (Bjola 2009, 76, 139). If truthfulness is fundamental to communicative action, it makes sense that it should be fundamental to securing legitimacy through deliberation (Mitzen

2005, 403). Securing a consensus means securing agreement among the participants in a debate, but leaders who gain that agreement dishonestly cannot claim a normative right to be obeyed. For our case, trying to gauge how truthful the Blair government was can help us understand both its normative and political failings. As the following chapters make clear, both ministers and officials consistently struggled to demonstrate truthfulness. The common accusation that Tony Blair lied to take Britain to war does not, in practice, entirely hold up. But we can and will find fault with his and his colleagues' commitment to truthfulness throughout the pre-invasion debate.

The second criterion, best described as 'openness', reflects the Habermasian belief that legitimacy "does not represent the *will* of all, but ... results from the *deliberation of all*" (Manin, Stein and Mansbridge 1987, 351–352, emphasis in original). For a public debate to generate the right sort of consensus, Habermasians argue, all "affected parties ... must be allowed to participate" (Bjola 2009, 76). Leaders are under a normative obligation not merely to permit but to encourage a wide range of actors to join in public debate. Failure to do so means whatever agreement they secure cannot possibly be described as a consensus. Consensus implies consent, which in turn implies at least the possibility of participation. Similarly, given we are defining public opinion in terms of publicness, it makes sense to adopt a definition of legitimacy that takes participation in public debate seriously. Again, the Blair government did not do a good job addressing this second criterion. Ministers and officials repeatedly sought to foreclose the discussion of plausible scenarios that conflicted with their preferred narrative. Blair, for example, maintained that "doing nothing" about Iraq was "not an option" (Blair 2002c, 2002d). There was "no doubt that the world would be a better place without Saddam". Only "the method of achieving that" was up for discussion (Hansard 2002, col. 12). As he told one press conference, "how we deal with [the alleged Iraqi threat] ... is an open question, but that we have to deal with it isn't" (Blair 2002f). Critics who tried to raise alternative scenarios found the government unwilling to engage. At the same time, members of the Downing Street inner circle took unprecedented steps to exclude doubters, even amongst Cabinet ministers, from crucial decisions.

The final criterion, which we will label 'flexibility', requires participants in public debate to place securing a mutually acceptable consensus ahead of 'winning' the argument in a conventional sense. For Habermas, communicative action only occurs when everyone involved is willing to revise their preferred stance in the face of superior logic and better evidence. As Risse noted, there is a practical dimension to this argument. If no one in a debate is willing to be persuaded, no one will be able to persuade (Risse 2000, 8). Again, this proved a tough standard for the Blair government to meet. Blair believed his personal view was right. He was not interested in being persuaded. He only wanted to persuade. In private meetings with officials he said "if the political context were right", the British people would support regime change in Iraq (Rycroft 2002). He urged critics to hear him out although "it might be not what some people want to hear" (Blair 2002g). He never seriously considered that his detractors might have better arguments. By early 2003 he conceded he was losing as he battled for public support, concluding "there are certain situations in which you have simply got to say to people look this is what I believe" (Blair 2003b). He apparently did not consider changing course. Instead he used all his power to try to change minds. As we have seen in Chapter 3, this worked to some extent. The support Blair's efforts generated did not, however, translate into legitimacy in a normative sense because the same determination that allowed him to press on in the face of criticism undermined his commitment to communicative action, despite his stated intention to secure a Habermasian deliberative consensus, in other words, he acted much more in line with Foucauldian expectations.

Categorizing the debate

Making sense of the British public debate over Iraq is tricky. Though its intensity varied, as we saw in Chapter 3, it lasted in some form for around 15 months. Hundreds of commentators participated through thousands of newspaper articles and dozens of parliamentary sessions. To make all this talk comprehensible, the following chapters break the debate down thematically, drawing on the wider legitimacy literature for guidance as well as allowing categories to emerge organically from what participants actually said (Clark 2005, 4, 207, 226; Reus-Smit 2007, 160; Finnemore 2003, 2; Hansen 2006, 34–35). The resulting framework allows us to consider arguments about the necessity of meeting the perceived Iraqi threat, matters of legality and the role of the UN, the morality of military intervention, and questions about domestic politics and where the authority to use force should properly lie.

Just War Theory

This is not the only framework we could conceivably use for this analysis. Just War Theory, for example, offers a set of external criteria for determining the legitimacy of a given use of force. According to the Just War Theory model, states seeking to use force must act with right intent and just cause, with proper authority and proportionate means, and as a last resort (Walzer 1977). We could quite clearly assess the Blair government's approach to Iraq according to these criteria. It would probably not fare well. For example, ministers framed their decision to go to war as a proportionate measure and, very much, a last resort. Perhaps the Chilcot Report's most damning passage addressed this point directly; "at the time of the Parliamentary vote of 18 March", Chilcot concluded, "diplomatic options had not been exhausted. The point had not been reached where military action was the last resort" (Chilcot 2016, 614).

The problem with basing our analysis entirely on Just War criteria, however, is that it would take us back to the clash between normative and political standards discussed above. Just War Theory establishes normative standards that take no account of the politics involved in a specific decision-making scenario. A war is either just or it is not. We are interested, however, in the politics, in the gaps between what our theoretical expectations say and what the British public thought. It probably did not help the Blair government that Iraq was not a Just War. But to achieve our goals we need to integrate a Just War framework into an approach tailored to the actual British debate. This is eminently doable. We can identify statements ministers made about the threat from Iraqi WMD and the moral case for regime change with the Just War standards of right intent and just cause. We can similarly link their efforts to assert UN Security Council approval and to engage MPs with right authority. Last resort and proportionality are more complicated. Chapters 6 and 8 talk about this dimension to some extent, highlighting the mismatch between the UN weapons inspection process and the US timetable for war. No one really considered proportionality. It seems evident in retrospect that the single biggest strategic error the Bush administration made in invading Iraq was employing means disproportionate to its goals. But the question of whether a full-scale land invasion seemed a sensible response to the perceived Iraqi threat or the moral case for war played little part in Britain's pre-invasion debate.

Doctrine of international community

We might similarly apply criteria derived from Tony Blair's own statements on the proper use of force. His 1999 'doctrine of international community' speech set five standards he pledged to use to judge military intervention; "are we sure of our case? ... have we exhausted all diplomatic options? ... are there military operations we can sensibly and prudently undertake? ... are we prepared for the long term? ... do we have national interests involved?" (Blair 1999). Again, his decisions in 2003 fare poorly when assessed against these criteria. Blair was himself sure of his case, that much is clear. He should not have been. The advice he received spoke repeatedly of uncertainty. Diplomacy, as Chilcot concluded, was not exhausted. There may have been sensible and prudent military options available, but invading Iraq with a force large enough to destroy the existing government, but too small to occupy the country successfully was not one of them. Britain was woefully under-prepared for a long-term commitment in Iraq and it did not, in the final analysis, have significant national interests at stake.

Again, these failures help explain the legitimacy deficit surrounding the war. But they also take us a step away from the actual contours of the pre-invasion debate. Oddly, or perhaps because he knew he would not meet them, Blair never explicitly revisited his five standards as he made the case for war in Iraq. Nor did anyone else. Questions of certainty arose repeatedly around the Iraqi threat and the legal arguments different actors made. They were relevant, also, to how far the government met the first Habermasian criterion of truthfulness. Several critics complained about the US administration's apparent willingness to short-circuit international diplomacy. But, again, prudence, long-term planning and national interest did not really form central parts of the arguments presented. This is probably because supporters of the decision to go to war assumed the government had these areas covered, while critics had bigger concerns to raise.

Conclusion

It is helpful, then, to be aware of how both Blair's past record, and the established Just War Theory approach can help inform our analysis. As we have discussed, it still seems more appropriate in terms of the questions we seek to answer to adopt an inductive approach and to use criteria echoed in the legitimacy literature. Over the next few chapters we will look to understand how the pre-invasion debate generated the legitimacy deficit that in Britain surrounds the decision to invade Iraq. We will analyse arguments about the Iraqi threat, the role of the UN and the legal grounds for war, the morality of regime change and the locus of decision-making authority at both international and domestic levels. Along the way we will assess how far the Blair government's approach met Habermasian criteria, and where the tone and the content of the claims it presented made its arguments more or less persuasive. We will also consider the relationship between logics of persuasion and communicative action, and suggest as Kornprobst does that in practice the two look similar, but not identical. Our ultimate goal is simple: To determine how the pre-invasion debate made possible the legitimacy deficit that followed.

References

Adler, Emanuel. 'Seizing the middle ground: constructivism in world politics.' *European Journal of International Relations* 3, no. 3 (1997): 319–363.

Bially Mattern, Janice. 'Why "soft power" isn't so soft: representational force and the sociolinguistic construction of attraction in world politics.' *Millennium: Journal of International Studies* 33, no. 3 (2005): 583–612.

Bjola, Corneliu. 'Legitimating the use of force in international politics: a communicative action perspective.' *European Journal of International Relations* 11, no. 2 (2005): 266–303.

Bjola, Corneliu. 'Legitimacy and the use of force: bridging the analytical-normative divide.' *Review of International Studies* 34, no. 4 (2008): 627–644.

Bjola, Corneliu. *Legitimising the Use of Force in International Politics: Kosovo, Iraq and the Ethics of Intervention.* London: Routledge, 2009.

Blair, Tony. 'The doctrine of international community.' 24 April 1999. www.pbs.org/newshour/bb/international-jan-june99-blair_doctrine4-23/ (accessed 22 August 2016).

Blair, Tony. 'Press conference with Vice-President Cheney.' 11 March 2002a. http://webarchive.nationalarchives.gov.uk/20080305120708/www.pm.gov.uk/output/Page1704.asp (accessed 24 November 2010).

Blair, Tony. 'Interview with NBC.' 4 April 2002b. http://webarchive.nationalarchives.gov.uk/+/www.number10.gov.uk/Page1709 (accessed 27 May 2010).

Blair, Tony. 'Press conference with President Bush.' 6 April 2002c. http://webarchive.nationalarchives.gov.uk/+/www.number10.gov.uk/Page1711 (accessed 27 May 2010).

Blair, Tony. 'Speech at the George HW Bush Presidential Library.' 7 April 2002d. www.theguardian.com/politics/2002/apr/08/foreignpolicy.iraq (accessed 22 September 2015).

Blair, Tony. *Hansard House of Commons Debates*, vol. 383, 10 April 2002e.

Blair, Tony. 'Prime Minister's monthly press conference.' 3 September 2002f. http://webarchive.nationalarchives.gov.uk/20061004051823/http://number10.gov.uk/page3001 (accessed 22 September 2015).

Blair, Tony. 'Speech to the TUC.' 10 September 2002g. http://webarchive.national archives.gov.uk/+/www.number10.gov.uk/Page1725 (accessed 19 May 2016).

Blair, Tony. 'Prime Minister's monthly press conference.' 13 January 2003a. http://webarchive.nationalarchives.gov.uk/20061004051823/http://number10.gov.uk/output/Page3005.asp (accessed 28 June 2016).

Blair, Tony. 'Prime Minister's monthly press conference.' 18 February 2003b. http://webarchive.nationalarchives.gov.uk/20061004051823/http://number10.gov.uk/page3006 (accessed 28 August 2015).

Blair, Tony. *Hansard House of Commons Debates*, vol. 401, 18 March 2003c.

British Government. *Iraq's Weapons of Mass Destruction: The Assessment of the British Government*. London: HMSO, 2002.

Checkel, Jeffrey. 'Social constructivisms in global and European politics: a review essay.' *Review of International Studies* 30, no. 2 (2004): 229–244.

Chilcot, John. *Report of the Iraq Inquiry: Volume 6*. London: HMSO, 2016.

Clark, Ian. 'Legitimacy in a global order.' *Review of International Studies* 29, no. 1 (2003): 75–95.

Clark, Ian. *Legitimacy in International Society*. Oxford: Oxford University Press, 2005.

Finnemore, Martha. *National Interests in International Society*. Ithaca, NY: Cornell University Press, 1996.

Finnemore, Martha. *The Purpose of Intervention: Changing Beliefs About the Use of Force*. Ithaca, NY: Cornell University Press, 2003.

Finnemore, Martha. 'Legitimacy, hypocrisy, and the social structure of unipolarity: why being a unipole isn't all it's cracked up to be.' *World Politics* 61, no. 1 (2009): 58–85.

Finnemore, Martha, and Kathryn Sikkink. 'International norm dynamics and political change.' *International Organization* 52, no. 4 (1998): 887–917.

Franck, Thomas. 'Legitimacy in the international system.' *American Journal of International Law* 82, no. 4 (1988): 705–759.

Grafstein, Robert. 'The failure of Weber's conception of legitimacy: its causes and implications.' *The Journal of Politics* 43, no. 2 (1981): 456–472.

Habermas, Jurgen. *The Theory of Communicative Action: Volume 1: Reason and the Rationalisation of Society*. Translated by Thomas McCarthy. London: Heinemann Educational Books Ltd, 1981.

Hansard. *House of Commons Debates*, vol. 383, 10 April 2002.

Hansard. *House of Commons Debates*, vol. 401, 18 March 2003.

Hansen, Lene. *Security as Practice: Discourse Analysis and the Bosnian War*. Abingdon: Routledge, 2006.

Hurd, Ian. 'Legitimacy and authority in international politics.' *International Organization* 53, no. 2 (1999): 379–408.

Hurrell, Andrew. 'Legitimacy and the use of force: can the circle be squared?' *Review of International Studies* 31, no. 1 (2005): 15–32.

Katzenstein, Peter. 'Alternative perspectives on national security.' In *The Culture of National Security: Norms and Identity in World Politics*, by Peter Katzenstein, 1–32. New York, NY: Columbia University Press, 1996.

Kornprobst, Markus. 'International relations as a rhetorical discipline: toward (re-)newing horizons.' *International Studies Review* 11, no. 1 (2009): 87–108.

Kornprobst, Markus. 'From political judgements to public justifications (and vice versa): how communities generate reasons upon which to act.' *European Journal of International Relations* 20, no. 1 (2014): 192–216.

Kratochwil, Friedrich. *Rules, Norms and Decisions: on the Conditions of Practical and Legal Reasoning in International Relations and Domestic Affairs.* Cambridge: Cambridge University Press, 1989.

Kratochwil, Friedrich. 'The embarrassment of changes: neo-realism as the science of Realpolitik without politics.' *Review of International Studies* 19, no. 1 (1993): 63–80.

Krebs, Ronald, and Patrick Thaddeus Jackson. 'Twisting tongues and twisting arms: the power of political rhetoric.' *European Journal of International Relations* 13, no. 1 (2007): 35–66.

Manin, Bernard, Elly Stein, and Jane Mansbridge. 'On legitimacy and political deliberation.' *Political Theory* 15, no. 3 (1987): 338–368.

Milliken, Jennifer. 'The study of discourse in international relations: a critique of research and methods.' *European Journal of International Relations* 5, no. 2 (1999): 225–254.

Mitzen, Jennifer. 'Reading Habermas in anarchy: multilateral diplomacy and global public spaces.' *American Political Science Review* 99, no. 3 (2005): 401–417.

Muller, Harald. 'Arguing, bargaining and all that: communicative action, rationalist theory and the logic of appropriateness in international relations.' *European Journal of International Relations* 10, no. 3 (2004): 395–435.

Onuf, Nicholas. *World of Our Making: Rules and Rule in Social Theory and International Relations.* Columbia, SC: University of South Carolina Press, 1989.

Reus-Smit, Christian. 'Human rights and the social construction of sovereignty.' *Review of International Studies* 27, no. 4 (2001): 519–538.

Reus-Smit, Christian. 'Imagining society: constructivism and the English School.' *British Journal of Politics and International Relations* 4, no. 3 (2002): 487–509.

Reus-Smit, Christian. 'International crises of legitimacy.' *International Politics* 44, no. 2 (2007): 157–174.

Reus-Smit, Christian. 'Reading history through constructivist eyes.' *Millennium: Journal of International Studies* 37, no. 2 (2008): 395–414.

Risse, Thomas. 'Let's argue!: Communicative action in world politics.' *International Organization* 54, no. 1 (2000): 1–39.

Rycroft, Matthew. 'Iraq: Prime Minister's meeting, 23 July.' 23 July 2002. www.iraqinquiry.org.uk/media/232630/2002-07-23-letter-rycroft-to-manning-iraq-prime-ministers-meeting-23-july.pdf#search=rycroft (accessed 20 July 2016).

Searle, John. *The Construction of Social Reality.* New York, NY: The Free Press, 1995.

Steffek, Jens. 'The legitimation of international governance: a discourse approach.' *European Journal of International Relations* 9, no. 2 (2003): 249–275.

Stephen, Matthew. '"Can you pass the salt?" The legitimacy of international institutions and indirect speech.' *European Journal of International Relations* 21, no. 4 (2015): 768–792.

Stothard, Peter. *30 Days: A Month at the Heart of Blair's War.* London: Harper Collins, 2003.

Walzer, Michael. *Just and Unjust Wars: A Moral Argument with Historical Illustrations.* New York, NY: Basic Books, 1977.

Weldes, Jutta. 'Constructing national interest.' *European Journal of International Relations* 2, no. 2 (1996): 275–318.

5 Threat and WMD

This chapter discusses the debate over the threat that Iraq posed to British national security. According to the Blair government, Britain invaded Iraq to dismantle two distinct risks relating to its chemical, biological and nuclear weapons programmes. First, ministers feared that Iraqi weapons might reach terrorists looking to attack the West. Second, they thought Iraq might use its capabilities to destabilize the Middle East. An official 'dossier' published in September 2002 asserted the case in stark and certain terms. Iraq developed and used so-called 'Weapons of Mass Destruction' (WMD) during the 1980s. As a condition of the ceasefire that ended the Gulf War in 1991, the UN Security Council required Iraq to disarm. It failed to comply with UN weapons inspectors, who withdrew in 1998, prompting a brief US-led bombing campaign. Western intelligence agencies believed that Iraq reconstituted its programmes between 1998 and 2002, and that considerable stocks of banned materials survived. Shocked to action by the 11 September attacks, both Washington and London felt the need to do something. They knew that might mean war.

Framing Iraq as a threat to Britain should have helped the Blair government legitimize its invasion (Hayes 2016, 2–4). Democratic publics may dislike military aggression, but they generally support the use of force in self-defence (Finnemore 2003, 2; Hansen 2006, 34–35). Instead, however, ministers' efforts to frame Iraq as a security priority stalled. While the 'dossier' went down fairly well, it changed few minds. Both parliament and the press questioned the claims it made. Few disputed that Iraq was in violation of its UN-imposed disarmament obligations. But, as the government itself failed to appreciate sufficiently, that did not necessarily make it dangerous. Too many in Britain thought the risk of WMD reaching terrorists was too remote and hypothetical to make intervention necessary, proportionate and just. That was bad enough. But despite their relative lack of impact on the pre-invasion debate, after March 2003 the claims ministers earlier made about the Iraqi threat became, in Chilcot's words, "the baseline against which the Government's good faith and credibility were judged" (Chilcot 2016d, 283). Those judgements were rarely favourable.

Three shortcomings in the government's approach help us understand how its arguments about the Iraqi threat helped make possible the legitimacy deficit surrounding the war. First, ministers and officials misjudged the Iraqi threat. Iraq

72 *Legitimacy*

was not in fact developing WMD. It no longer possessed significant WMD stocks. It was not in league with *al-Qaeda*. It was not about to trigger a regional war. Considering the contemporary intelligence picture, Iraq's past record and the post-11 September atmosphere, it makes some sense that both the US and UK governments got this particular judgement wrong (Jervis 2010, 124). Being wrong is still damaging, however. To make matters worse, the Chilcot Report shows that SIS downplayed weaknesses in its evidence, that the JIC fell victim to 'groupthink' and that ministers held and publicly expressed beliefs that exaggerated or contradicted the advice they received (Chilcot 2016d). None of this did much for the invasion's legitimacy, especially once it became public knowledge. Second, the government's communication efforts downplayed caveats surrounding the intelligence services' judgements about Iraq's capabilities. Lord Butler's review of Britain's intelligence on Iraqi WMD concluded that a "changed calculus of threat" in the aftermath of the 11 September attacks led ministers to reinterpret risks previously thought manageable in a more urgent, threatening light (Butler 2004, 34). At the same time, their lack of direct knowledge about Iraq's WMD activities left officials operating amidst considerable uncertainty and over-reliant on extrapolation from past Iraqi behaviour. Engaging in communicative action means being honest about the basis for the claims one makes. That was not the Blair government's approach. Though it did have grounds for fearing its critics would not listen to nuanced arguments, its claim to Habermasian legitimacy suffered. Finally, ministers proved unable not to exploit the information advantage they enjoyed. Downing Street received secret, intelligence-derived information other actors could not safely see. That made the Iraq debate unequal, a significant issue given communicative action can take place only among equals. While the government framed the dossier as an attempt to reduce the resulting information gap, in reality it exploited its advantage to promote the use of force.

Judgement

Two misjudgements undermined the Blair government's arguments about the Iraqi threat. First, ministers believed Iraq was developing banned WMD. It was not. Second, they thought those WMD threatened Britain. They did not. The fact that both claims were wrong goes to the heart of the legitimacy deficit surrounding the war. Understanding where they came from will help us see how it was possible for ministers to base the case for their invasion on incorrect information. To begin with, it seems clear the JIC fell victim to "groupthink", with the result that it exaggerated how much it knew about Iraq in giving advice to ministers (Janis 1982; Butler 2004, 16; Chilcot 2016a, 57). Britain's top intelligence analysts failed to appreciate, let alone to question, the extent to which they viewed new information about Iraq's WMD capabilities through the lens of its past conduct. They failed to revisit, let alone to revise, their views in response to new information. Second, ministers themselves believed things the JIC did not. Blair framed Iraqi WMD as a "current and serious threat to the UK national interest" in his foreword to the 'dossier' (British Government 2002). Chilcot found that Blair did indeed believe this statement, but also that it "did not reflect the view of the JIC (Chilcot 2016d, 247). No wonder the threat dimension of the Iraq debate raised issues in the long term.

Defining the threat

The problem began with how the government defined the Iraqi threat. Within weeks of the 11 September attacks, the Bush administration embarked upon a rhetorical, political and literal 'war on terrorism' (Hoijer *et al.* 2004, 7; Jackson 2005, 31; Burke 2011, 46). Tony Blair bought into it wholeheartedly. He referred in public to the prospect of an all-out battle "between the free and democratic world and terrorism" (Blair 2001a). He warned MPs that the very values of Western society were at stake (Blair 2001b, col. 604). He wrote in his autobiography that 11 September was indeed "a declaration of war", one to which the West had no choice but to respond (Blair 2010, 342). Extending the point, Jack Straw warned that

> people who have the fanaticism and the capability to fly an airliner laden with passengers and fuel into a skyscraper will not be deterred by human decency from deploying chemical or biological weapons, missiles or nuclear weapons if they are available to them
>
> (Straw 2001a, col. 619)

This was vivid imagery, and in the febrile aftermath of 11 September far from unusual. It also directly contradicted the advice both Straw and Blair received. John Scarlett and Stephen Lander told Blair on 11 September that *al-Qaeda* was unlikely to associate with "rogue governments" (Campbell and Stott 2007, 560). A briefing prepared for David Manning, Blair's foreign policy advisor, ahead of a visit to the US in December 2001 underlined the point which noted that Iraq "has no responsibility for the 11 September attacks and no significant links to UBL/Al Qaida", even if there was "real reason for concern about Iraq's WMD programmes" in a general sense (McDonald 2001).

Eliza Manningham-Buller offered similar advice ahead of Blair's trip to Texas in March 2002. MI5 believed "Saddam is only likely to order terrorist attacks if he perceives that the survival of his regime is threatened". Even then, Manningham-Buller went on, the "Iraqi capability to mount attacks in the UK is currently limited". In any event, Saddam's "preferred option would be to use conventional military delivery systems [for chemical weapons] against targets in the region, rather than terrorism" (Manningham-Buller 2002). As the Chilcot Report put it, "Saddam Hussein's regime had the potential to proliferate material and know-how to terrorist groups, but it was not judged likely to do so ... there was no basis in the JIC Assessments to suggest that Iraq ... represented such a threat" (Chilcot 2016e, 610–611). Key ministers, especially Straw and Blair, effectively internalized the US 'war on terrorism' narrative despite the JIC's conclusion that Iraq was not a direct threat to Britain (Joint Intelligence Committee 2002b). This apparently was not simply a rhetorical tactic. Blair actually believed that Iraqi WMD could reach terrorists who would use them on the West. As he put it in his autobiography, "I certainly thought so. Actually, I still think so" (Blair 2010b, 386). Others within government were more circumspect. During a meeting in Downing Street on 23 July 2002, Straw observed that "the case was thin. Saddam was not threatening his neighbours, and his WMD capability was less than that of Libya, North Korea or Iran". Richard Dearlove warned at the same time that "the intelligence and facts were being fixed around the policy" in the US (Rycroft 2002), a comment he later confirmed related specifically to the suggestion that Iraq might work with terrorists (Chilcot 2016c, 63). Attorney-General Lord Goldsmith followed up the 23 July meeting with a note to the Prime Minister warning "on the basis of the material which I have been shown ... there would not be any grounds for regarding an Iraqi use of WMD as imminent" (Goldsmith 2002). Blair held firm.

Limited intelligence

Two key intelligence errors during the course of 2002 undermined the advice the intelligence services provided. First, the JIC focused its attention on the narrow question of whether Iraq was developing banned WMD, allowing ministers quietly to forget the doubts it previously expressed about whether Iraq actually threatened Britain. Straw and Goldsmith apparently recognized the distinction. Blair seemingly did not. Compounding the issue, the JIC then answered its narrower question incorrectly. It repeatedly failed to consider alternative hypotheses, never considered that Iraq might have disarmed, and interpreted new intelligence on the assumption that Saddam Hussein was doing something wrong. For example, JIC analysts interpreted Saddam's order that Iraqi officers should ensure that UNMOVIC saw no grounds for complaint as evidence he intended to circumvent the inspection process. As Chilcot points out, the same intelligence might also indicate a desire to co-operate. Iraq repeatedly lied about its WMD activities during the 1990s, and UNMOVIC did find evidence of proscribed activities during early 2003. Chilcot admitted that the JIC's judgements have to be "considered in the context that past Iraqi statements had often been shown to be untrue" (Chilcot 2016d, 290, 304, 416). They were nevertheless wrong.

Blair, Campbell, Powell, and Straw all told the Chilcot Inquiry that, in their view, few people in government, the public, or the wider international community doubted that Iraq possessed deployable WMD prior to the invasion (Blair 2010a, 78; Campbell 2010a, 94; Powell 2010, 50; Straw 2011, 54). Everts and Isernia (2005, 273) found that "most people in countries where polls were held on the issue" agreed. Members of the Defence Intelligence Staff within the MoD complained internally about the phrasing of the 'dossier'. They still believed Iraq could develop a nuclear bomb in under a year, though only if it successfully circumvented Western sanctions (Defence Intelligence Staff 2002). Chief of the Defence Staff Admiral Mike Boyce, Head of the Diplomatic Service Lord Jay and UNMOVIC chairman Hans Blix all told Anthony Seldon they believed Iraq had WMD (Seldon *et al.* 2007, 138). Blix confirmed as much to Chilcot, recalling that "I, like most people at the time, felt that Iraq retains weapons of mass destruction" (Blix 2010, 29–30). Both the Blair government itself and its advisors in the intelligence community erred by answering a different question to the one they ostensibly posed. Asked whether Iraq threatened Britain, they replied that it was probably developing WMD; a better-evidenced but less dramatic conclusion than the government's public communications had implied.

Second, some members of the intelligence community apparently lost their objectivity. Richard Dearlove and SIS come in for particular criticism in the Chilcot Report. Chilcot noted that Dearlove travelled extensively with Blair in the aftermath of 11 September "and got to know the Prime Minister and the Prime Minister got to know him" (Chilcot 2016b, 279). Chilcot implies, without stating as much directly, that Dearlove grew too close to Blair, and began to advocate a particular policy line rather than simply offering impartial advice. This mattered. At one stage, late in the Iraq debate, Blair told Dearlove "Richard, my fate is in your hands". Dearlove apparently responded to the Prime Minister's expectations. He personally intervened in JIC deliberations to advocate for new SIS material to be included in the dossier while downplaying the fact that it "had not been properly evaluated" and "should have been treated with caution", as Chilcot observed. He complained to Straw that the draft dossier "was weakened by the JIC doctrinaire approach to drafting" and stated he would be happier "if SIS made its own in-house judgements on the release of material" (Chilcot 2016d, 322, 239–240, 149). Straw did not take up the suggestion, which turned out to be a good thing. SIS did not exactly cover itself with glory in the pre-Iraq period. It received new information in August 2002 that it attributed to an "established and reliable line of reporting" which went on to impact the dossier significantly (Hutton 2004, 112). SIS did not tell the JIC that none of the fresh material it presented was actually "based on first-hand knowledge", and it refused to give other agencies access to its sources, citing the need to ensure secrecy. Doubts emerged within SIS about the information presented even before the end of 2002. It became clear that one source was a fantasist. His description of a nerve gas delivery system drew heavily on a technically-inaccurate fictional portrayal in the Hollywood movie *The Rock*. SIS did not report these doubts to the rest of the JIC, and only formally withdrew the relevant intelligence reports after the invasion. Even then, "Mr Blair and Mr Hoon became aware that the reporting had been withdrawn as a result of the Butler Review" rather than because SIS brought the issue to their attention (Chilcot 2016d, 164, 312–313, 387). To some extent SIS was simply following standard operating procedures like a good bureaucracy. Nevertheless, the consequences damaged the government.

John Scarlett told Chilcot these reports were among several received at around the same time that "led to a firming up of what were already quite firm judgments" that Iraq retained WMD it was prepared to use (Scarlett 2009, 59). In particular, they underpinned the JIC assessment on 9 September 2002 that Iraq's "chemical and biological munitions could be with military units and ready for firing within 20–45 minutes" (Joint Intelligence Committee 2002b). This judgement in turn informed the statement in the dossier that "the Iraqi military are able to deploy chemical and biological weapons within 45 minutes of an order to do so" (British Government 2002, 19). It attracted particular notoriety in the aftermath of the invasion when a BBC journalist alleged that Downing Street inserted the claim against the wishes of the JIC, an incident discussed in Chapter 9. Though Blair and his inner circle were cleared of this specific charge by Lord Hutton, and indeed by the Chilcot Report (Chilcot 2016d, 281), the '45-minute claim' still stands as an example of how problematic the government's use of flawed information about Iraqi WMD actually was. For one thing, the wording of the dossier did not precisely follow that of the JIC assessment. The JIC referred specifically to 'munitions', meaning battlefield artillery shells deployable over a relatively short range. The dossier talked more vaguely of 'weapons', implying a greater threat than the JIC actually identified (Chilcot 2016d, 8). Several observers thought 'weapons' meant missiles capable of hitting long-range targets, including RAF Akrotiri in Cyprus or even mainland Europe. The front cover of the *Evening Standard* on the day of the dossier's release featured an image of rows of bombs supposedly containing nerve gas under the headline "45 minutes from attack", implying a direct threat to Britain (Reiss 2002). Alastair Campbell told Chilcot that just "one or two" British newspapers interpreted the statement in the dossier as a reference to ballistic missiles (Campbell 2010a, 112). This study identified at least nine separate articles across the following day's *Daily Mail*, *Daily Telegraph*, *Guardian*, *Independent*, *Mirror*, *Sun* and *The Times* that repeated either the dossier's ambiguous reference to "weapons" or the *Standard*'s more specific description of Iraqi missiles. No less an expert than former chief UN weapons inspector Charles Duelfer commented in *The Times* that the inclusion of the '45-minute claim' in the dossier suggested "that concrete intelligence has now been obtained" of something UNSCOM "strongly suspected", namely "that the regime had the ability to launch a chemical or biological attack" (Duelfer 2002). Only the *Guardian*'s expert commentators noted the claim was "a bit vague" as to whether it referred to missiles or artillery, and concluded that if it meant munitions then it was credible but unsurprising. Of course, Iraq could launch artillery shells carrying chemical agents. It did so in the 1980s, which was how it gained its reputation for using WMD in the first place (Pallister and Watt 2002). The difference therefore mattered a great deal.

Campbell insisted to Chilcot that governments couldn't possibly correct every single misunderstanding that appeared in the press (Campbell 2010b, 4). He further maintained that no one in Downing Street sought to draw journalists' attention to the 45-minute claim (Campbell 2010a, 111). Lord Butler spoke to "some 60 editors of national and regional print and broadcast media" to check this. He found "some journalists had had their attention drawn *after* its publication to passages in the Prime Minister's Foreword" but that "the '45-minute' story attracted attention because it was of itself an eye-catching item" in an otherwise dry document (Butler 2004, 127, emphasis in original). Jonathan

Powell asked Campbell on 19 September "what will the *Standard* headline be [on the day of the dossier's release]? What do we want it to be?" (Powell 2002b), implying a deliberate effort at media manipulation. But Powell told Chilcot that this "relates back to an in-joke from opposition time [relating to Campbell's poor record of predicting *Standard* headlines] ... so it was a bit of a sort of a dig, I am afraid, rather than a serious point" (Powell 2010, 63). Geoff Hoon, meanwhile, told Chilcot that he requested a special briefing when he read the 45-minute claim, which he noted was "the only thing in the draft that I had not seen before in terms of my familiarity with the intelligence". He, however, admitted that he did not pay attention to the media reaction, and did not see the *Standard* front page until "shortly before Lord Hutton reported" in 2004 (Hoon 2010, 120). David Omand concluded that "with hindsight, one can see that adding a bit of local colour like that is asking for trouble", highlighting the point that the statement was at the conservative end of the JIC's actual assessment. He insisted, however, that "we didn't really spot that at the time" (Omand 2010, 25). It was a damaging mistake.

Nuance

Being wrong was bad enough. But the Blair government also exaggerated. It deliberately downplayed how nuanced its understanding of the Iraqi threat was. Britain did not know what was going on in Iraq during 2002 and early 2003. Chilcot found that SIS had "no sources of human intelligence with reliable first-hand knowledge of Iraq's WMD capabilities or Saddam Hussein's intentions" (Chilcot 2016d, 405). Against the backdrop of the 11 September attacks, however, this uncertainty looked ominous. Jack Straw later described a heightened "perception of risk" amongst decision-makers at this time (Straw 2010a, 7). High-impact risks that were once thought too improbable to worry about suddenly seemed more concerning. As Straw told Blair in March 2002, "objectively, the threat from Iraq has not worsened.... What has however changed is the tolerance of the international community (especially that of the US)" (Straw 2002a). The tolerance of the US had indeed changed. Over the course of 2002 President Bush set out a new doctrine for the use of force. He asserted a right to act pre-emptively against potential threats, rather than waiting for them to crystallize. The Blair government bought into this narrative, though ministers disagreed over how far to prioritize Iraq. It tried not to advertise it. Most British commentators found the Bush doctrine too aggressive. Too many distrusted Bush, and his motives. Managing public debate proved difficult enough without trying to win a difficult hypothetical argument about what really constituted a threat in the post-11 September world. So, the government largely did not do it.

The Bush doctrine

President Bush first introduced his new doctrine in a speech to cadets at West Point during June 2002. "We must take the battle to the enemy", he declared, "disrupt his plans and confront the worst threats before they emerge" (Bush 2002b). Following up in October he maintained "we cannot wait for the final proof – the smoking gun – that could come in the form of a mushroom cloud" (Bush 2002c). Blair echoed the point to the Trades Union Congress in September, emphasizing the potential threat posed by Iraq (Blair 2002e).

No one in Britain was surprised that the Bush administration turned its attentions to Iraq. During the initial Afghan campaign, one observer noted Washington still regarded Iraq as "the quintessential terrorist state" (Almond 2001). Another noted "a new argument" developing across the Atlantic: "Since the Iraqi regime is building weapons of mass destruction, and is known to consort with terrorists, and since Osama bin Laden made clear his desire to acquire such weapons, the US is entitled to take action against Iraq" (MacIntyre 2001). That was indeed the argument Bush made. His first State of the Union Address saw him denounce Iraq, Iran and North Korea "and their terrorist allies" as "an axis of evil, arming to threaten the peace of the world" (Bush 2002a). Linking 'rogue states' to terrorism both allowed Bush to propose conventional military solutions to the threats the US faced and facilitated a shift in focus to Iraq, one driven by deeper pressures within his administration. Britain sympathized with the thrust of Bush's claims, but ministers worried privately about how to "de-link" the three very different states he named (Straw 2002a). Defence Secretary Hoon told Blair shortly before the Crawford meeting that "in objective terms, Iran may be the greater problem for the UK" (Hoon 2002a). The first version of the document that eventually became the WMD 'dossier' covered all three 'axis of evil' states. It was shelved in part to avoid confusing the issue (Straw 2011, 48) and in part because Straw became convinced it lacked sufficient evidence to persuade critics (Chilcot 2016a, 71).

Bush's speech directly affected British public debate. The morning before, the British right-wing press stuck to their established script, arguing that while action was needed to curb Saddam Hussein's ability to challenge Western power, direct efforts to root out international terrorism were a greater priority (*The Times* 2002a). The morning after, they hailed the speech as evidence of a welcome "paradigm shift" in US thinking about international security (Harnden 2002). Theirs was not, however, the majority view. Critics complained that "tragedy does not give America a free hand", and attacking the 'axis of evil' concept as "nonsense" or "ludicrous tripe" (*Guardian* 2002a; Maddox 2002a; Routledge 2002a). Ministers anticipated such a reaction. One of the earliest 'war cabinet' meetings after 11 September predicted the US would at some point turn its attentions to Baghdad. It was "possible to be sympathetic", the meeting concluded, but "the political consequences" of rash action were "all too obvious" (Campbell and Stott 2007, 567). Blair told Bush in December 2001 "I have no doubt we need to deal with Saddam. But if we hit Iraq now, we would lose the Arab world, Russia, probably half the EU ... we just don't need it debated too freely in public" (Blair 2001c).

Blair's reluctance reflected political as well as diplomatic realities. Criticized after the 'axis of evil' speech, Downing Street hinted that it would publish evidence of the Iraqi threat. In response, the chairman of the newly-formed Stop the War coalition asked if ministers could really "be trusted when it comes to war and peace" (Murray 2002). Journalists talked of "New Labour's declining reputation for probity" (Glover 2002) while MPs responded sarcastically, with one Labour backbencher predicting "we will read that some such weapons are more sophisticated than those in the Pentagon" (Mahon 2002, col. 77WH). Pro-war Conservatives seized the opportunity to attack the good faith of a Labour prime minister, despite the fact many agreed with the substance of what he was apparently doing. When the government announced its decision to delay the publication, critics pointed to "mendacious spin", "incompetence" or "negligence at a very high level" as likely causes (D'Ancona 2002; Pilger 2002; Oborne 2002). To understand the Blair government's reluctance to express the nuances in its arguments openly, we need to appreciate the degree of distrust it faced.

Pressure from the press

Three factors made the Blair government's news management efforts especially challenging. To begin with, as Robin Cook complained, newspapers, "terrified that they will be the last to get in on the storyline", repeatedly published speculative claims that military action was imminent (Cook 2003, 113). During his 20 June press conference, journalists demanded that Blair accept that reports of imminent US military action that were published by the *New York Times* were "certain to be correct" (Blair 2002c). They were not. On the same day, Bernard Jenkin and Tam Dalyell challenged Geoff Hoon to explain apparently bellicose comments by the US Chairman of the Joint Chiefs on BBC radio. General Myers did not work for Hoon. On 5 July, the first of a series of Pentagon information 'leaks' took place, with details appearing in the *New York Times* of a planned "massive military assault on Iraq" drawn from an internal Bush Administration paper (Schmitt 2002). The *Independent on Sunday*'s coverage observed that "this sort of document never surfaces by accident", implying (probably rightly) that it reflected arguments taking place behind the scenes in Washington (Cornwell and Brown 2002). Commentators began to view "the volume and density of the leaks, to say nothing of their frequency" as decisive evidence that the US was about to go to war (Hitchens 2002). This speculation increased further following the 15 July announcement that Blair would again visit the US in September. British newspapers responded by warning against the country "sleepwalking" into an invasion, and began to speculate that military action would begin before the US mid-term elections on 5 November, if not earlier (*Mirror* 2002a; Routledge 2002b; *Daily Mail* 2002a). This was incorrect, if not entirely implausible. British ministers insisted that no decisions had been taken as to what would be done, and no military action was imminent (Hoon 2002b, col. 413; Blair 2002d, col. 36). Their claims fell on deaf ears.

A second issue concerned the ease with which observers incorporated government claims about the Iraqi threat into their preconceived policy positions. *The Times* of 29 August, for example, argued before seeing the dossier that:

no reasonable person doubts that Saddam is actively pursuing weapons of mass destruction, no neutral observer would contest that his motives for that quest are either to blackmail his neighbours or sponsor attacks on others, and no rational figure could believe that he will abandon this effort of his own volition.

(*The Times* 2002b)

By contrast, four separate newspapers (from both the left and right of the political spectrum) carried leading articles describing the government's statements up to that point as an inadequate justification for war (*Daily Mail* 2002b; *Daily Telegraph* 2002; *Guardian* 2002b; *Independent* 2002a). They, too, remained unmoved by ministerial efforts to respond. Given the amount of information already publicly available about Iraq's WMD, some observers worried that Blair risked "setting up expectations he is unlikely to fulfil" by promising to prove that Iraq was a threat. "Those who are already deeply alarmed will feel vindicated", they warned, "but those who are critical or uneasy about an attack on Iraq are unlikely to find enough to convince them" (Maddox 2002b). Alastair Campbell expressed similar concerns (Campbell and Stott 2007, 633). Sceptics generally did admit that "the case for war could be made", given that "Saddam has acquired chemical and biological weapons in the past and tried to acquire nuclear weapons" (*Independent* 2002). They maintained, however, that there was insufficient evidence of a new or immediate threat to justify war.

How journalists interpreted the International Institute for Strategic Studies report on Iraqi WMD, released in early September 2002, offered a taste of their likely response to the government 'dossier'. On one level, by providing an authoritative but apolitical discussion of evidence already in the public domain, the IISS reinforced the government's credibility. Indeed, as both Jack Straw and Alastair Campbell pointed out to the Chilcot Inquiry, the IISS report went further than the government did in describing the Iraqi nuclear threat (Campbell 2010a, 102; Straw 2011, 57). Most press coverage incorporated the IISS findings into established editorial lines. The *Daily Mail* concluded that "nothing in the IISS report is a surprise", insisting that the threat was already well known, and maintaining that no further action was required to contain it (*Daily Mail* 2002c). The *Independent* thought the IISS contribution was "interesting ... but by no means ... particularly decisive" in terms of the broader debate over Iraqi disarmament (*Independent* 2002c). Most revealingly, the IISS assessment that Iraq was several years from nuclear capacity under sanctions, but could put together a weapon in months if it was able to illicitly obtain enriched uranium, received highly selective coverage. The *Mirror* reported that "Saddam Hussein is years away from developing his own nuclear weapons" (Blackman 2002) and the *Sun* reported that "Saddam Hussein could have nuclear weapons within months" (Hughes 2002). Both of these articles were, ostensibly, objective news reports. Both in fact presented descriptions of the IISS report heavily skewed by their respective publications' editorial positions. The government could expect similar treatment for its own dossier.

Finally, press critics repeatedly moved the goalposts in terms of what information they expected the government to produce. Information was not, in other words, what they really wanted. One commentator complained in March that any document the government released would contain "little new or surprising evidence" (Rufford 2002). It did not matter how dangerous Iraq was, what mattered was novelty. With the IISS report having undermined the most hostile critical attacks, opponents of military action shifted from claiming the dossier would contain "spin" or "propaganda" (Routledge 2002c; Lewis-Smith 2002) to demanding "something really unexpected" to convince them to change their view (*Mirror* 2002c). In the process, they accepted the claim underpinning the government's threat narrative, that "Saddam's not a very nice guy and has some rather unpleasant weapons" but still argued that because "we knew that when we pulled back from Baghdad in 1991", military action to deal with those weapons could not possibly be justified, regardless of how dangerous they were (*Mirror* 2002b; *Guardian* 2002c). Though supportive publications insisted the document would be "sober in tone" and that it would "directly reject Iraqi claims" (T. Jones 2002; Bone and Webster 2002), no one really expected a 'smoking gun'. This was a problem. The government's whole argument was that the risk of waiting for a smoking gun was too great to take. Faced with public hostility, ministers failed to press their case.

Parliament's response to the dossier echoed the press debate. Jon Owen Jones, a Labour MP, argued that "few in the House or outside would disagree … that Saddam Hussein's regime represents a threat" (J.O. Jones 2002, col. 20). Conservative Leader of the Opposition, Iain Duncan Smith agreed that making claims about Iraq's ability to enrich uranium went beyond the government's, insisting "Saddam has the motive to strike against Britain" and implying that meant he also possessed the means (Duncan Smith 2002, cols. 7–8). Most of those who spoke accepted that Iraq retained some WMD capacity, but a majority thought military action was not yet a practical or proportionate response. Only a handful critiqued the government's arguments directly, and they were mostly the 'usual suspects' like George Galloway who could easily be ignored. Press commentators expressed disappointment with both the dossier itself and the parliamentary discussion surrounding it. Many focused on the document's failure to offer the new evidence of an imminent Iraqi threat they had previously accepted it would not provide (*Daily Mail* 2002d; *Independent* 2002d). The *Mirror* stuck to its critical stance, calling Blair's speech "as good a defence of the indefensible as was possible" and printing several articles expressing distrust of Blair and accusing the government of propagandizing (*Mirror* 2002d). The *Sun* meanwhile called the evidence presented "overwhelming and – except to the most blinkered minds – irrefutable" (*Sun* 2002). As Butler later concluded, the dossier was regarded in September 2002 as "cautious, and even dull" because it lacked smoking guns (Butler 2004, 76). It changed few minds and made little impact on opinion polls, though Chilcot found that the Cabinet "absorbed it and accepted it" (Chilcot 2016d, 261). As Chapter 3 argues, the dossier's main contribution was that it answered critics' demands for information, and so dampened speculation for a time.

82 *Legitimacy*

The key point here is that the Blair government struggled to persuade critics even when it downplayed nuances in its argument and failed to admit shortcomings in the evidence underpinning it. A more balanced approach emphasizing the hypothetical but unlikely possibility that Iraqi WMD might wind up in the hands of terrorists would probably not have worked. This in turn points to one key reason why this strand of the case for war helped undermine its legitimacy in the long term. To secure legitimacy through public deliberation, leaders must be open and honest about the bases for statements they make. They must also be willing to adjust course if it transpires that their claims lack sufficient weight. That was not what the Blair government did. Instead, it repeatedly reiterated its case, despite lacking good evidence, downplaying more nuanced arguments about the uncertainty surrounding Iraq's WMD activities from 1998 onwards and suggesting instead that Iraq threatened Britain directly.

Evidence

As foreign policy decision-makers often do, the Blair government enjoyed a considerable information advantage over its critics throughout the Iraq debate. Ministers saw secret intelligence assessments not available to MPs, let alone journalists and ordinary citizens. This imbalance was inevitable to some extent. Governments always know things their constituents do not, especially in more remote arenas like foreign policy (Holsti 1996, 215). Public actors lack independent information sources and must rely on what governments see fit to reveal. Once a conflict starts, journalists can, over time, narrow the information gap, which indeed happened after the invasion of Iraq (Baum and Groeling 2010). But getting unrestricted access to potentially hostile territory can be tricky, especially in the build-up to a war. Given the Blair government's stated commitment to legitimizing its plans for war through an open public debate, the extent of the information advantage it enjoyed was problematic. Achieving legitimacy through communicative action means ensuring public debate remains both open and well-informed (Bjola 2009, 76, 139). It is difficult to meet these criteria when the government's case for action depends on evidence the public cannot safely see (Hurrell 2005, 22; Kaufmann 2004, 42). British ministers found it impossible to inform public debate over Iraq without giving vital secrets away. This is a common shortcoming. More damningly, it also did a bad job of presenting the evidence it felt able to publish in a fair and balanced fashion.

Judgement and evidence

Warning signs appeared right at the start of the 'war on terrorism'. After the 11 September attacks the government released a 'dossier' asserting that "Usama Bin Laden and Al Qaida, the terrorist network which he heads, planned and carried out the atrocities on 11 September 2001" (British Government 2001). It was an uncontroversial claim, well-supported by evidence available publicly. Its presentation still raised concerns. Menzies Campbell warned that the government was putting its credibility on the line by making statements parliament could not independently verify (Campbell 2001, cols. 704–705). This was not an issue in 2001, but became one after 2003. Most commentators ignored the document entirely. Those who did read it noted it presented "not 'evidence', so much as a convincing argument" (Robertson 2001). This was an important distinction to make. It proved more important still after the WMD 'dossier' emerged, but it was not widely recognized in either government or public debate.

As the Iraq debate got under way, ministers tried to avoid the issue of evidence. Blair told MPs early on that "of course it is important that we act on the basis of evidence" with respect to Iraq (Blair 2001b, col. 679). He gave no indication of what, in practice, that might mean. Robin Cook remarked that much of the early demand for information (from the press, in particular) was self-generated and speculative. But he also observed "it is true that, whenever he gets the opportunity, Tony fails to kill the mounting speculation" (Cook 2003, 113). It *was* true. Blair missed repeated opportunities to clarify his position in the months before Crawford. During the joint press conference with Vice-President Cheney on 11 March, he maintained that "no decisions of course have been taken yet" about the possible use of force, yet also agreed that *something* had to be done about Iraq. Someone asked whether there was evidence that Saddam Hussein posed a threat to Britain. The danger was "not in doubt at all", he replied, contradicting the advice he received privately. He did not elaborate (Blair 2002a). Pressed, similarly, about the IAEA's clean rating of the Iraqi nuclear programme, he maintained that there was "no doubt" that Saddam was "still trying to acquire nuclear capability and ballistic missile capability" (Blair 2002b, col. 32). Clearly, there *was* doubt if the IAEA doubted it.

Introducing the dossier, Blair noted the publication of intelligence information was "unprecedented", but maintained that "in light of the debate about Iraq ... I wanted to share with the British public the reasons why I believe this issue to be a current and serious threat". He framed the dossier as a neutral public information exercise, in other words, claiming that it faithfully reflected the views of the JIC (British Government 2002, 3). This was a deliberate strategy. Chilcot concluded that Downing Street "intended the information and judgements in the Iraq dossier to be seen to be the product of the JIC in order to carry authority with Parliament and the public" (Chilcot 2016d, 281). Relying on formal authority in this way is problematic from a communicative action perspective. Either an argument makes logical sense and builds on strong evidence, or it does not. It should not matter who makes it.

Despite Blair's claims, the dossier did not in fact reflect precisely the intelligence advice he received. Instead, Chilcot concluded, it "conveyed more certainty than the JIC Assessments about Iraq's proscribed activities and the potential threat they posed" (Chilcot 2016d, 8). Part of the problem stemmed from the fact that the dossier exercise truly was 'unprecedented'. There was no clear process for producing an intelligence-based assessment for public consumption. Officials had to make things up as they went along. David Omand told Chilcot "I didn't see it in any different a light really than an ordinary JIC assessment". He recalled that "two members of the assessment staff were detailed to write it essentially, supervised by the Chief of the Assessments Staff, superintended by the Chairman of the JIC". Omand thought John Scarlett's personal involvement ensured that sensitive material was "being handled in the right way" (Omand 2010, 18). The JIC, however, had no experience of preparing documents for public release. Jon Williams told Chilcot that Scarlett sought the help of a "golden pen", and that he himself volunteered, but Alastair Campbell turned him down (Chilcot 2016d, 153). Most FCO personnel were occupied with preparations for the UN General Assembly during the period between Blair's 3 September press conference and the dossier's publication date (Straw 2011, 50). Campbell ruled that the JIC should take ownership, with Downing Street advising on presentation (Campbell and Stott 2007, 636). The fact this ruling was necessary underlines the ad hoc nature of the exercise.

Information and advocacy

Campbell's involvement raised questions after the invasion. Lord Hutton later concluded it was "wholly appropriate" for the JIC to take presentational advice (Hutton 2004, 108). Omand echoed Hutton's conclusion, strongly rejecting the suggestion that communications advisors were involved in intelligence discussions – "they certainly don't get into the JIC" – while arguing "their views were sought perfectly properly" on their area of expertise (Omand 2010, 19, 20). Hutton concluded that Campbell requested changes to the text to 'firm up' the argument presented, noting that "10 Downing Street ... was concerned that the intelligence ... should be presented in a way which made as strong a case against Saddam Hussein as the intelligence properly permitted". He thought this acceptable because "Mr Scarlett did not accept drafting suggestions emanating from 10 Downing Street unless they were in keeping with the intelligence available to the JIC and he rejected any suggestions which he considered were not supported by such intelligence" (Hutton 2004, 132, 141). Omand reinforced the point, telling Chilcot:

> I think by then I knew John Scarlett well enough, and he knew me well enough, that, if he had felt under pressure [from No. 10], he would have put his head round my office door and said, "Can you help me fend these people off?" But he didn't.
>
> (Omand 2010, 23)

Indeed, Campbell wrote that he told Scarlett "the drier the better, cut the rhetoric", an account the Chilcot Report later confirmed (Campbell and Stott 2007, 637; Chilcot 2016d, 185–186).

However proper it may have been, Campbell's involvement inevitably transformed the dossier from a neutral public information exercise into an act of policy advocacy underpinned by the JIC. Blair claims Lord Hutton cleared the government of 'spinning' the intelligence picture it presented (Blair 2010b, 463).

Blair's interpretation is not entirely accurate. Hutton concluded the government did not deliberately lie, but did intend the dossier to make the case for war rather than simply informing public debate (Hutton 2004, 144). Officials in the Ministry of Defence "had no doubt at that time this was exactly its purpose and these very words ['make the case for war'] were used" (Laurie 2010). Chilcot concluded the dossier was indeed "designed to 'make the case' and secure parliamentary (and public) support for the government's policy" (Chilcot 2016a, 18). Neither Hutton nor Chilcot identified how significant the distinction was between how the government framed the dossier exercise and what it was actually supposed to do. Ministers described the dossier as an attempt to close the information gap. In fact, it formed part of an exercise in "organized political persuasion" (Herring and Robinson 2014, 552). It was an example of strategic persuasion, not communicative action, in a Habermasian sense.

Hutton also acknowledged the possibility

> that the desire of the Prime Minister to have a dossier which ... was as strong as possible in relation to the threat posed by Saddam Hussein's WMD, may have subconsciously influenced Mr Scarlett and the other members of the JIC to make the wording of the dossier somewhat stronger than it would have been.
>
> (Hutton 2004, 152–153)

Freedman went further, attributing the dossier's deviation from the staid format common to JIC assessments to the fact "the JIC were aware that they had to produce a document that was stronger than normal" (Freedman 2004, 27). Lord Butler agreed with Freedman, noting that "the dossier did not follow the format of JIC assessments" but concluding "nor should it have done" given "it was written for a different purpose and a different audience" (Butler 2004, 79–80). Robin Cook, however, expressed concern at the "violence" the dossier did to the "craft" of writing intelligence assessments (Cook 2003, 220). Chilcot concluded that "the JIC accepted ownership of the dossier and agreed its content" and that "there is no evidence that intelligence was improperly included in the dossier or that No. 10 improperly influenced the text". But that was not the point. The point was that the entire exercise conflated policy advocacy and neutral intelligence advice, not least because it juxtaposed the Prime Minister's heavily slanted foreword with more neutral, if still somewhat biased, analysis. Several in government believed the formal distinction between the two parts of the document mattered. One MoD official commented that "the foreword can be as loaded as we like in terms of the political message". Chilcot however concluded it was "unlikely that parliament and the public would have distinguished" between the JIC's judgements and the Prime Minister's comments (Chilcot 2016d, 115, 209, 282). Jonathan Powell reflected that "in hindsight, you'd have been better to just have published the JIC reports" instead of producing a separate dossier (Powell 2010, 65). At least that way the government could not be accused of manipulation, while the JIC would not appear tainted by association with failed political judgements. The intelligence services preferred the dossier approach (Omand 2010, 33).

A final problem stemmed from the way the government talked about the limitations of its information. Jack Straw later conceded that the dossier was incorrect, yet argued that it reflected the underlying intelligence picture. He insisted that "all the little bits of information, however patchy and sporadic, all pointed in one direction", towards Iraq possessing WMD (Straw 2010b, 67). JIC assessments from the period do however describe the information available about Iraq as "sporadic and patchy" and "limited" (Joint Intelligence Committee 2002a, 2002b). Chilcot concluded that the dossier "conveyed certainty without acknowledging the limitations of the intelligence" (Chilcot 2016e, 612). In Parliament, Blair described the intelligence picture as "extensive, detailed and authoritative" (Blair 2002f). The JIC called it "limited" and emphasized "that many of its judgements were inferential" (Chilcot 2016d, 240). Anthony Seldon quotes Butler describing "the three words – extensive, detailed, authoritative" as "the closest Blair came to the 'lie direct'" (Seldon *et al.* 2007, 140).

In his foreword to the dossier, Blair said "I believe the assessed intelligence has established beyond doubt" that Iraq possessed WMD (British Government 2002, 3). The statement involved a problematic rhetorical trick. At Chilcot, Blair insisted this statement was correct. Regardless of what the evidence *objectively* showed, he *subjectively* believed the claims he advanced (Blair 2010a, 80). As Chilcot concluded, the "assessed intelligence had *not* established beyond doubt either that Saddam Hussein had continued to produce chemical and biological weapons or that efforts to develop nuclear weapons continued" (Chilcot 2016d, 116, emphasis added). Blair's view was incorrect. Straw then exacerbated the issue, pointing to what the dossier "shows", "reveals", or "sets out" about the threat. He even referred back to what "the Prime Minister spelt out", as if Blair's assertions themselves constituted evidence. Straw did not refer to belief, judgement, or assessment (Straw 2002b, cols. 27–30). Both Blair and Straw furthermore hinted that there was further evidence not included in the dossier (Butler 2004, 82). Chilcot concluded that these statements did not offer "an accurate description of the intelligence" and that while "there may be evidence which is 'authoritative' or which puts an issue 'beyond doubt' ... there are unlikely to be many circumstances when those descriptions could properly be applied to inferential judgements relying on intelligence" (Chilcot 2016d, 275). Phrases that were included in the foreword because they worked well rhetorically ultimately undermined its accuracy. To make things worse, this exaggeration apparently did not even work.

Downing Street's final failure occurred in February 2003, with the release of a further 'dossier' intended to emphasize concerns that Iraq was successfully circumventing the UN inspection process. Unlike the first document, written by the JIC, this paper emerged from the Coalition Information Centre, a central communications hub devised by Campbell to co-ordinate US, UK and allied press operations during the Afghan campaign. Journalists identified Campbell's secretary, two junior Downing Street press officers, and the Foreign Office "head of story development" as its authors (Wilson 2003). Scarlett and Campbell both approved the document for release, but neither took responsibility for quality control. That proved a mistake, and led to what Campbell described as "a bad own goal" (Campbell and Stott 2007, 664–665). Though it was generally accurate, journalists quickly spotted that the document plagiarized material from a recently-published academic paper (Al-Marashi 2002). Most of the subsequent coverage focused on what this said about the government's trustworthiness in general. Very little discussed the substantive claims the document made. Robin Cook, never a great supporter of Campbell or his techniques, expressed amusement at "this bungling incompetence", but nevertheless worried that "the serious consequence is to damage Tony's credibility when he asks the public to trust him" (Cook 2003, 287). Cook was right to be concerned. Even war supporters complained that "the Number 10 culture of spin is undermining a perfectly good case" (*Daily Telegraph* 2003), while anti-war voices spoke of "a deliberate attempt to hoodwink and mislead the public [which] will undermine trust in anything the government says about the Iraqi threat" (*Observer* 2003; *Independent on Sunday* 2003). An 'own goal' indeed.

Conclusion

Tony Blair describes criticism of statements he made about the Iraqi threat as little more than "*ex post facto* wisdom" (Blair 2010b, 406). As this chapter shows, there is more to it than that. In theory, claiming that Iraq posed at least a potential threat to the United Kingdom should have helped strengthen the Blair government's case for war. In practice, the dossier had a small but noticeable effect on opinion polls and a larger but more short-lived impact on public debate. Two points combined to undermine its credibility. First, though ministers claimed they sought only to level the debating field by informing the public, in reality, they explicitly conceived of the dossier as a persuasive device. The dossier framed intelligence judgements in ways that stretched the limits of the underlying evidence and downplayed its shortcomings. To gain legitimacy through communicative action, leaders need to make honest, accurate and complete claims (Bjola 2009, 76). This is especially true when governments enter a debate with an information advantage relative to other participants, as is often the case in the foreign policy field.

The Blair government, by putting a positive 'spin' on the dossier, prioritized persuasion over information. It engaged in a form of "deception" by implying its policy arguments reflected neutral intelligence assessments (Herring and Robinson 2014). As Chilcot observed, this approach "produced a damaging legacy", making it harder for governments to justify foreign policy decisions "where the evidence depends on inferential judgements drawn from intelligence" (Chilcot 2016d, 116). Parliament's veto of military action in Syria underlines this finding. During the debate in August 2013, several MPs pointed to the JIC's conclusion that the Assad regime probably carried out chemical attacks on civilians in Damascus as evidence that the regime could not possibly be responsible. Once a mark of credibility, the JIC's imprimatur no longer confers authority. Hostile critics probably would have eviscerated a weaker argument in 2002 and 2003. They gave the dossier itself a hard time. But that does not justify the approach the Blair government adopted. If you seek legitimacy through public debate, and you lose, you cannot proceed regardless and expect that lost legitimacy to reappear.

That the judgements underpinning the dossier were also wrong exacerbated these shortcomings. Since Iraq did not in fact threaten the West, the invasion was not a 'Just War'. Nor did it meet the first test from Blair's 'doctrine of international community' speech: "are we sure of our case?" (Blair 1999). Britain was not sure of its case. That was the whole basis of the arguments ministers made, that they could not tolerate uncertainty around dangers as great as WMD. Blair repeatedly made statements that were technically true but dishonest in spirit. His hair-splitting at the Chilcot Inquiry around the significance of the word 'believe' in the foreword to the dossier underlines the point. More broadly, several parts of government got the Iraqi threat wrong, often in a manner that could have been avoided. SIS placed too much weight on untested sources. The JIC failed to reassess its own assumptions as new information arrived. Ministers adopted a definition of the Iraqi threat that went beyond the advice they received, and further exaggerated that definition publicly. It did not have to be this way. Reflecting on Robin Cook's resignation on the eve of war, Chilcot observed that "it was possible for a minister to draw different conclusions from the same information" that Blair and Straw received (Chilcot 2016a, 46). Cook left a security briefing in early 2003 convinced "that Saddam probably does not have weapons of mass destruction in the sense of weapons that could be used against large-scale civilian targets" (Cook 2003, 299). He said as much during his resignation speech. By the start of the invasion the IAEA was on the verge of declaring Iraq nuclear-free (Blix 2004, 211). None of this made any difference to the policy. By asserting a commitment to public deliberation and then exploiting its information advantage to try to persuade its constituents to support war in Iraq, the Blair government damaged its normative claim to legitimacy. By relying heavily on arguments that subsequently turned out to be untrue, it lost legitimacy in political terms, too. What should have been a strong dimension of the case for war in Iraq wound up seriously undermining it. Our analysis of the pre-invasion debate is off to a difficult start.

References

Al-Marashi, Ibrahim. 'Iraq's security and intelligence network: a guide and analysis.' *Middle East Review of International Affairs* 6, no. 3 (2002): 1–13.

Almond, Mark. 'Is Saddam the next target?' *Daily Mail*, 8 October 2001.

Baum, Matthew, and Tim Groeling. 'Reality asserts itself: public opinion and the elasticity of reality.' *International Organization* 64, no. 3 (2010): 443–479.

Bjola, Corneliu. *Legitimising the Use of Force in International Politics: Kosovo, Iraq and the Ethics of Intervention.* London: Routledge, 2009.

Blackman, Oonagh. 'Saddam weapons: this proves nothing.' *Mirror*, 10 September 2002.

Blair, Tony. 'The doctrine of international community.' 24 April 1999. http://webarchive.nationalarchives.gov.uk/+/www.number10.gov.uk/Page1297 (accessed 30 September 2015).

Blair, Tony. 'Statement on the terrorist attacks in the United States.' 11 September 2001a. http://news.bbc.co.uk/1/hi/uk_politics/1538551.stm (accessed 19 May 2016).

Blair, Tony. *Hansard House of Commons Debates*, vol. 372, 4 October 2001b.

Blair, Tony. 'Letter to President Bush.' 11 October 2001c. www.iraqinquiry.org.uk/media/243721/2001-10-11-letter-blair-to-bush-untitled.pdf (accessed 15 July 2016).

Blair, Tony. 'Press conference with Vice President Cheney.' 11 March 2002a. http://webarchive.nationalarchives.gov.uk/20020926165953/www.pm.gov.uk:80/textonly/Page4598.asp (accessed 15 February 2016).

Blair, Tony. *Hansard House of Commons Debates*, vol. 383, 10 April 2002b.

Blair, Tony. 'Prime Minister's monthly press conference.' 20 June 2002c. http://webarchive.nationalarchives.gov.uk/20061101012618/http://number10.gov.uk/page2999 (accessed 16 May 2016).

Blair, Tony. *Hansard House of Commons Debates*, vol. 388. 1 July 2002d.

Blair, Tony. 'Speech to the TUC.' 10 September 2002e. www.tuc.org.uk/about-tuc/congress/congress-2002/congress-2002-prime-ministers-speech (accessed 19 May 2016).

Blair, Tony. *Hansard House of Commons Debates*, vol. 390, 24 September 2002f.

Blair, Tony. 'Evidence to the Chilcot Inquiry.' 29 January 2010a. www.iraqinquiry.org.uk/media/229766/2010-01-29-transcript-blair-s1.pdf (accessed 6 August 2016).

Blair, Tony. *A Journey*. London: Hutchinson, 2010b.

Blix, Hans. *Disarming Iraq: The Search for Weapons of Mass Destruction*. London: Bloomsbury, 2004.

Blix, Hans. 'Evidence to the Chilcot Inquiry.' 27 July 2010. www.iraqinquiry.org.uk/media/95406/2010-07-27-Transcript-Blix-S2.pdf (accessed 17 August 2016).

Bone, James, and Philip Webster. 'Blair dossier proves Baghdad "lies".' *The Times*, 21 September 2002.

British Government. *Responsibility for the Terrorist Attacks in the United States*. London: HMSO, 2001.

British Government. *Iraq's Weapons of Mass Destruction: The Assessment of the British Government*. London: HMSO, 2002.

Burke, Jason. *The 9/11 Wars*. London: Allen Lane, 2011.

Bush, George W. 'The State of the Union.' 29 January 2002a. http://georgewbush-whitehouse.archives.gov/news/releases/2002/01/20020129-11.html (accessed 15 February 2016).

Bush, George W. 'Speech at West Point.' 1 June 2002b. https://georgewbush-whitehouse.archives.gov/news/releases/2002/06/20020601-3.html (accessed 25 October 2016).

Bush, George W. 'Speech in Cincinnati.' 7 October 2002c. http://edition.cnn.com/2002/ALLPOLITICS/10/07/bush.transcript/ (accessed 18 May 2016).

Butler, Lord. *The Butler Report*. London: HMSO, 2004.

Campbell, Alastair. 'Evidence to the Chilcot Inquiry, morning session.' 12 January 2010a. www.iraqinquiry.org.uk/media/95142/2010-01-12-Transcript-Campbell-S1-am.pdf (accessed 6 August 2016).

Campbell, Alastair. 'Evidence to the Chilcot Inquiry, afternoon session.' 12 January 2010b. www.iraqinquiry.org.uk/media/95146/2010-01-12-Transcript-Campbell-S1-pm.pdf (accessed 17 August 2016).

Campbell, Alastair, and Richard Stott. *The Blair Years: Extracts from the Alastair Campbell Diaries*. London: Arrow Books, 2007.

90 *Legitimacy*

Campbell, Menzies. *Hansard House of Commons Debates*, vol. 372, 4 October 2001.
Chilcot, John. *Report of the Iraq Inquiry: Executive Summary*. London: HMSO, 2016a.
Chilcot, John. *Report of the Iraq Inquiry: Volume 1*. London: HMSO, 2016b.
Chilcot, John. *Report of the Iraq Inquiry: Volume 2*. London: HMSO, 2016c.
Chilcot, John. *Report of the Iraq Inquiry: Volume 4*. London: HMSO, 2016d.
Chilcot, John. *Report of the Iraq Inquiry: Volume 6*. London: HMSO, 2016e.
Cook, Robin. *The Point of Departure*. London: Simon & Schuster, 2003.
Cornwell, Rupert, and Colin Brown. 'Blair under renewed pressure over US plans to oust Saddam.' *Independent on Sunday*, 7 July 2002.
Daily Mail. 'Leading article', 20 July 2002a.
Daily Mail. 'Leading article', 4 September 2002b.
Daily Mail. 'Leading article', 10 September 2002c.
Daily Mail. 'Leading article', 25 September 2002d.
Daily Telegraph. 'Leading article', 4 September 2002.
Daily Telegraph. 'Leading article', 8 February 2003.
D'Ancona, Matthew. 'Bush and Blair could not be closer – or further apart.' *Sunday Telegraph*, 7 April 2002.
Defence Intelligence Staff. 'What does Iraq need to do to get the bomb quickly?' 20 March 2002.
Duelfer, Charles. 'Only through threat of regime change can Saddam be disarmed.' *The Times*, 25 September 2002.
Duncan Smith, Iain. *Hansard House of Commons Debates*, vol. 390, 24 September 2002.
Everts, Philip, and Pierangelo Isernia. 'The polls – trends: the war in Iraq.' *Public Opinion Quarterly* 69, no. 2 (2005): 264–323.
Finnemore, Martha. *The Purpose of Intervention: Changing Beliefs About the Use of Force*. Ithaca, NY: Cornell University Press, 2003.
Freedman, Lawrence. 'War in Iraq: selling the threat.' *Survival* 46, no. 2 (2004): 7–50.
Glover, Stephen. 'We cannot go to war on one man's say-so.' *Daily Mail*, 5 March 2002.
Goldsmith, Lord. 'Memo to Tony Blair: Iraq.' 30 July 2002. www.iraqinquiry.org.uk/media/75931/2002-07-30-Minute-Attorney-General-to-Prime-Minister-Iraq.pdf (accessed 16 August 2016).
Guardian. 'Leading article', 31 January 2002a.
Guardian. 'Leading article', 4 September 2002b.
Guardian. 'Leading article', 13 September 2002c.
Hansen, Lene. *Security as Practice: Discourse Analysis and the Bosnian War*. Abingdon: Routledge, 2006.
Harnden, Toby. 'We must realise Bush meant what he said: this is war.' *Daily Telegraph*, 7 February 2002.
Hayes, Jarrod. 'Identity, authority and the British war in Iraq.' *Foreign Policy Analysis*, 2016: 1–20.
Herring, Eric, and Piers Robinson. 'Report X marks the spot: the British Government's deceptive dossier on Iraq and WMD.' *Political Science Quarterly* 129, no. 4 (2014): 551–584.
Hitchens, Christopher. 'Bush will launch an attack on Iraq by November.' *Mirror*, 15 July 2002.
Hoijer, Birgitta, Stig Nohrstedt and Rune Ottosen. 'Media and the "War on Terror".' In *U.S. and the Others: Global Media Images in 'The War on Terror'*, by Stig Nohrstedt and Rune Ottosen, 7–22. Goteborg, Sweden: NORDICOM, 2004.

Holsti, Ole. *Public Opinion and American Foreign Policy.* Ann Arbor: University of Michigan Press, 1996.

Hoon, Geoff. 'Iraq: memo to Tony Blair.' 22 March 2002a. www.iraqinquiry.org.uk/media/75847/2002-03-22-Minute-Hoon-to-Prime-Minister-Iraq.pdf (accessed 17 August 2016).

Hoon, Geoff. *Hansard House of Commons Debates*, vol. 387. 20 June 2002b.

Hoon, Geoff. 'Evidence to the Chilcot Inquiry.' 19 January 2010. www.iraqinquiry.org.uk/media/232462/2010-01-19-transcript-hoon-s1.pdf (accessed 17 August 2016).

Hughes, Simon. 'Tyrant to get nuke bomb "in months".' *Sun*, 10 September 2002.

Hurrell, Andrew. 'Legitimacy and the use of force: can the circle be squared?' *Review of International Studies* 31, no. 1 (2005): 15–32.

Hutton, Lord. *The Hutton Report.* London: HMSO, 2004.

Independent. 'Leading Article', 4 September 2002a.

Independent. 'Leading Article', 9 September 2002b.

Independent. 'Leading Article', 10 September 2002c.

Independent. 'Leading Article', 25 September 2002d.

Independent on Sunday. 'Leading article', 9 February 2003.

Jackson, Richard. *Writing the War on Terrorism: Language, Politics and Counter-Terrorism.* Basingstoke: Palgrave, 2005.

Janis, Irving. *Groupthink.* Boston, MA: Wadsworth, 1982.

Jervis, Robert. *Why Intelligence Fails: Lessons from the Iranian Revolution and the Iraq War.* Ithaca, NY: Cornell University Press, 2010.

Joint Intelligence Committee. 'The status of Iraqi WMD programmes.' 15 March 2002a. www.iraqinquiry.org.uk/media/242501/2002-03-15-cig-assessment-the-status-of-iraqi-wmd-programmes.pdf (accessed 17 August 2016).

Joint Intelligence Committee. 'Iraqi use of chemical and biological weapons: possible scenarios.' 9 September 2002b. www.iraqinquiry.org.uk/media/224483/2002-09-09-JIC-Assessment-Iraqi-use-of-biological-and-chemical-weapons-possible-scenarios.pdf (accessed 17 August 2016).

Jones, Jon Owen. *Hansard House of Commons Debates*, vol. 390, 24 September 2002.

Jones, Terry. 'The audacious courage of Mr Blair: you cannot help but admire the Prime Minister's steadfast refusal to be intimidated by facts and figures.' *Observer*, 22 September 2002.

Kaufmann, Chaim. 'Threat inflation and the failure of the marketplace of ideas: the selling of the Iraq War.' *International Security* 29, no. 1 (2004): 5–48.

Laurie, Michael. 'Statement to the Chilcot Inquiry.' 27 January 2010. www.iraqinquiry.org.uk/media/96006/2010-01-27-Statement-Laurie.pdf (accessed 17 August 2016).

Lewis-Smith, Victor. 'More fuel you, Bush.' *Mirror*, 21 September 2002.

MacIntyre, Donald. 'What will Mr Blair do if the US extends the war to Iraq?' *Independent*, 29 November 2001.

Maddox, Bronwen. 'Why America may have to go it alone.' *The Times*, 31 January 2002a.

Maddox, Bronwen. 'Blair dossier may tell us what little we already know.' *The Times*, 4 September 2002b.

Mahon, Alice. *Hansard House of Commons Debates*, vol. 381, 6 March 2002.

Manningham-Buller, Eliza. 'Memo to John Gieve.' 22 March 2002. www.iraqinquiry.org.uk/media/75843/2002-03-22-Letter-Manningham-Buller-to-Gieve-Iraq-Possible-Terrorist-Response-to-a-US-Attack.pdf (accessed 17 August 2016).

92 Legitimacy

McDonald, Simon. 'Letter to Michael Tatham.' 3 December 2001. www.iraqinquiry.org.uk/media/177424/2001-12-03-Letter-McDonald-to-Tatham-Iraq-Options.pdf (accessed 17 August 2016).

Mirror. 'Leading article', 18 July 2002a.

Mirror. 'Leading article', 11 September 2002b.

Mirror. 'Leading article', 24 September 2002c.

Mirror. 'Leading article', 25 September 2002d.

Murray, Andrew. 'Spinning to war on Iraq.' *Guardian*, 4 March 2002.

Oborne, Peter. 'While the Prime Minister's away.' *Observer*, 7 April 2002.

Observer. 'Leading article', 9 February 2003.

Omand, David. 'Evidence to the Chilcot Inquiry.' 20 January 2010. www.iraqinquiry.org.uk/media/95182/2010-01-20-Transcript-Omand-S2.pdf (accessed 17 August 2016).

Pallister, David, and Nicholas Watt. 'Iraq dossier: sifting the old claims from new and suspicions from as-sertions of fact.' *Guardian*, 25 September 2002.

Pilger, John. 'Not in our name.' *Mirror*, 5 April 2002.

Powell, Jonathan. 'Email to John Scarlett and Alastair Campbell.' 19 September 2002. http://webarchive.nationalarchives.gov.uk/20090128221546/www.the-hutton-inquiry.org.uk/content/evidence/cab_11_0103.pdf (accessed 19 May 2016).

Powell, Jonathan. 'Evidence to the Chilcot Inquiry.' 18 January 2010. www.iraqinquiry.org.uk/media/95166/2010-01-18-Transcript-Powell-S1.pdf (accessed 17 August 2016).

Reiss, Charles. '45 minutes from attack.' *Evening Standard*, 24 September 2002. http://i.dailymail.co.uk/i/pix/2014/06/24/1403629726293_Image_galleryImage_EVENING_STANDARD_FRONT_PA.JPG (accessed 19 May 2016).

Robertson, Geoffrey. 'Lynch mob justice or a proper trial: the government statement does not add up to conclusive proof.' *Guardian*, 5 October 2001.

Routledge, Paul. 'Nod, nod, it's poodle Blair: Bush is taking him for a ride.' *Mirror*, 1 February 2002a.

Routledge, Paul. 'Please sir, can I have some war?' *Mirror*, 19 July 2002b.

Routledge, Paul. '10 questions for you, Tony.' *Mirror*, 20 September 2002c.

Rufford, Nicholas. 'Blair rebuff over Iraq's terror links.' *Sunday Times*, 10 March 2002.

Rycroft, Matthew. 'Memo to David Manning: Iraq: Prime Minister's meeting.' 23 July 2002. www.iraqinquiry.org.uk/media/210955/2002-07-23-minute-rycroft-to-manning-iraq-prime-mi-nisters-meeting-23-july.pdf (accessed 6 August 2016).

Scarlett, John. 'Evidence to the Chilcot Inquiry.' 8 December 2009. www.iraqinquiry.org.uk/media/94850/2009-12-08-Transcript-Scarlett-S3.pdf (accessed 17 August 2016).

Schmitt, Eric. 'US plan for Iraq is said to include attack on 3 sides.' *New York Times*, 5 July 2002.

Seldon, Anthony, Peter Snowdon and Daniel Collings. *Blair Unbound.* London: Simon & Schuster, 2007.

Straw, Jack. *Hansard House of Commons Debates*, vol. 372, 14 September 2001.

Straw, Jack. 'Crawford/Iraq: memo to Tony Blair.' 25 March 2002a. www.iraqinquiry.org.uk/media/195509/2002-03-25-minute-straw-to-prime-minister-crawford-iraq.pdf#search=straw (accessed 29 July 2016).

Straw, Jack. *Hansard House of Commons Debates*, vol. 390, 24 September 2002b.

Straw, Jack. 'Evidence to the Chilcot Inquiry: written statement.' 21 January 2010a. www.iraqinquiry.org.uk/media/194013/2010-01-xx-statement-straw-1.pdf (accessed 17 August 2016).

Straw, Jack. 'Evidence to the Chilcot Inquiry.' 21 January 2010b. www.iraqinquiry.org.uk/media/95186/2010-01-21-Transcript-Straw-S1.pdf (accessed 17 August 2016).
Straw, Jack. 'Evidence to the Chilcot Inquiry.' 2 February 2011. www.iraqinquiry.org.uk/media/95414/2011-02-02-Transcript-Straw-S1.pdf (accessed 17 August 2016).
Sun. 'The Sun says', 25 September 2002.
The Times. 'Leading article', 29 January 2002a.
The Times. 'Leading article', 29 August 2002b.
Wilson, Graeme. 'Cheats of Downing Street.' *Daily Mail*, 8 February 2003.

6 Legality and the UN

This chapter considers the debate over the legal case for British military action in Iraq, and the role of the UN. It begins by discussing the different ways contributors to public debate understood the authority of the UN Security Council. It continues by considering the procedural ambiguities surrounding Security Council Resolution (SCR) 1441 and the role of UNMOVIC. It concludes by highlighting the critical clash between the US military timetable and the UN weapons inspection process.

Legality and legitimacy are linked but separate concepts (Hurd 1999, 381). An independent commission famously described the 1999 Kosovo conflict as "illegal, but legitimate" (Independent International Commission on Kosovo 2000, 186). NATO's actions upheld the UN's founding spirit but violated its rules. Britain's then-Ambassador to the UN, Jeremy Greenstock, similarly described the Iraq War as "legal, but of questionable legitimacy" (Greenstock 2009a, 38). Greenstock believed the US-led 'coalition of the willing' followed the rules but failed to uphold their spirit. Most legally-minded observers doubt that the Blair government's actions complied with international law. Jason Ralph, for example, calls the underlying reasoning "strained and unconvincing" (Ralph 2011, 124). Chilcot refused to comment on the substance, but described the process through which the government secured legal backing "far from satisfactory" (Chilcot 2016a, 62). This was strong criticism. As one senior legal expert put it, "far from satisfactory" is "a career-ending phrase" in the staid language of British civil servants (Sands 2016).

Critics argue that the invasion lacked legitimacy as a result of these legal shortcomings. What constitutes international law is, however, a matter of some debate. Legality is a discursive construct at the best of times (Onuf 1989, 77). The effect is magnified at the international level, where competing claims about sovereignty, human rights and security clash (Reus-Smit 2001, 519). During the Iraq debate these difficulties crystallized around the specific question of the UN Security Council's proper role, and the degree to which Britain's actions in Iraq implemented or circumvented its authority. That the Security Council has a privileged position as an arbiter of international legitimacy is well-established (Claude 1966, 370; Franck 1988, 725). It is also controversial. Where the Council speaks with one voice, its judgments carry considerable weight. The picture gets more problematic when it is divided. Under the UN Charter, the Security Council holds various quasi-executive and quasi-judicial powers. It remains, however, a political body at heart. Its judgements reflect compromises amongst its members, especially the veto-wielding 'permanent' great powers (Bjola 2005, 267). For this reason, different observers place different amounts of weight on Security Council approval as a sign of compliance with international law.

The Blair government needed a clear basis in international law before it could use force in Iraq. Proceeding otherwise would trigger official resignations and Cabinet divisions. Both Jeremy Greenstock and Jack Straw told the Chilcot Inquiry that they could not have supported an invasion without some sort of legal mandate (Greenstock 2009a, 8; Straw 2010a, 7, 24). What this meant in practice remained remarkably open. Blair repeatedly insisted publicly that "whatever we do we will do in line with international law" while refusing to comment on specifics (Blair 2002b). Privately, Lord Goldsmith advised that the "most secure, and preferred, legal basis for military action" would be "a new Security Council resolution explicitly authorizing the use of force" (Goldsmith 2002). Goldsmith's view mattered greatly. Days before the invasion Ministry of Defence legal adviser Martin Hemming told Chief of the Defence Staff Admiral Mike Boyce that "his order to commit UK armed forces ... would be a lawful order by him" provided "the Attorney General has advised that he is satisfied" (Hemming 2003). Goldsmith's office confirmed that was the case (Brummell 2003b), and Boyce relayed the order to go to war. Blair told Chilcot he recognized that Britain might have been unable to join the invasion if Goldsmith withheld his support (Blair 2011, 67).

Goldsmith may ultimately have been satisfied. But many in Britain were not. The idea that the invasion of Iraq was illegal continues to haunt not just Tony Blair's legacy, but the entire practice of military intervention abroad. Three problems prevented the government winning the legal argument. To begin with, different groups of public actors understood the UN's role in radically different and even contradictory ways. Each could plausibly project their views onto unambiguous Security Council approval. But considerable scope for conflict remained in the presence of ambiguity. Ministers believed they acted on behalf of the Security Council. Chilcot found instead that "the UK [undermined] the authority of the Security Council" (Chilcot 2016c, 570). Second, ministers failed to spell out, with sufficient clarity, their understanding of the UN process. Rather than trying to maximize the public's understanding of its position, the government refused repeatedly to engage with hypothetical but plausible questions about what would happen in the event of a stalemate. Finally, ministers proved unable to reconcile the clash between the US political and military timetables for action, and the Iraqi regime's partial compliance with UNMOVIC. Iraq never met the disarmament obligations placed upon it by successive SCRs dating back to the Gulf War in 1991. But nor was the US willing to give it every possible opportunity to avoid war. Reconciling Iraqi reticence, US belligerence and a commitment to uphold international law proved too great a task for even Tony Blair's considerable persuasive powers.

Defining the UN's role

Three distinct interpretations of the UN's role in international affairs emerged during the British public debate preceding the Iraq war. Each shared the view Jack Straw had reported to Vice President Cheney in January 2003, that the UN was "a legitimator of action" (Chilcot 2016e, 111). Problematically, from the Blair government's perspective, the three differed dramatically in terms of how they thought the UN's legitimating role worked. Tony Blair appeared to believe that the public would accept military action launched on clear legal grounds, backed by express multinational support and possessed of at least the semblance of being a last resort (Kampfner 2003, 257). He genuinely thought the "international community" could act collectively, decisively and effectively to address Iraq's WMD (Dyson 2011, 64). At the same time, as Buzan and Gonzalez-Pelaez rightly observed, invoking the "international community" in this way has "an important political function in generating legitimacy" for foreign policy interventions (Buzan and Gonzalez-Pelaez 2005, 31). Blair told David Manning in September 2002 that Britain and the US needed "to play Iraq cleverly", to "look reluctant to use force" and to recognize that "if we appeared to be riding roughshod over the UN or taking it for granted, opinion would be very difficult to shift" (Chilcot 2016b, 177). Blair went down the 'UN route', in other words, because he believed it was the right thing to do, because he thought others believed it was too, and because he thought it would work. These beliefs had merit. Even in the US, most survey respondents prefer multilateral to unilateral action, and want their governments to seek UN approval before using force abroad (Eichenberg 2005, 145). UN approval typically matters even more in weaker states, like the UK, whose survival depends to a greater degree on effective international institutions and laws (Voeten 2005, 532; Everts and Isernia 2005, 275). Yet no matter how often ministers argued that the UN itself, rather than the US or UK, placed Iraqi WMD on the agenda of international politics (Blair 2003b), this remained demonstrably untrue. Contemporary commentators recognized that "Iraq is a crisis today only because the US had made it so" (Cornwell 2003).

Three interpretations

A first group of British public actors regarded the UN, and the Security Council in particular, as the ultimate arbiter of international law (Scott and Ambler 2007, 83). Proponents of this interpretation generally rejected the notion that an organization affording considerable clout to human rights violators, like Russia and China, might reasonably hold any great *moral* authority. An *Observer* editorial, for example, warned "it might be difficult for some to accept a sole veto from Beijing autocrats, for example, on action which might restore democracy to another nation" (*Observer* 2003). They nevertheless thought Security Council approval carried the force of law. Former Scottish National Party MP Jim Sillars argued that "no one could pretend for a moment that the UN Security Council can claim great moral authority. What it does claim, in international law, is LEGAL authority" (Sillars 2002).

A second group downplayed the legal dimension, noting that the UN lacked the capacity to enforce its decisions directly having to out-source any actual fighting to its member states. These commentators instead framed the Security Council as a kind of moral authority. To some extent their views reflected the distinction between the "substantive" and "procedural" dimensions of international law (Bjola 2005, 270). Whereas advocates of the legal position focused on substantive outcomes, those who took the moral view emphasized procedural aspects. For them, working through the UN was a point of principle, a matter of the right way things should be done. As Richard Norton-Taylor put it, although the US "always considered itself above any tenet of international law", both it and the UK were "corrupting the Security Council" by reducing it to little more than a forum for political bargaining amongst great powers (Norton-Taylor 2003). Just as there are right and wrong ways for governments to win public support, so too there were right and wrong ways to secure Security Council approval.

A final group of commentators framed the Security Council as a forum for political bargaining amongst great powers, as an arena where states with conflicting views on and interests in the management of international peace and security could meet to forge agreements. As Daniel Finkelstein put it, "the Security Council is not a panel of disinterested philosophers. Its decisions all too often are based on national prejudice, imperial adventurism, the vanity of individuals and the murderous impulses of dictators". Its role was to provide "a forum for countries" to work together despite their differences (Finkelstein 2003). Advocates of this third view praised international consensus as a political good while denying UN approval offered any sort of "moral cover" for war (*Independent* 2002). A *Sunday Telegraph* editorial, for example, described the UN unflatteringly as "a venue for horse-trading, rather than a font of ethical purity" (*Sunday Telegraph* 2003). Speaking in the House of Commons, the Conservative MP Douglas Hogg warned the government "not to invest the Security Council with undue moral authority", insisting that its resolutions were "political statements [that] ... cannot make just or moral a war which otherwise is not" (Hogg 2003, col. 39).

For a government seeking legitimacy through public deliberation, these different understandings of the UN raised problems. None of their proponents seemed willing to consider alternative viewpoints, and in any event talking through each approach would take more time and energy than ministers could spare. Even the most open and flexible deliberative approach might not have generated consensus. Only one result offered a plausible route to public agreement: unambiguous Security Council approval for military action.

Compliance with international law

Crucially, this was also the Attorney General's main criterion for judging how far any action complied with international law. Shortly after the 23 July 2002

Downing Street planning meeting on Iraq, Goldsmith wrote an unprompted and, he later thought, not "terribly welcome" memo to Blair (Goldsmith 2010, 23) setting out the legal basis for military action as he then saw it. It was far from the only time he felt compelled to take such an unusually pro-active step (Chilcot 2016e, 56). His starting point, and a position he stuck to throughout the pre-invasion period, was that the legality of any use of force depended on UN Security Council approval. Acknowledging the advice his predecessor gave at the time of Operation Desert Fox in 1998, Goldsmith accepted the general validity of the so-called "revival argument" under which the authorization for the use of force against Iraq which is contained in SCR 678, the resolution that approved the Gulf War, and suspended but not lifted by SCR 687, which set out the terms of the ceasefire, might be revived by a subsequent breach of the conditions that SCR 687 set down. There was a problem, however. Operation Desert Fox followed a period of Iraqi interference with UN weapons inspectors. It was a direct response to a report from UNSCOM that it was no longer able to do its job. Absent a similar crisis moment, Goldsmith warned, it would be far harder to justify reviving the authorization in SCR 678. A fresh Security Council Resolution was required (Goldsmith 2002). Jonathan Powell subsequently wrote to both the Ministry of Defence and the Foreign Office asking them to burn their copies of this memo "to avoid further leaks". Only Downing Street's version was retained (Powell 2002).

For a government concerned with both legitimacy and legality, going the UN route was both politically prudent and practically necessary. So far, its different interests aligned. But even setting aside the different understandings of the UN's role circling in public debate, ministers still faced significant challenges as they sought to legitimize military action in Iraq by framing it as a UN-sanctioned response to Iraqi violations of international law. To begin with, their Bush administration allies held to a far more expansive understanding of how international law worked. SCRs 1368 and 1373 required states to prevent terrorist groups using their territory to organize and launch attacks abroad, and authorized the international community to use force against those who refused. Writing to the Security Council to announce its decision to use force in Afghanistan, the US pointed to the combined effect of these resolutions. It also invoked Article 51 of the UN Charter, under which every state has the right to self-defence. So far, so orthodox. Though some in Britain warned that "retaliation is not self-defence by any legal measure" (Campbell 2001, col. 625), most accepted that Article 51 applied. Indeed, the (British) Secretary-General of NATO played a key role in its invocation on 12 September 2001 of Article 5 of the Washington Treaty, under which an attack on one NATO member counts as an attack on all. More problematic was the assertion in the US notification that it reserved the right to use force "against other organizations and other states" beyond *Al-Qaeda* and Afghanistan (Negroponte 2001). This prompted complaints in the UK that "America has neither a moral nor a legal right to take such momentous decisions by itself without proper recourse to the international community" (*Guardian* 2001), though some observers disagreed. A *Times* editorial in late 2001 called on the US to pursue the "unfinished business" of Iraqi disarmament, arguing existing SCRs offered all the legal authority required (*The Times* 2001).

This *Times* piece proved prescient. As Goldsmith told Chilcot, the US did not share the UK's legal concerns (Goldsmith 2010, 87). Under the Clinton-era Iraq Liberation Act, US domestic law not only permitted but required the Bush administration to pursue regime change in Iraq. Through the 'Bush doctrine', the US asserted a new legal right to pre-empt potential as well as imminent threats (Bush 2002a; US Government 2002). This posed a problem for Britain. In public, ministers insisted that no difficulty existed. Geoff Hoon told MPs that "pre-emptive action is no more than modern jargon to deal with the ancient right of self-defence" (Hoon 2003, col. 39). In private the picture looked different. Foreign Office Legal advisers confirmed the 'Bush doctrine' was incompatible with international law as Britain saw it (Wood 2002). As ministers began to rely more heavily on claims that they were 'going the UN route' to legitimize efforts to disarm Iraq, British Ambassador to Washington Christopher Meyer warned London that "the UK's and the US's views of what exhausting the UN process means could suddenly diverge" (Meyer 2002, 2009, 54). Robin Cook echoed the warning in the Cabinet (Cook 2003, 204–205). Publicly the government glossed over genuine disagreements about the importance of Security Council approval between Britain and the United States. And that was before ambiguities in the process itself kicked in.

David Manning warned Secretary of State Powell and National Security Adviser Rice in the Summer of 2002 that "it was impossible for the United Kingdom to take part in action against Iraq unless it were through the United Nations" (Manning 2009, 19). Powell and Rice convinced the President, and a meeting between Tony Blair and Vice-President Cheney at Camp David in early September clinched Bush's agreement. The US would at least try to work through the UN (Greenstock 2009a, 9; Campbell 2010, 44). On 12 September Bush spoke at the General Assembly. Asking "will the United Nations serve the purpose of its founding or will it be irrelevant?", he announced the US "will work with the UN security council for the necessary resolutions" in order to resolve outstanding issues relating to Iraq (Bush 2002b). The plural, "resolutions", was an error; the wrong version of Bush's speech was placed on the teleprompter, and he had to ad-lib the line, misspeaking in the process (Meyer 2005, 253). It was a potentially costly error, as the question of whether the US sought one resolution, or two, came to dominate the following debate.

Procedural ambiguities

Initially, the Bush administration's decision to work through the UN worked in the Blair government's favour. At the Labour Party conference in October 2002, Blair promised delegates that he would proceed through "the UN route" (Blair 2002c). As one observer noted, promising to work "in the name of the UN, which they all revere" was a good way to win Labour Party members over (Freedland 2002). As Chapter 3 shows, the shift in focus to the Security Council dramatically reduced the intensity of public opposition to the government's Iraq policy. There remained two problems, however. First, Blair was never totally committed to the UN process. He repeatedly warned that "the UN route ... has got to be the way of dealing with this issue, not the way of avoiding dealing with it" (Blair 2002a). He envisioned a scenario from the outset in which Saddam Hussein refused to co-operate fully with a UN-led disarmament process, and member states were forced to choose whether to act or to delay. He was entirely frank about this. The caveat appeared almost every time he talked about going the UN route. Few observers noticed, which made sense to some extent. After all, the US and UK defied critics' expectations by deciding to work through the UN. No one seems to have anticipated, at least not publicly, that working through the UN could mean very different things to different people.

UN Security Council 1441 and the question of the 'second' resolution

On 8 November 2002, the Security Council unanimously approved Resolution 1441, condemning Iraq for its WMD violations, mandating a new inspection regime and giving Saddam Hussein "a final opportunity to comply" or face "serious consequences" (United Nations Security Council 2002). British observers hailed "a diplomatic triumph for the Bush-Blair approach" (*Daily Telegraph* 2002). Several previous critics of the government's policy expressed cautious support. Labour's Gerald Kaufman, for example, told MPs that the resolution "has changed the position from the summer" (Kaufman 2002, col. 92). A number still spoke out against what Alice Mahon called "a war resolution ... mined with trip wires to trigger a war" (Mahon 2002, col. 439). A *Guardian* editorial, for instance, called an early US draft "a blueprint for invasion" (*Guardian* 2002). Robin Cook worried in Cabinet that the plan was "to contrive an assault on Iraq whatever Saddam does" (Cook 2003, 209), while David Manning felt the need to tell Condoleezza Rice that the UK was "not in the business of manufacturing a casus belli" (Chilcot 2016b, 216). In general, however, most commentators accepted if Iraq failed to grasp its final chance military action would follow. Fergal Keane, writing in the anti-war *Independent*, remarked "the nations who have signed the resolution know that it paves the way for war if Saddam refuses to disarm".

Critically, however, Keane also argued that "the devil is not in the detail of the resolution" (Keane 2002). He was wrong. The final text contained a number of "deliberate ambiguities" (Chilcot 2016b, 199), ambiguities that were "necessary to get a consensus", as Christopher Meyer put it, but that left the whole agreement "fatally undermined" (Meyer 2009, 68). Chief among them was the unanswered question of whether SCR 1441 authorized the use of force in the event Iraq failed to comply, or whether the Council would have to vote again. France and Russia pushed hard for a 'two-stage' process, under which a first resolution re-established the UN inspections regime while a second was required to approve the resort to arms. The Bush administration, however, was "dead against" constraining its freedom of action in this way. Involving the UN at all was problematic enough for Washington 'hawks' (Adams 2002). Impasse followed, as each side struggled over several weeks to identify a compromise approach the other could live with (Straw 2010c, 43). At the heart of the dispute was the issue of 'automaticity', and in effect the question of who would decide when enough inspections were enough. France and Russia did not want to give *carte blanche* to the US to launch an invasion without allowing the inspection process a decent amount of time to work. Neither particularly expected Iraq to comply, but both worried about allowing the US a free hand (Goldsmith 2010, 41–42). In the end, Britain and France worked out a compromise, later presented to the rest of the Security Council as a *fait accompli* (Adams 2003). Though the US and UK would not back down on substance, they were prepared to offer what Jack Straw later described to Goldsmith as a degree of "procedural comfort" (Straw 2003c). In the event that Iraq failed to comply with its obligations, the Security Council would have to meet "to consider the situation" before any military action could take place (United Nations Security Council 2002, OP 12). SCR 1441 did not, in other words, grant automatic authorization for the use of force. Not, at least, until after a further Security Council discussion. Whether this also meant a further resolution remained deliberately unclear.

In public, the government put out mixed messages on this point. Just before SCR 1441 passed, Straw told MPs that "whether military action is justified in international law, with or without a second resolution, depends on the circumstances" (Straw 2002b, col. 439). Greenstock echoed this point on *Channel 4 News*, telling presenter Krishnan Guru-Murthy that "our huge preference is for the Security Council to stay together on this". He ducked a question about whether Britain and the US would proceed in the event of disagreement amongst Council members (Greenstock 2002b). Straw told Russian Foreign Minister Ivanov that the Security Council would "decide what action was required" if Iraq failed to comply (Chilcot 2016b, 331). He later said "the preference of the Government ... is that there should be a second Security Council resolution" while insisting "we must reserve our position" and that the key passage in paragraph 12 of SCR 1441 "does not stipulate that there has to be a second Security Council Resolution to authorize military action" (Straw 2002c, col. 53). Blair proved even more reticent, telling journalists who were asking about the prospect of a further SCR that "there are certain questions frankly ... it is not very helpful to speculate on" (Blair 2002a); "unhelpful for him", as Peter Riddell put it in *The Times* (Riddell 2002).

Riddell was right, probably more so than he realized. Though Blair enjoyed a brief period of relative calm in the immediate aftermath of SCR 1441, his inner circle was soon divided over whether or not Britain required a further resolution before taking military action. These divisions began even before the final Security Council vote. Straw told Goldsmith during a telephone conversation on 18 October that "he accepted that we would need a second resolution" on the basis of the draft then under discussion (Sedwill 2002). He confirmed as much in a diplomatic cable to Greenstock in New York three days later, noting "further action will be for the Council" (Straw 2002a). Goldsmith, whose opinion really mattered, was not kept fully informed about developments in the negotiation process, nor was he asked for his opinion on the final draft until early 2003 (Chilcot 2016b, 368). This proved problematic. Chilcot found that different ministers and officials believed quite different things about what SCR 1441 allowed, and that ultimately the government "didn't really know what it was voting for" (Chilcot 2016b, 373). Blair's public statements in October explicitly aligned Britain with the Bush administration position that no second resolution could be required. This directly contradicted advice he received from Straw and Manning (Chilcot 2016b, 388, 288). Straw, for example, wrote to Blair on 16 October urging him to "give some clear messages to Bush that we'll have to settle for a two resolution approach" (Straw 2002a). Blair however commented "I don't accept this in all circs", a point Straw seemingly did not grasp until a summit meeting between the two on 12 March (Chilcot 2016b, 289, 2016e, 166). On 11 November Goldsmith warned Powell that "he was not at all optimistic" about the legal position in the absence of a second SCR (Brummell 2002a). The following day he told Straw "it seemed implicit in Resolution 1441 that ... it would be for the Security Council to decide" (Brummell 2002b), a point David Manning later echoed back to him in a meeting in Downing Street (Brummell 2002c). Goldsmith sent a first draft of his formal legal advice to Blair on 14 January, confirming "my opinion is that resolution 1441 does not revive the authorization to use of force contained in resolution 678 in the absence of a further decision of the Security Council" (Goldsmith 2003a). Neither Straw nor Hoon received this document (Chilcot 2016e, 164). Goldsmith repeated the point on 30 January, maintaining "the correct legal interpretation of resolution 1441 is that it does not authorize the use of military force without a further determination by the Security Council". Blair underlined the statement, scribbling "I just don't understand this" in the margin (Goldsmith 2003b). But understanding Goldsmith's tentative conclusion was not the problem. It was consistent with every piece of advice Goldsmith gave from October 2002 onwards (Chilcot 2016e, 57). Blair simply disagreed.

This was a problem. As Blair's comment suggests, he was surprised by Goldsmith's stance, and concerned. Straw told Goldsmith on 6 February that he had "doubts about the negotiability" of an SCR explicitly authorizing military action (Straw 2003c). If Goldsmith ruled that Britain could not act legally without a further resolution, it might be unable to act at all. Straw was right to be concerned. On 24 January, FCO Legal Adviser Sir Michael Wood wrote to warn him that there was "no doubt" a further resolution would be required (Wood 2003). Neither Blair nor Straw accepted the advice they received. Straw replied to Wood a few days later, stating "I note your advice, but I do not accept it" and arguing that international law was "uncertain" and that "the issue is an arguable one, capable of honestly and reasonably held differences of view". The problem, Straw argued, was one of legitimacy rather than legality, of what sort of further role the British public envisioned for the Security Council in response to SCR 1441. Britain might yet seek a second resolution "for political reasons". It did not need one in law (Straw 2003b). In a private meeting, he told Vice President

Cheney that the British "would need bullet-proof jackets if we did not even try" to get a second SCR (Chilcot 2016c, 111). As early as October, Blair told Bush a second resolution was desirable but not necessary (Chilcot 2016b, 257).

In public, Blair maintained both that "if there is a breach the United Nations will agree to another resolution" and that if it failed to do so, perhaps because of an "unreasonable" veto, the US and Britain might have to act regardless (Blair 2003b). He told MPs that if "an unreasonable veto is put down ... we would still act" (Blair 2003c, col. 678). Chilcot observed that "these statements were at odds with the draft [legal] advice he had received" (Chilcot 2016e, 43). Both Goldsmith and Wood advised that there was no such thing in law as an "unreasonable" veto. A veto was a veto. If a permanent member vetoed a Security Council resolution, Britain could not legally use force (Brummell 2002b; Wood 2003). Jack Straw held the public line at the time. He later accepted at the Chilcot Inquiry that it did not stand up (Straw 2010c, 47). Even Blair told Chilcot he knew he might have to pull out if Goldsmith's advice remained unchanged. He reasoned, simply, that France and Russia were less likely to approve a further resolution if he admitted in public that he needed one legally. But that in turn raises questions about the legitimacy of Blair's approach, and specifically about the truthfulness and openness he showed in seeking to make the legal dimension of his case. It was probably a sensible diplomatic approach, to refuse to acknowledge the strength of the French and Russian position. But it also meant presenting an unrealistic picture of the legal position to the British public. As Chapter 10 concludes, the greatest challenge the Blair government faced during this period was the imperative to consider both the international and the domestic implications of the things it said.

Asked at the Chilcot Inquiry to explain the discrepancy between his private and public statements, Blair gave a somewhat convoluted explanation, arguing: "I was less making a legal declaration, as it were, because I could not do that, but a political point" (Blair 2011, 74). The exchange said a great deal about Blair's approach to public deliberation, and points towards a crucial reason why he struggled to legitimize his war. It is vital, as we have seen, for actors seeking legitimacy through public deliberation to make their case honestly and openly (Bjola 2009, 76). Blair was generally honest and open about what he personally believed the legal position to be, just as he was in talking about WMD. He was much more reticent about the weakness of his case. Both Blair and Straw showed an additional unwillingness to shift stance in the face of advice that did not meet their preferences. During the 19 December, Downing Street meeting, Jonathan Powell suggested that Goldsmith should meet Greenstock, "to get a fuller picture of the history of the negotiation of Resolution 1441" (Brummell 2002c). Having spoken to Greenstock and further to Straw, Goldsmith "thought it would be helpful" to meet his effective US counterpart, State Department Legal Adviser William Taft IV. He met Taft in Washington in early February alongside several other officials including Rice and US Attorney General Ashcroft (Goldsmith 2010, 109–111). The combined effect of these conversations led him to change his mind. Downing Street instructed Greenstock ahead of the negotiations that led to SCR 1441 that it was "important that the draft should provide legal cover for military action without further Council action" (McDonald 2002). Greenstock acknowledged in early September that his negotiating objective was "to justify the use of force (without a further SCR)" (Greenstock 2002a). Goldsmith's interlocutors in Washington reported similar instructions from the White House. He told Chilcot he ultimately struggled "to believe ... that all these experienced lawyers, and negotiators in the United States could actually have stumbled into doing the one thing that they had been told mustn't happen" (Goldsmith 2010, 127). On 12 February he wrote to Blair again. Noting "a number of ambiguities in the drafting" of SCR 1441, including differences of interpretation between the US and UK, he ultimately concluded that a "reasonable case can be made that resolution 1441 revives the authorization to use force in resolution 678". His advice remained finely balanced. He maintained "that the safest legal course would be to secure the adoption of a further Council decision" (Goldsmith 2003c). But from the government's perspective, it was enough.

This, however, was where the discrepancy between legality and legitimacy really hit home for the government. By the time Goldsmith changed his mind, bringing his private legal advice into line with Blair and Straw's public statements, public opinion had settled on the question of a second resolution as a key test of ministers' commitment to obeying international law (Dunne 2008, 354). Blair recalled having realized by the end of January 2003 that he "might be unable to survive the expected House of Commons vote" without a second resolution (Blair 2010b, 412). Manning reported as much to Rice, warning that "the US must not promote regime change in Baghdad at the price of regime change in London" (Chilcot 2016c, 136). Alastair Campbell noted that "everyone [Blair] was speaking to was saying they needed a second resolution or they wouldn't get support" (Campbell and Stott 2007, 658). During a *BBC Newsnight* interview on 6 February Blair told Jeremy Paxman: "I think if there were a second UN resolution then I think people would be behind me. I think if there's not then there's a lot of persuading to do" (Blair 2003d). As Bronwen Maddox pointed out in *The Times*, Blair was increasingly committed to producing "some kind of 'second resolution' ... to the point where it does not matter too much what the piece of paper says, so long as he can produce it" (Maddox 2003). So much for Goldsmith's legal advice.

Public pressure, in other words, forced the Blair government to seek a 'second' SCR, even as Goldsmith's change of heart lifted the legal obligation to do so. Having repeatedly argued that a second resolution was unnecessary, the government wound up pursuing one anyway. This further complicated its argument. It also raised significant practical difficulties. President Bush used his second State of the Union address on 28 January to declare "the course of this nation does not depend on the decisions of others" (Bush 2003a). Confronted with his ally's domestic difficulties during a meeting on 31 January, Bush "realised that no second resolution might mean ... no Britain" (Seldon *et al.* 2007, 147). Blair did not tell Bush about Goldsmith's legal advice, wanting to avoid appearing wobbly at a crucial moment. But he did make the political case for a final UN push (Chilcot 2016c, 171). Bush agreed to support British efforts to negotiate a further vote "to help Mr Blair, but there were major reservations within the US administration about the wisdom of that approach" (Chilcot 2016c, 176). Given the strength of his assertions just a few days before, Bush faced domestic pressure too (Meyer 2009, 55). He remained visibly lukewarm about the prospect of further negotiation, telling journalists at a joint press conference that "should the United Nations decide to pass a second resolution, it would be welcomed", while maintaining that "1441 gives us the authority to move without any second resolution" (Bush 2003b). So stark was the difference of emphasis between Bush and Blair on this point, and so focused was the media on reporting it, that the Prime Minister felt compelled to travel to the press section of his plane during the return flight to London. As the then-ITV political editor Nick Robinson put it, this was "a journey he makes only when told that the media thinks his day went badly" (Robinson 2003).

The decision to seek a second resolution served primarily to encourage critics who already believed that SCR 1441 did not provide legal grounds for the use of force. It had the added benefit, though, of preventing the Security Council from discussing a Franco-Russian counter-resolution supporting inspections, forcing the US and UK into an embarrassing veto. Even a vetoed resolution would destroy Goldsmith's newly-minted legal argument (Greenstock 2009a, 13; Straw 2010b, 82). In the end, though, the divisions on the Council proved impossible to overcome. Blair assured Cabinet, parliament (Chilcot 2016c, 196, 356) and President Bush that he could obtain a second resolution relatively easily (Cook 2003, 276). This was unrealistic given France's stated objections to the use of force (Marfleet and Miller 2005, 338). Considerable tension developed between the US and France after Dominique de Villepin's 20 January "ambush" of Colin Powell at the UN, in which the French Foreign Minister used an impromptu press conference during an unrelated ministerial summit to attack US posturing over Iraq (Straw 2010c, 74). The publication on 30 January and 6 February of letters of support for the US from a range of EU member and candidate states further underscored European divisions (Ehrenberg *et al.* 2010, 124–126). Chapter 8 discusses these issues in more detail. In the end, the gaps proved too large to close. In the final weeks before the invasion, Blair ordered Greenstock to keep working for a second SCR. Blair informed neither Greenstock nor Goldsmith that he had himself already given up (Chilcot 2016c, 486, 2016e, 166).

The role of UNMOVIC

Ambiguity also surrounded the role of UNMOVIC, the UN weapons inspection regime formally established by SCR 1284 in 1999 but not deployed until SCR 1441 backed it with the implicit threat of force. British officials assumed Iraq would either refuse entirely to co-operate with UNMOVIC, thus "provoking an indisputable example of Iraqi intransigence" (Greenstock 2002a) or that the inspectors, once allowed back into Iraq, would quickly find enough banned material to demonstrate a further material breach of SCR 687. No one, as a result, gave much thought to how best to present the inspection process to the

British public, a "tactical error" from a communications perspective, as commentators put it in early 2003 (Gedye *et al.* 2003). Iraq was obliged to declare its WMD capabilities and then to dismantle them. UNMOVIC's role was to validate both the declaration and the dismantling. It was quite explicitly not supposed to have to search out WMD. As UNMOVIC chairman Hans Blix put it, "self-declaration is as basic to arms control as it is to income tax systems. The weapons inspector or tax man should not need to go and find what you have" (Blix 2004, 99). This was significant. Downing Street apparently thought UNMOVIC "didn't have a cat's chance in hell of finding anything" (Kampfner 2003, 257) in Iraq. That was fine. UNMOVIC was meant to verify, not to find. Iraq would breach SCR 1441 and face the 'serious consequences' it promised if it failed to satisfy UNMOVIC that it was co-operating fully, whether in fact it still had WMD or not.

British ministers failed to explain that the burden of proof lay on Iraq and not on UNMOVIC. In part this was their own fault, for sending mixed messages. Though Blair, for example, told journalists the inspection process "is not a game of hide and seek" (Blair 2002d), he also told MPs that "it is for the inspectors to examine *whether there is evidence* of weapons of mass destruction" in Iraq, a statement that made UNMOVIC sound like more of a detective agency (Blair 2003a, cols. 164–168, emphasis added). Critics seized upon this ambiguity to place the burden of proof on the US and UK. Conservative MP Peter Tapsell argued that "if they [UNMOVIC] are unable to find any such weapons ... we could not ... justify an attack on Iraq" (Tapsell 2002, col. 70). Richard Norton-Taylor wrote in the *Guardian* that "if it is a question of peace or war, surely the advocates of war must provide evidence of Iraqi guilt" (Norton-Taylor 2002). Some observers, like Matthew D'Ancona in the *Sunday Telegraph*, did accept that the "resolution ... does not require the UN weapons inspectors to provide proof of Saddam's weapons of mass destruction. The onus is explicitly upon Iraq", but even he complained in the same sentence that "having worked so hard to secure UN Resolution 1441, the Prime Minister has failed so conspicuously to sell it to the British public" (D'Ancona 2003). Having gained some ground with the WMD 'dossier' in September 2002, the government lost it again from November onwards by losing the framing battle over the role of UNMOVIC.

On 8 December Iraq submitted a dossier of its own to UNMOVIC and its 12,000 pages of documents intended to support its claim that it retained no WMD capabilities. Hans Blix recalls being "hopeful" that Iraq would use the declaration as an opportunity to answer the questions left unresolved when UNSCOM pulled out in 1998. He was "disappointed" with the result (Blix 2010, 38). Blair told his staff the declaration was "the defining moment. This was his big opportunity. He's blown it" (Seldon *et al.* 2007, 143). The JIC warned immediately after SCR 1441 that "Iraq could try to overload UNMOVIC" by producing piles of irrelevant documentation (Chilcot 2016d, 303). Its declaration fit an expected pattern of obfuscation and partial co-operation. By 14 December a number of British newspapers were recycling off-the-record Bush administration quotes published by the *New York Times* claiming that Iraq's declaration contained holes "big enough to drive a tank through" (Simpson 2002; Paveley and Lowther 2002). Even the metaphor that was used sent a message. On 18 December, the JIC reported that Iraq's declaration left a number of questions unanswered, including critical issues raised by UNSCOM's final report. From a UK perspective, it was particularly significant that "the declaration makes no attempt to deal with the points made in the UK dossier" (Joint Intelligence Committee 2002). Chilcot remarked that this use of the dossier as a "baseline" helps explain both Britain's impatience with UNMOVIC and the JIC's subsequent failure to reassess its assumptions (Chilcot 2016d, 116).

None of this helped the government. By early 2003 it was clear, as a *Times* editorial put it, that a significant segment of British public opinion thought UNMOVIC would "postpone the prospect of a military campaign indefinitely". For many, it noted, the fact "that the inspectors might become irrelevant if Baghdad failed to provide a credible inventory of its materials has come as an unwelcome surprise" (*The Times* 2003). Hans Blix observed as early as September 2002 the belief amongst journalists that "inspection was the alternative to war" (Blix 2004, 79). A handful of critics made it clear that they would never support the use of force, even with UN sanction. As Scottish Socialist MSP Tommy Sheridan put it in the *Mirror*, "with or without the backing of the UN, a war for oil that will kill tens of thousands of children would be immoral" (Sheridan 2003). Veteran anti-war campaigner Tony Benn refused to sign the *Mirror*'s anti-war petition because it implied he would support a UN-sanctioned war; "I wouldn't" (*Mirror* 2003). Some commentators never anticipated that the Bush administration would follow a UN process at all (Watkins 2002). Others accepted that Iraq was "in breach of hair-trigger UN resolution 1441" while arguing that "wars should not be fought on technicalities" (*Guardian* 2003). Some even suggested that a "smoking gun" would mean only that "the investigations are working" (Tisdall 2003), underlining the importance of the government's failure to get its understanding of UNMOVIC's role widely accepted. Pro-war commentators noted that this sort of circular argument disguised a more visceral belief that invading Iraq was fundamentally wrong (Hames 2003).

Ambiguity, then, about both the nature of SCR 1441 and the role of UNMOVIC undermined the Blair government's efforts to frame the use of force in Iraq as an effort to comply with and, indeed, uphold international law. Ministers could do nothing about those who argued about second resolutions and inspection results when in reality they were not prepared to support the use of force under any circumstances. But it does appear they lost potential backers by failing to clarify early enough how the UNMOVIC regime and the SCR process were supposed to work. Going the UN route was a popular policy. But leaving unclear what it meant in practice proved damaging.

Clashing timetables

By September 2002 British officials knew the Bush administration had a reasonably well worked-out military plan involving action in early 2003, and little interest in waiting on further diplomacy (Greenstock 2009b, 76; Meyer 2009, 55). Britain was not yet totally committed to military action. But there was more to the Blair government's military preparations than simple contingency planning, and domestic critics knew it. The *Independent on Sunday* complained that Britain was "being dragged into a conflict on the grounds of inevitability, all previous concerns brushed aside by the momentum of the military build-up" (*Independent on Sunday* 2002). Echoing this concern, Labour MP Peter Kilfoyle raised the spectre of "A.J.P. Taylor's theory on mobilization" during a debate with Defence Secretary Hoon, asking "is not there a certain inevitability about military action?" (Kilfoyle 2002, col. 854). Taylor famously argued the start of the First World War was "imposed on the statesmen of Europe by railway timetables", that the process of troop mobilization soon took on a logic of its own and outstripped the ability of governments to control it (Taylor 1969).

Crucially, key officials within the Blair government agreed that this was indeed what happened during early 2003. Meyer raised Taylor's thesis in a memo to Manning as early as October 2002 (Meyer 2002). Manning warned Blair at the end of January 2003 that "Bush is in danger of being driven by the tempo of his own military build-up" (Manning 2003). Omand and Greenstock told the Chilcot Inquiry that the "American political timetable" dictated the "window for invasion", and that the deployment of forces as a 'contingency' developed "huge momentum of [its] own" by early 2003 (Omand 2010, 57; Greenstock 2009b, 76). Ministers were far from frank in public about the extent of the pressure they faced to fit US military timetables. As early as 17 October, Blair, Straw and Hoon agreed that "the only way to keep the US on the UN route was if ... action would be taken even if a second resolution could not be agreed" (Chilcot 2016b, 307). By delaying Goldsmith's advice until British troops were already deployed, Downing Street put the Attorney General in an impossible position. For Goldsmith "to have advised that the conflict would have been unlawful without a second resolution would have been very difficult at that stage without handing Saddam Hussein a massive public relations advantage" (Wilmshurst 2010, 25). Again, we see the government struggling with the challenge of balancing domestic and international pressures. Once troops are deployed, the pressure to use them can overwhelm the diplomatic process.

Iraq never complied fully with SCR 1441. It never satisfied UNMOVIC that it was willing to co-operate. On 27 January 2003 Hans Blix delivered an initial report to the Security Council. Although later he thought the phrase "perhaps was a bit too harsh" (Blix 2010, 81), at the time he stated that "Iraq appears not to have come to a genuine acceptance – not even today – of the disarmament, which was demanded of it" (Blix 2003a). In effect, he accepted the US argument that Iraq had yet to make a "strategic decision" in favour of disarmament. As he later recalled, "it appeared from our experience that Iraq had decided in principle to provide cooperation on process, notably access. A similar decision on substance, I said, was indispensable" (Blix 2004, 139). He was not willing to give up just yet. As he told *Channel 4 News*, "there is something odd about having had eight years of inspections, then four years without, and then only two months, and then write it off". However, he went on, "I cannot say in good conscience that I see signs of co-operation" (Blix 2003b). Yet when Blix returned to the Security Council on 14 February, his tone was less critical. Though issues remained, Iraq was engaging more pro-actively (Blix 2003c). There was hope for a peaceful resolution, in other words. But the US was visibly unwilling to give UNMOVIC sufficient time to reach conclusions of its own. As Christopher Meyer put it, this meant "you had to short-circuit the inspection process by finding the notorious smoking gun" (Meyer 2009, 52). There had to be some indication that the UNMOVIC process was not working, could not work and should not continue beyond the target start date for war. This was a problem. Dearlove told Blair that he "estimated the chance of a successful operation to produce a defector or a smoking gun at about 20 percent" (Chilcot 2016c, 53). By early January, Straw warned Blair of the need for a "strategy if inspections produce no early and large smoking gun" (Straw 2003a). That meant denigrating the inspectors just months after celebrating their deployment.

British anti-war commentators warned that the first sign of a push for war would be efforts by the pro-war camp to discredit the inspection process (Fisk 2002). Sure enough, when Iraq submitted its declaration on 8 December, some British newspapers attacked Blix as "complacently bureaucratic" and "bumbling" because he insisted on reading it before dismissing it as false (*Sunday Telegraph* 2002; *Sun* 2002). Several reported that Condoleezza Rice pressed Blix to be "more aggressive" in his efforts during January (Watson and Bone 2003). Blix himself recalls Rice doing nothing of the sort, and suggests "information might have been passed to the media on what some policy hub wanted or expected her to say – without caring to check what she actually *did* say" (Blix 2004, 195). A crunch point arrived after the 14 February update. Robin Cook called Blix's more benign comments Blair's "nightmare come true" (Cook 2003, 293–294). Blix himself argues that his change of tone simply reflected changes in Iraqi behaviour, arguing "if you are asked to report about the weather, your reports must be different when the weather changes" (Blix 2004, 178). But the Blair government did not, perhaps could not, see things that way. Blair told Chilcot that "Hans Blix obviously takes a certain view now … in my conversations with him then it was a little different" (Blair 2010a, 120). In his autobiography he wrote that Blix wanted to be honest about Iraq's shortcomings but did not want to be responsible for war. Greenstock thought "part of his [Blix's] judgment on what he said publicly on 14 February was affected by the reaction of the Americans to what he said on 27 January". He claims Blix "was tougher on the Iraqis and their lack of cooperation in private than he had been in public" (Greenstock 2009b, 71). Jack Straw implied that Blix subsequently applied "gloss" to what he said in 2003 (Straw 2010b, 88). Underpinning these judgments is an implicit claim that Blix should not be seen as a neutral arbiter, but rather as a political player every bit as much as Blair and Bush.

Blix understood the power his office held to confer legitimacy on war (Blix 2004, 136). US and British official efforts to undermine him rather proved the point. Yet Blix emerged largely unscathed in the wider public debate. So central was the notion of 'going the UN route' to the Blair government's case for confronting Iraq that its efforts to circumvent the inspection process did more harm than good. Iraq was co-operating on process, which in practice meant inspectors were permitted to visit potential WMD production sites at will. They did not find a 'smoking gun', an important point the JIC never really thought about properly (Chilcot 2016d, 290). Though UNMOVIC was never satisfied by Iraqi compliance, it could have been. Blix apparently kept an open mind, as the differences between his 27 January and 14 February statements suggest. The problem with UNMOVIC was that it worked both too well and not well enough. Iraq's compliance was sufficient to avoid creating an insurmountable breach in relations, but the inspectors were unable to conclude quickly that there was no case to answer. The resulting delay put pressure on the US military timetable, and the Blair government, rather than abandoning the UN route entirely, opted instead to try to downplay UNMOVIC's importance to it.

In early February, Downing Street released its second 'dossier' describing Iraq's alleged 'infrastructure of concealment, deception and intimidation' (British Government 2003). Its purpose was clear: to argue that UNMOVIC could not possibly do its job properly, given the Iraqi state's capacity for misdirection and organized untruth. As Chapter 5 discusses, it failed badly, damaging rather than shoring up the official case for war. From the US side, Colin Powell made a similar presentation to the Security Council on 5 February, alleging that Iraq was successfully evading the inspectors' work (C. Powell 2003). These efforts were significant because they showed how far the US and UK governments lost the argument about UNMOVIC's role. Iraqi concealment should not have been a problem in and of itself. If UNMOVIC followed its mandate, and pushed for evidence of the absence of WMD rather than just observing the absence of evidence, there would be no problem. But that would take more time than the US was willing to wait. As Blix put it, "while rejecting any need for a 'smoking gun' to find Iraq in 'material breach', the US and UK realized that to convince the public and the world ... they needed to show concrete cases of violations". He concluded

> it is hard to avoid the reflection that Colin Powell had been charged with the thankless task of hauling out the smoking guns that in January were said to be irrelevant and that, after March, turned out to be non-existent.
>
> (Blix 2004, 152, 156)

It is difficult to argue simultaneously that smoking guns do not matter to the inspection process and that the inspection process does not matter because you have found a smoking gun. That was what the Blair government attempted. It did not work.

Conclusion

The Blair government claimed it would use force against Iraq only to uphold UN Security Council Resolutions, and in line with international law. But the way it approached the UN process made clear it would act even if the weapons inspectors reported Iraqi compliance or if the Security Council said no (Ralph 2011, 130). Consulting the UN probably did more harm than good to the invasion's domestic legitimacy, as a result. Matters that might have remained ambiguous gained a public airing, and not to ministers' benefit. At the same time, the government clearly faced an impossible trade-off. Public opinion expected, even demanded, UN involvement. Attorney General Lord Goldsmith did too. Though public pressure and private legal advice often pulled ministers in different directions, the two converged on this basic point. Public actors held a range of different views about the UN's importance. An unambiguous Security Council Resolution authorizing the use of force against Iraq would probably have satisfied them all. But, in light of the ambiguity surrounding the UN process, especially around whether SCR 1441 envisioned a further Security Council decision, and the role of UNMOVIC, these differences mattered. Those opponents who regarded the Council as a forum for political deal-making focused on the fact that Britain ultimately failed to do a deal. Those who vested it with moral authority complained about the bargains offered and struck along the way. And those who saw the Security Council as the ultimate arbiter of international law were not satisfied by uncertainty. One of the government's most senior international legal experts called the invasion a "crime of aggression", and resigned (Wilmshurst 2003). When even government lawyers remained unconvinced, winning public approval was always going to be hard.

Uncertainty remained the watchword. In a final failure to comply with the requirements of communicative action, Straw asked Goldsmith to downplay the nuances in his advice before making his conclusions public. Though Goldsmith told aides he was satisfied, by March 2003, that Britain could legally use force in Iraq without a 'second' SCR (Brummell 2003a), he warned Blair he could not "be confident that [a] court would agree with this view". The "safest legal course", he maintained, "would be to secure the adoption of a further resolution" (Goldsmith 2003d). During a meeting with Straw on 13 March, Goldsmith himself apparently recognized that "in public he needed to explain his case as strongly and unambiguously as possible". He planned to write to Foreign Affairs Committee Donald Anderson to confirm his stance, that "1441 is sufficient". But he also "thought he might need to tell Cabinet when it met on 17 March that the legal issues were finely balanced". This was more problematic. The FCO note of the meeting records that Straw suggested Goldsmith "needed to be aware of the problem of leaks from the Cabinet", and that "it would be better, surely, if the Attorney General distributed the draft letter ... and then made a few comments" (McDonald 2003). This was problematic. Chilcot concluded "Cabinet was not misled" about the legal position, but also that it "should have been made aware of the legal uncertainties" (Chilcot 2016e, 168). By releasing only a condensed summary of Goldsmith's ultimate judgment, the Blair government suppressed information about the detailed and finely-balanced reasoning process underpinning it, concealing Goldsmith's doubts even from Cabinet itself. As with their approach to the alleged Iraqi threat, senior ministers honestly presented their conclusions, but omitted their uncertain grounds. They also excluded interested actors from key deliberations and repeatedly refused to revise their own stance

112 *Legitimacy*

in the face of concerted and authoritative opposition. This is simply not how leaders who are interested in securing legitimacy through communicative action behave. It looks much more like strategic persuasion.

These shortcomings ensured the legal dimension of the Blair government's case for war in Iraq failed to meet the normative standards set for securing legitimacy through communicative action. Over time they contributed to the wider legitimacy deficit surrounding the invasion. Goldsmith's full legal advice leaked shortly before the 2005 general election, revealing the caveats supressed in the final public version. This damaging incident is discussed in Chapter 9. Ministers' failure to secure a sufficient UN consensus to satisfy the public's different interpretations of the Security Council's role exacerbated the problem, as did the ambiguity surrounding the whole process. When it proved impossible to reconcile US military plans and UNMOVIC's inspection timetable, the legal dimension of the case for war wound up on rocky ground.

References

Adams, Cathy. 'Memo to Lord Goldsmith.' 14 October 2002. www.iraqinquiry.org.uk/media/242576/2002-10-14-minute-adams-to-ag-iraq-meeting-with-david-manning-14-october.pdf (accessed 17 August 2016).

Adams, Cathy. 'Letter to David Manning.' 28 January 2003. www.iraqinquiry.org.uk/media/244291/2003-01-28-letter-adams-to-manning-iraq.pdf (accessed 17 August 2016).

Bjola, Corneliu. 'Legitimating the use of force in international politics: a communicative action perspective.' *European Journal of International Relations* 11, no. 2 (2005): 266–303.

Bjola, Corneliu. *Legitimising the Use of Force in International Politics: Kosovo, Iraq and the Ethics of Intervention.* London: Routledge, 2009.

Blair, Tony. "Press conference with President Bush." 6 April 2002a. http://webarchive.nationalarchives.gov.uk/+/www.number10.gov.uk/Page1711 (accessed 27 May 2010).

Blair, Tony. *Hansard House of Commons Debates*, vol. 383, 10 April 2002b.

Blair, Tony. 'Speech to the Labour Party conference.' 1 October 2002c. www.britishpoliticalspeech.org/speech-archive.htm?speech=185 (accessed 23 October 2015).

Blair, Tony. 'Prime Minister's monthly press conference.' 25 November 2002d. http://webarchive.nationalarchives.gov.uk/20060715135117/http://number10.gov.uk/page3004 (accessed 4 June 2016).

Blair, Tony. *Hansard House of Commons Debates*, vol. 397, 8 January 2003a.

Blair, Tony. 'Prime Minister's monthly press conference.' 13 January 2003b. http://webarchive.nationalarchives.gov.uk/20040105034004/number10.gov.uk/page3005 (accessed 2 June 2016).

Blair, Tony. *Hansard House of Commons Debates*, vol. 397, 15 January 2003c.

Blair, Tony. Interview by Jeremy Paxman. *BBC Newsnight.* (6 February 2003d).

Blair, Tony. 'Evidence to the Chilcot Inquiry.' 29 January 2010a. www.iraqinquiry.org.uk/media/229766/2010-01-29-transcript-blair-s1.pdf (accessed 6 August 2016).

Blair, Tony. *A Journey.* London: Hutchinson, 2010b.

Blair, Tony. 'Evidence to the Chilcot Inquiry.' 21 January 2011. www.iraqinquiry.org.uk/media/230337/2011-01-21-transcript-blair-s1.pdf (accessed 17 August 2016).

Blix, Hans. 'UNMOVIC chairman's report to the UN Security Council.' 27 January 2003a. www.un.org/Depts/unmovic/new/pages/security_council_briefings.asp#5 (accessed 4 June 2016).

Blix, Hans. Interview by Jon Snow. *Channel 4 News* (30 January 2003b).

Blix, Hans. 'UNMOVIC chairman's briefing to the Security Council.' 14 February 2003c. www.un.org/Depts/unmovic/new/pages/security_council_briefings.asp#6 (accessed 4 June 2016).

Blix, Hans. *Disarming Iraq: The Search for Weapons of Mass Destruction*. London: Bloomsbury, 2004.

Blix, Hans. 'Evidence to the Chilcot Inquiry.' 27 July 2010. www.iraqinquiry.org.uk/media/95406/2010-07-27-Transcript-Blix-S2.pdf (accessed 17 August 2016).

British Government. *Iraq: Its Infrastructure of Concealment, Deception and Intimidation*. London: HMSO, 2003.

Brummell, David. 'Iraq: note of telephone conversation between Attorney General and Jonathan Powell.' 11 November 2002a. www.iraqinquiry.org.uk/media/76075/2002-11-11-Note-Brummell-AGO-Iraq-note-of-telephone-conversation-between-the-Attorney-General-and-Jonathan-Powell-Monday-11th-November-2002.pdf (accessed 17 August 2016).

Brummell, David. 'Iraq: note of telephone conversation between the Foreign Secretary and the Attorney General.' 12 November 2002b. www.iraqinquiry.org.uk/media/76079/2002-11-12-Note-Brummell-AGO-Iraq-note-of-telephone-conversation-between-the-Foreign-Secretary-and-the-Attorney-General-on-Tuesday-12-November-2002.pdf (accessed 17 August 2016).

Brummell, David. 'Iraq: note of meeting at No. 10 Downing Street.' 19 December 2002c. www.iraqinquiry.org.uk/media/242591/2002-12-19-minute-brummell-ago-note-of-meeting-at-no-10-downing-street-400-pm-19-december-2002.pdf (accessed 17 August 2016).

Brummell, David. 'Iraq: legal basis for use of force: note of discussion with Attorney General.' 13 March 2003a. www.iraqinquiry.org.uk/media/244316/2003-03-13-minute-brummell-iraq-legal-basis-for-use-of-force-note-of-discussion-with-ag-thursday-13-march-2003.pdf (accessed 17 August 2016).

Brummell, David. 'Letter to Martin Hemming'. 14 March 2003b. www.iraqinquiry.org.uk/media/76311/2003-03-14-Letter-Brummell-to-Hemming-Iraq-Position-Of-The-CDS.pdf (accessed 17 August 2016).

Bush, George W. 'Speech to the Graduating Class of West Point Military Academy.' 1 June 2002a. https://georgewbush-whitehouse.archives.gov/news/releases/2002/06/20020601-3.html (accessed 2 June 2016).

Bush, George W. 'Speech to the UN General Assembly.' 12 September 2002b. https://georgewbush-whitehouse.archives.gov/news/releases/2002/09/20020912-1.html (accessed 3 June 2016).

Bush, George W. 'The State of the Union.' 28 January 2003a. https://georgewbush-whitehouse.archives.gov/news/releases/2003/01/20030128-19.html (accessed 3 June 2016).

Bush, George W. 'Press conference with Prime Minister Blair.' 31 January 2003b. https://georgewbush-whitehouse.archives.gov/news/releases/2003/01/20030131-23.html (accessed June 3, 2016).

Buzan, Barry, and Ana Gonzalez-Pelaez. 'International community after Iraq.' *International Affairs* 81, no. 1 (2005): 31–52.

Campbell, Alastair, and Richard Stott. *The Blair Years: Extracts from the Alastair Campbell Diaries*. London: Arrow Books, 2007.

Campbell, Alastair. 'Evidence to the Chilcot Inquiry, afternoon session.' 12 January 2010. www.iraqinquiry.org.uk/media/95146/2010-01-12-Transcript-Campbell-S1-pm.pdf (accessed 17 August 2016).

Campbell, Menzies. *Hansard House of Commons Debates*, vol. 372, 14 September 2001.

Chilcot, John. *Report of the Iraq Inquiry: Executive Summary.* London: HMSO, 2016a.

Chilcot, John. *Report of the Iraq Inquiry: Volume 2.* London: HMSO, 2016b.

Chilcot, John. *Report of the Iraq Inquiry: Volume 3.* London: HMSO, 2016c.

Chilcot, John. *Report of the Iraq Inquiry: Volume 4.* London: HMSO, 2016d.

Chilcot, John. *Report of the Iraq Inquiry: Volume 5.* London: HMSO, 2016e.

Claude, Inis. 'Collective legitimization as a political function of the United Nations.' *International Organization* 20, no. 3 (1966): 367–379.

Cook, Robin. *The Point of Departure.* London: Simon & Schuster, 2003.

Cornwell, Rupert. 'This weird little dude has caught the US on the hop.' *Independent*, 3 January 2003.

Daily Telegraph. 'Leading article', 8 November 2002.

D'Ancona, Matthew. 'I agree with Blair on Iraq. And, boy, do I feel lonely.' *Sunday Telegraph*, 12 January 2003.

Dunne, Tim. 'Britain and the gathering storm over Iraq.' In *Foreign Policy: Theories, Actors, Cases*, by Steve Smith, Amelia Hadfield and Tim Dunne, 339–358. Oxford: Oxford University Press, 2008.

Dyson, Stephen. 'New Labour, leadership, and foreign policy-making after 1997.' In *British Foreign Policy: The New Labour Years*, by Oliver Daddow and Jamie Gaskarth, 63–83. Basingstoke: Palgrave Macmillan, 2011.

Ehrenberg, John, J. Patrice McSherry, Jose Ramon Sanchez, and Caroleen Marji Sayej (Eds.) *The Iraq Papers.* Oxford: Oxford University Press, 2010.

Eichenberg, Richard. 'Victory has many friends: US public opinion and the use of military force 1981–2005.' *International Security* 30, no. 1 (2005): 140–177.

Everts, Philip, and Pierangelo Isernia. 'The polls – trends: the war in Iraq.' *Public Opinion Quarterly* 69, no. 2 (2005): 264–323.

Finkelstein, Daniel. 'Abdication crisis: how we gave our conscience to the UN.' *The Times*, 28 January 2003.

Fisk, Robert. 'We are being set up for a war against Saddam.' *Independent*, 4 December 2002.

Franck, Thomas. 'Legitimacy in the international system.' *American Journal of International Law* 82, no. 4 (1988): 705–759.

Freedland, Jonathan. 'The subtle art of sugaring bitter pills goes down well.' *Guardian*, 2 October 2002.

Gedye, Robin, Toby Harnden, and Toby Helm. 'The damning of Saddam: Iraq still has biological and chemical weapons, says Blix.' *Daily Telegraph*, 28 January 2003.

Goldsmith, Lord. 'Memo to Tony Blair.' 30 July 2002. www.iraqinquiry.org.uk/media/75931/2002-07-30-Minute-Attorney-General-to-Prime-Minister-Iraq.pdf (accessed 17 August 2016).

Goldsmith, Lord. 'Iraq: interpretation of Resolution 1441.' 14 January 2003a. www.iraqinquiry.org.uk/media/76099/2003-01-14-Minute-Goldsmith-to-Prime-Minister-Iraq-Interpretation-Of-Resolution-1441.pdf (accessed 17 August 2016).

Goldsmith, Lord. 'Iraq: memo to Tony Blair.' 30 January 2003b. www.iraqinquiry.org.uk/media/76159/2003-01-30-Minute-Goldsmith-to-Prime-Minister-Iraq.pdf (accessed 17 August 2016).

Goldsmith, Lord. 'Iraq: interpretation of Resolution 1441.' 12 February 2003c. www.iraqinquiry.org.uk/media/76187/2003-02-12-Paper-Attorney-General-Iraq-Interpretation-Of-Resolution-1441.pdf (accessed 17 August 2016).

Goldsmith, Lord. 'Iraq: legal advice: memo to Tony Blair.' 7 March 2003d. http://image.guardian.co.uk/sys-files/Guardian/documents/2005/04/28/legal.pdf (accessed 20 August 2015).

Goldsmith, Lord. 'Evidence to the Chilcot Inquiry.' 27 January 2010. www.iraqinquiry.org.uk/media/235686/2010-01-27-transcript-goldsmith-s1.pdf (accessed 17 August 2016).

Greenstock, Jeremy. 'Iraq: handling in the Security Council: letter to Michael Jay.' 3 September 2002a. www.iraqinquiry.org.uk/media/75959/2002-09-03-Letter-Greenstock-to-Jay-Iraq-Handling-in-the-Security-Council.pdf (accessed 17 August 2016).

Greenstock, Jeremy. Interview by Krishnan Guru-Murthy. *Channel 4 News.* (8 November 2002b).

Greenstock, Jeremy. 'Evidence to the Chilcot Inquiry: written statement.' 27 November 2009a. www.iraqinquiry.org.uk/media/242305/2009-11-xx-statement-greenstock.pdf (accessed 17 August 2016).

Greenstock, Jeremy. 'Evidence to the Chilcot Inquiry.' 27 November 2009b. www.iraqinquiry.org.uk/media/94798/2009-11-27-Transcript-Greenstock-S1.pdf (accessed 17 August 2016).

Guardian. 'Leading article', 10 October 2001.

Guardian. 'Leading article', 3 October 2002.

Guardian. 'Leading article', 5 February 2003.

Hames, Tim. 'Blair needs a weapon of mass persuasion.' *The Times*, 13 January 2003.

Hemming, Martin. 'Letter to David Brummell.' 12 March 2003. www.iraqinquiry.org.uk/media/76279/2003-03-12-Letter-Hemming-to-Brummell-Iraq-Position-Of-The-CDS.pdf (accessed 17 August 2016).

Hogg, Douglas. *Hansard House of Commons Debates*, vol. 398, 20 January 2003.

Hoon, Geoff. *Hansard House of Commons Debates*, vol. 398, 20 January 2003.

Hurd, Ian. 'Legitimacy and authority in international politics.' *International Organization* 53, no. 2 (1999): 379–408.

Independent. 'Leading article', 8 November 2002.

Independent International Commission on Kosovo. *The Kosovo Report: Conflict, International Response, Lessons Learned.* Oxford: Oxford University Press, 2000.

Independent on Sunday. 'Leading article', 22 December 2002.

Joint Intelligence Committee. 'An initial assessment of Iraq's WMD declaration.' 18 December 2002. www.iraqinquiry.org.uk/media/76087/2002-12-18-Assessment-JIC-An-initial-assessment-of-Iraqs-WMD-declaration.pdf (accessed 17 August 2016).

Kampfner, John. *Blair's Wars.* London: Free Press, 2003.

Kaufman, Gerald. *Hansard House of Commons Debates*, vol. 395, 25 November 2002.

Keane, Fergal. 'Dominant at home and abroad, but it could all go quickly wrong for Mr Bush.' *Independent*, 9 November 2002.

Kilfoyle, Peter. *Hansard House of Commons Debates*, vol. 396, 18 December 2002.

Maddox, Bronwen. 'Alliance with US could make Blair first war casualty.' *The Times*, 15 February 2003.

Mahon, Alice. *Hansard House of Commons Debates*, vol. 394, 7 November 2002.

Manning, David. 'Memo to Tony Blair.' 3 January 2003. www.iraqinquiry.org.uk/media/213639/2003-01-03-minute-manning-to-prime-minister-iraq.pdf (accessed 18 July 2016).

Manning, David. 'Evidence to the Chilcot Inquiry.' 30 November 2009. www.iraqinquiry.org.uk/media/94802/2009-11-30-Transcript-Manning-S1.pdf (accessed 17 August 2016).

Marfleet, B. Gregory, and Colleen Miller. 'Failure After 1441: Bush and Chirac in the UN Security Council.' *Foreign Policy Analysis* 1, no. 3 (2005): 333–360.

McDonald, Simon. 'Iraq: ultimatum: letter to David Manning.' 27 August 2002. www.iraqinquiry.org.uk/media/75939/2002-08-27-Letter-McDonald-to-Manning-Iraq-ultimatum-attaching-Draft-SCR.pdf (accessed 17 August 2016).

McDonald, Simon. 'File note: Foreign Secretary's meeting with the Attorney General, 13 March.' 17 March 2003. www.iraqinquiry.org.uk/media/76327/2003-03-17-Note-McDonald-Iraq-Meeting-With-The-Attorney-General.pdf (accessed 12 August 2016).

Meyer, Christopher. 'Telegram to David Manning.' 11 October 2002. www.iraqinquiry.org.uk/media/210455/2002-10-11-telegram-1326-washington-to-fco-london-us-iraq-will-the-president-go-to-war.pdf (accessed 15 July 2016).

Meyer, Christopher. *DC Confidential.* London: Widenfield & Nicolson, 2005.

Meyer, Christopher. 'Evidence to the Chilcot Inquiry.' 26 November 2009. www.iraqinquiry.org.uk/media/94794/2009-11-26-Transcript-Meyer-S1.pdf (accessed 17 August 2016).

Mirror. 'Benn in Iraq trip', 25 January 2003.

Negroponte, John. 'Letter to the president of the Security Council.' 7 October 2001. http://avalon.law.yale.edu/sept11/un_006.asp (accessed 2 June 2016).

Norton-Taylor, Richard. 'Bush has little intention of playing by the book: Saddam's gameplan may yet succeed in dividing his opponents.' *Guardian*, 9 December 2002.

Norton-Taylor, Richard. 'If only he would listen, this could be Blair's finest hour.' *Guardian*, 6 January 2003.

Observer. 'Leading article', 19 January 2003.

Omand, David. 'Evidence to the Chilcot Inquiry.' 20 January 2010. www.iraqinquiry.org.uk/media/44187/20100120pm-omand-final.pdf (accessed 4 June 2016).

Onuf, Nicholas. *World of Our Making: Rules and Rule in Social Theory and International Relations.* Columbia, SC: University of South Carolina Press, 1989.

Paveley, Rebecca, and William Lowther. '6,500 UK troops may be sent to Gulf next month.' *Daily Mail*, 14 December 2002.

Powell, Colin. 'Presentation to the UN Security Council.' 5 February 2003. http://2001-2009.state.gov/secretary/former/powell/remarks/2003/17300.htm (accessed 6 June 2016).

Powell, Jonathan. 'File note.' 31 July 2002. www.iraqinquiry.org.uk/media/210871/2002-07-31-note-for-no10-file-powell.pdf (accessed 15 July 2016).

Ralph, Jason. 'A difficult relationship: Britain's "doctrine of international community" and America's "war on terror".' In *British Foreign Policy: The New Labour Years*, by Oliver Daddow and Jamie Gaskarth, 123–138. Basingstoke: Palgrave Macmillan, 2011.

Reus-Smit, Christian. 'Human rights and the social construction of sovereignty.' *Review of International Studies* 27, no. 4 (2001): 519–538.

Riddell, Peter. 'UN's umbrella is protection against backbench revolt.' *Times*, 4 October 2002.

Robinson, Nick. 'Nick Robinson's notebook.' *The Times*, 7 February 2003.

Sands, Philippe. 'A grand and disastrous deceit.' *London Review of Books*, 28 July 2016: 9–11.

Scott, Shirley, and Olivia Ambler. 'Does legality really matter? Accounting for the decline in US foreign policy legitimacy following the 2003 invasion of Iraq.' *European Journal of International Relations* 13, no. 1 (2007): 67–87.

Sedwill, Mark. 'Iraq: Foreign Secretary's conversation with Attorney General.' 18 October 2002. www.iraqinquiry.org.uk/media/212919/2002-10-18-minute-sedwill-to-ricketts-iraq-foreign-secretarys-conversation-with-the-attorney-general-18-october.pdf (accessed 17 August 2016).

Seldon, Anthony, Peter Snowdon and Daniel Collings. *Blair Unbound*. London: Simon & Schuster, 2007.
Sheridan, Tommy. 'War on Iraq is same oil story after 12 years.' *Mirror*, 15 January 2003.
Sillars, Jim. 'UN has the power but not the morals.' *Sun*, 1 October 2002.
Simpson, John. 'Bush's peace and love sentiments unlikely to last until March.' *Sunday Telegraph*, 13 December 2002.
Straw, Jack. 'Cable to Jeremy Greenstock.' 21 October 2002b. www.iraqinquiry.org.uk/media/224518/2002-10-21-Telegram-602-FCO-London-to-UKMIS-New-York-Iraq-Draft-UNSCR.pdf (accessed 17 August 2016).
Straw, Jack. *Hansard House of Commons Debates*, vol. 392, 7 November 2002c.
Straw, Jack. *Hansard House of Commons Debates*, vol. 393, 25 November 2002d.
Straw, Jack. 'Memo to Tony Blair.' 3 January 2003a. www.iraqinquiry.org.uk/media/242601/2003-01-03-minute-straw-to-prime-minister-iraq-plan-b.pdf (accessed 18 July 2016).
Straw, Jack. 'Iraq: legal basis for the use of force.' 29 January 2003b. www.iraqinquiry.org.uk/media/218280/2003-01-29-Minute-Straw-to-Wood-Iraq-Legal-Basis-for-the-Use-of-Force.pdf (17 August 2016).
Straw, Jack. 'Iraq: letter to Lord Goldsmith.' 6 February 2003c. www.iraqinquiry.org.uk/media/76183/2003-02-06-Letter-Straw-to-Attorney-General-Iraq-Second-Resolution.pdf (accessed 17 August 2016).
Straw, Jack. 'Evidence to the Chilcot Inquiry (written statement).' 21 January 2010a. www.iraqinquiry.org.uk/media/43119/jackstraw-memorandum.pdf (accessed 6 June 2016).
Straw, Jack. 'Evidence to the Chilcot Inquiry.' 21 January 2010b. www.iraqinquiry.org.uk/media/95186/2010-01-21-Transcript-Straw-S1.pdf (accessed 17 August 2016).
Straw, Jack. 'Evidence to the Chilcot Inquiry.' 8 February 2010c. www.iraqinquiry.org.uk/media/95266/2010-02-08-Transcript-Straw-S2.pdf (accessed 17 August 2016).
Sun. 'The Sun says', 9 December 2002.
Sunday Telegraph. 'Leading article', 8 December 2002.
Sunday Telegraph. 'Leading article', 2 February 2003.
Tapsell, Peter. *Hansard House of Commons Debates*, vol. 395, 25 November 2002.
Taylor, A.J.P. *War by Timetable: How the First World War Began*. London: McDonald & Co Ltd., 1969.
The Times. 'Leading article', 25 October 2001.
The Times. 'Leading article', 8 January 2003.
Tisdall, Simon. 'Don't count on the UN to save us from going to war.' *Guardian*, 20 January 2003.
United Nations Security Council. 'Resolution 1441.' 8 November 2002. www.un.org/Depts/unmovic/documents/1441.pdf (accessed 3 June 2016).
US Government. 'The National Security Strategy of the United States of America.' 17 September 2002. www.state.gov/documents/organization/63562.pdf (accessed 2 June 2016).
Voeten, Erik. 'The political origins of the UN Security Council's ability to legitimize the use of force.' *International Organization* 59, no. 4 (2005): 527–557.
Watkins, Alan. 'Blair will lead a divided country into war.' *Independent on Sunday*, 24 November 2002.
Watson, Roland, and James Bone. 'Bush administration split over go-it-alone option if UN resists.' *The Times*, 16 January 2003.

Wilmshurst, Elizabeth. 'Memo to Michael Wood.' 18 March 2003. www.iraqinquiry.org.uk/media/242786/2003-03-18-minute-wilmshurst-to-wood-untitled.pdf (accessed 17 August 2016).

Wilmshurst, Elizabeth. 'Evidence to the Chilcot Inquiry.' 26 January 2010. www.iraqinquiry.org.uk/media/95214/2010-01-26-Transcript-Wilmshurst-S3.pdf (accessed 18 July 2016).

Wood, Michael. 'Memo to Stephen Wright'. 15 August 2002. www.iraqinquiry.org.uk/media/75935/2002-08-15-Letter-Wood-to-Wright-Iraq-legality-of-use-of-force.pdf (accessed 17 August 2016).

Wood, Michael. 'Iraq: legal basis for the use of force.' 24 January 2003. www.iraqinquiry.org.uk/media/226676/2003-01-24-minute-wood-to-ps-fco-iraq-legal-basis-for-use-of-force-with-manuscript-comment-mcdonald-to-wood-28-january.pdf (accessed 17 August 2016).

7 Morality and regime change

This chapter considers the debate over the morality of military action in Iraq, and the especially vexed issue of 'regime change'. It is both politically and theoretically difficult to claim the moral high ground for foreign policy actions that involve the use of force. Doing so is especially challenging in Britain, a country traditionally allergic to talk of international ethics (Gaskarth 2006, 326). Yet this is exactly what the Blair government attempted to do. To a significant degree its approach reflected public attitudes. Of course, Iraq was developing WMD. Even some of the war's most vocal critics agreed as much. As such, the Attorney General could credibly claim the invasion complied with international law. He was, after all, a highly experienced member of a profession that values the ability to grasp, elucidate and, above all, believe contradictory views, simultaneously. None of this won the argument, though it ensured the government did not lose. Opposition remained, as did deep unease, even amongst the government's supporters. Driving it was the more visceral belief that invading Iraq was simply the wrong thing to do. Many people in Britain felt that it was in some sense immoral, even if it was necessary and legal, to deploy the might of Western power against a closed, impoverished state no longer capable of, let alone engaged in, the sort of acts of aggression that warranted its isolation in the 1990s. However necessary or legal the use of force might be, innocent Iraqis would suffer. On the other side of the argument stood the Prime Minister, whose personal views dominated the moral dimension of the Iraq debate. Blair believed that removing Saddam Hussein from power was absolutely the right thing to do and that, if not quite a moral imperative, it was at least a moral good.

As the first part of this chapter sets out, Blair's faith carried him through the darkest days of early 2003, sustaining his belief in the need for action despite concerted and quite angry opposition. Understanding Britain's war in Iraq consequently means understanding Blair. It also means appreciating the very real difficulties he faced in making moral arguments publicly. For all their centrality to democratic debates on foreign policy legitimacy, questions about international morality remain complex and hard to resolve (Kratochwil 1993, 77). There is a direct clash between a universalist understanding of how the world *should* work and a more pluralist account of relations among states based on international law. True to his preferred approach to apparently insoluble conceptual challenges, Blair met this clash by proposing a 'third way', arguing that law should be contingent on morality rather than opposed to it. As the second part of this chapter discusses, Blair never really confronted, let alone resolved, the underlying difficulty: the question of whether he sought 'regime change' consequently dogged the fraught debate over the moral grounds for war. Blair believed that removing Saddam Hussein from power and replacing him with a democratic government was the right thing to do. He could not, however, say so publicly without contradicting his parallel commitment to obeying international law. Nor, in turn, could he bring himself to downplay the benefits of regime change, or to resist defending it in principle. In many ways, as this chapter's final section concludes, this strand of the moral case for war epitomized the strengths and weaknesses of the Blair government's entire approach to Iraq.

Responding directly to the mass street protests of 15 February 2003, Blair launched into a 'moral turn', increasingly playing up the benefits of regime change while still (just about) holding the line that it was a welcome side effect of military action aimed at disarmament, rather than its central goal. Finally able to make in public the arguments he believed most passionately in private, Blair quickly dispelled suggestions that he was acting solely because President Bush told him to. His sheer conviction rallied supporters and impressed critics. Though it did not win him the debate, it helped him survive the final parliamentary vote. At the same time, the 'moral turn' undermined the invasion's longer term legitimacy. It underlined how little the government's public case for war reflected its private reasoning, especially Blair's. This cast doubt on ministers' commitment to explaining their position honestly and completely. It also made clear how unwilling Blair was to take seriously opponents' views. At a conceptual level, these factors limited the scope for the government to secure legitimacy through communicative action. At a practical level, they reinforced public distrust, convincing many that the government withheld the 'real' reasons for war in favour of arguments it thought were easier to sell. David Chandler argued that governments make ethical or moral arguments to justify foreign policy because they know they can win support without being held accountable subsequently (Chandler 2003, 295). To some extent the Blair government did win support by making the moral case for war in Iraq. But it *was* ultimately held accountable, and once again arguments that worked initially hurt it after the invasion.

Understanding Tony Blair

It is odd, in a sense, that Tony Blair became identified so totally in the public imagination with foreign policy. He came to office knowing and caring little about the wider world. His electoral successes look all the more astonishing in retrospect after years of close-fought contests and parliamentary fragmentation. His domestic legacy, while disappointing in comparison to the scale of his political victories, nevertheless remains substantial. Yet it is in practice unsurprising that Blair is so often and so completely associated personally with foreign policy, and with Iraq in particular, far more than with any other issue, policy or event. As the moral dimension of the Iraq debate reveals, Blair possessed a perfect storm of psychological predilections and experience-based beliefs, a storm that both sustained and ultimately undermined his approach through 2002 and early 2003. Appreciating how both his personality and his previous record influenced the moral dimension of the Iraq debate means understanding what it was that drove Tony Blair on.

Personality: the 'Messiah complex'

Blair admits in his autobiography to "a somewhat weirdly optimistic view of the power of reason, of the ability to persuade if an argument is persuasive" (Blair 2010b, 117). On the surface, this faith in the power of reason should have inclined him towards communicative action as a path to legitimacy. Indeed, it explains in large part why he chose a communicative course in the first place, and why he remained so certain in the face of opposition that he would ultimately win critics over. Blair's self-analysis, however, falls short when set alongside accounts others offer of how his personality affected his approach to Iraq. It leaves out a crucial point. Not only did Blair believe in the power of reason, in the abstract, but he also believed in his own powers of reasoning. Although he claimed he did not "pretend to have a monopoly of wisdom in these issues" (Blair 2003f), he acted very much as if he did. He believed both that well-reasoned arguments could affect public debate, and that his own arguments were, by definition, the most well-reasoned available. Jonathan Powell labelled this his "Messiah complex" (Blair 2010b, 157; Powell 2010b, 56). Powell's choice of a biblical metaphor proved prescient. One Downing Street aide told Seldon that:

> this is a man who, in terms of the judgement of right and wrong, would think that his own judgement was at least as good as that of the Archbishop of Canterbury, of the Cardinal of Westminster, and of the Pope combined
> (Seldon *et al.* 2007, 153–154)

No sooner had Blair begun to lay out the moral case for war with Iraq than Archbishop Rowan Williams, Cardinal Cormac Murphy-O'Connor and Pope John Paul II challenged it publicly. Anti-war commentators thought the ecclesiastical intervention "makes a mockery of Tony Blair's claim that it would be immoral not to wage war on Iraq" and that it cast "doubt on the legitimacy of his logic" (*Mirror* 2003; *Independent* 2003a). Blair remained unmoved.

Tony Blair was (and is) a deeply religious man. As the leader of a predominantly secular country, possessing deep and sincere religious beliefs could occasionally be problematic. Alastair Campbell once famously interrupted a *Vanity Fair* interview with the then-Prime Minister to prevent the subject turning to Blair's faith. "I'm sorry", he told the interviewer, "we don't do God" (Margolick 2003). Blair's approach to Iraq reflected his faith to some extent, in that it involved dividing international politics into black and white worlds of evil and good. But, in part, it reflected the sense that religion plays poorly in British politics and, which Campbell's remark presaged, he never really talked about it publicly. That made sense. The British rarely even say 'God save the Queen' any more, other than when singing the national anthem. It is true that we don't really 'do' God. When Sir David Frost asked Blair if he and President Bush prayed together, he meant to catch the Prime Minister saying something his audience would find, if not shocking, at least somewhat strange (Frost 2002). But the resistance Blair put up in the face of opposition from significant Christian leaders both underlines the debt he owed to his Oxford friend, Peter Thomson, and the non-conformist "Christian socialism" of John MacMurray (Crampton 1995) and hints at a broader psychological basis to his approach.

Building on Margaret Hermann's "leadership trait analysis" (Hermann 1980), Stephen Dyson conducted a useful series of reviews of Blair's underlying psychological make-up. His conclusions are significant in this context. Blair, Dyson finds, possessed a "high belief in his ability to control events, a low conceptual complexity, and a high need for power" (Dyson 2006, 289). He was psychologically predisposed to interpret information about international affairs simplistically and moralistically (Dyson 2007, 2009, 235–236, 2011, 64, 71). This disposition helps us understand to a significant degree why Blair took such an absolute stance on the question of war with Iraq, as well as why he stuck to it in the face of concerted opposition (Kramer 2003; Bromund 2009). During the final months before the invasion Blair repeatedly acknowledged that he might lose his job over Iraq, or at least the broad coalition of public support on which his government depended (Blair 2003c; Campbell and Stott 2007, 669–672). By late February, as one chronicler recalled, "there was talk of mass resignations from party activists, of meltdown in the local elections, of several resignations from the Cabinet – perhaps even of Blair having to stand down" (Kampfner 2003, 283). He was not oblivious to this, as Robin Cook later suggested he might have been (Cook 2003, 314). He was simply unperturbed. He made his choice, and he planned to see it through. Blair was never so incautious when public opinion questioned his domestic agenda (Chandler 2003, 302–303). But on Iraq he was a "true believer" (Cox 2005, 218). At the Labour Party spring conference in February 2003, he concluded to the delegates that "sometimes unpopularity is the price of leadership and the cost of conviction" (Blair 2003c). President Bush told reporters at a joint press conference during Blair's Crawford visit that "the thing I admire about this Prime Minister is he doesn't need a poll or a focus group to convince him the difference between right and wrong" (Bush 2002). Blair echoed these sentiments at home, telling British journalists "I do what I think is the right thing, whether on foreign or domestic policy" (Blair 2002d), and "polls or no polls, my job in a situation like this is sometimes to say the things that people don't want to hear" (Blair 2003b). These were not the words of a man willing to revisit his personal views in response to criticism – a problem, in terms of his commitment to communicative action.

Experience

Blair's moral certainty did not emerge in a vacuum, even if it did owe much to his underlying psychological makeup. Iraq was not his first war. Between 1997 and 2003 he ordered British troops into combat four times, in Iraq itself in 1998, Kosovo in 1999, Sierra Leone in 2000 and Afghanistan in 2001. These experiences affected him. Apparent success in Kosovo, in particular, hardened his underlying instincts (Daddow 2009). Having defied considerable criticism, from both the establishment and the broader public, he felt emboldened. The experience reinforced his faith in his own superior judgment (Kennedy-Pipe and Vickers 2007, 210). It directly informed his approach to Iraq. Having faced down public doubters before, and won, Blair was better prepared psychologically to do so again, even if that meant rejecting credible challenges to his moral claims. Chilcot quoted David Manning noting that "Iraq fits into a pattern" of interventionism, that Blair was "very much an activist ... very comfortable with his own convictions" and someone who "believed he had a capacity to influence the international system in quite profound ways ... that he could actually act for the good, he could change things" (Chilcot 2016a, 515).

Blair gave an early account of the reasoning that later underpinned his approach to Iraq during the Kosovo conflict. Speaking at the Economic Club in Chicago, ostensibly to an audience of local business figures but indirectly addressing the Clinton administration, Blair set out what he called a "doctrine of international community". Humanitarian intervention was a moral good, he argued with specific reference to the ongoing NATO campaign. But it was also more than that. It was an act of what he later termed "enlightened self-interest" (Blair 2010b, 228). In an interdependent world, as he put it:

> [national] values and [national] interests merge. If we can establish and spread the values of liberty, the rule of law, human rights and an open society then that is in our national interests too. The spread of our values makes us safer.
>
> (Blair 1999)

It was difficult, in other words, to disentangle the moral and self-interested grounds for international action in Blair's mind. He believed it made little sense to try to distinguish between invading Iraq to disarm Saddam Hussein and invading Iraq because it was the right thing to do. For Blair, the two arguments were fundamentally linked. He implied as much in his response to the 11 September attacks, telling the Labour Party conference "this is a moment to seize ... the kaleidoscope has been shaken. The pieces are in flux. Soon they will settle again. Before they do, let us re-order this world around us" (Blair 2001a). The right response to mass terrorism was not just an effort to improve global security, but a more fundamental campaign of moral renewal. These, then, were the lessons Blair drew on in approaching Iraq.

Opposition

Blair's 2001 conference speech elicited a mixed response among commentators. Some observers noted that it smacked of imperialism (Hensher 2001). Others praised it as a "remarkable and remarkably grandiloquent" contribution (*Sunday Telegraph* 2001). Left-wingers welcomed the "mission to conquer world poverty and build international peace and a world based upon justice, equality and human rights" Blair seemed to be declare (Hain 2001). One major advantage Blair enjoyed in making the moral case for action in Afghanistan was that most observers believed that he meant what he said. Bronwen Maddox observed the impact in Whitehall of "the personal conviction that Blair has brought to the fight", though Matthew Parris distinguished between "the bad news", that Blair probably did believe the more expansive moral claims he made, and the "better news" that usually "he doesn't do it, once he's said it" (Maddox 2001; Parris 2001). That Blair preferred making moral arguments to arguing about intelligence or international law helped him in the final weeks of the pre-invasion debate. The media claim, that he was acting like President Bush's 'poodle', grew increasingly untenable as he risked everything politically, and exhausted himself physically, seeking converts to the pro-war party line. The *Times* remarked that "Blair's very conviction ... is persuasive in itself" (*The Times* 2003). Peter Riddell concluded that on this issue if not necessarily on others "the public Blair is the true Blair" (Riddell 2003). On the day of the final parliamentary debate, the *Independent* called the decision to go to war "a failure of potentially catastrophic proportions". Yet in the same breath it wrote of Blair that "his patent sincerity has impressed, banishing his reputation as a fickle politician without convictions" (*Independent* 2003b). Honesty can be popular even if the views a leader expresses are not. Pursuing communicative action can make an argument more persuasive in turn.

In the final weeks before the invasion, Downing Street launched what Alastair Campbell later called the "masochism strategy", seeking to maximize the boost to Blair's reputation by facing down critics publicly (Campbell 2010, 39). The approach worked, at least in that it reinforced the growing sense in the country that the Prime Minister genuinely believed invading Iraq was the right thing to do. Writing after a particularly brutal televised Q&A session with anti-war members of the public, Nick Robinson explained the extraordinary journalistic appeal of the situation: "Blair believes in the rightness of his cause, the logic of his case and his ability to convert people to it. And, for once, there is little downside for the media. The public wants to watch him try" (Robinson 2003). Andrew Marr, wondering at the Prime Minister's willingness to endure the punishment meted out by hugely hostile crowds, asked whether "he is still convinced by his ability, whatever the odds, to win people round? Or is it subtler – that he will gain respect for tackling the genuine critics and not ducking arguments?" (Marr 2003). To an extent it was both, but Blair did gain respect. Andrew Rawnsley remained agnostic about the prospect of military action in Iraq. He still observed that "never again will it be possible to portray this Prime Minister as a politician who would not put on a tie without first consulting a focus group" (Rawnsley 2003). Deborah Orr, who opposed the war, nevertheless marvelled at Blair's "pure, unadulterated conviction", noting it was "mesmerising ... to watch such awesome blind integrity in action" (Orr 2003). Though a handful of cynics dismissed the moral case for war as another act of "spin" (Hitchens 2003), most commentators agreed with the *Observer* that "even [Blair's] critics should acknowledge the remarkable leadership he is exhibiting" by sticking quite literally to his guns in the face of widespread and vocal hostility (*Observer* 2003).

It helped that the opposition struggled to cohere around a single moral counter-argument. During the Afghan campaign, supporters and critics divided over whether the military action taken was "restrained, small and targeted" or indiscriminate "carpet bombing" (Mercer 2001, col. 1123; *Independent* 2001). Neither side could realistically know what was happening on the ground. Some initial supporters of action in Afghanistan immediately reversed themselves and began to criticize the action as soon as it started (Salmond 2001, col. 852). They demanded a "pause" in the bombing campaign to allow aid into Afghanistan, and refugees out (Tonge 2001, col. 1094). This was patently unrealistic. Ministers responded that civilians were not being targeted, and that any reduction in the intensity of the assault would only prolong the fighting by allowing Taliban forces time to regroup. Though Blair accepted that "no one who raises doubts is an appeaser" (Blair 2001b), the spectre of Munich, a familiar trope of British public debates on war, occasionally crept into government statements at this time (Straw 2001b, col. 690). There was no 'pause'. Some of those who might ordinarily have opposed military action instead adopted what the *Guardian* writer Polly Toynbee described as a "hard liberal" argument, under which "promoting liberal values everywhere from Burma to Saudi Arabia, Iraq to Chechnya is not neo-colonialism, but respect for a universal right to freedom from oppression" (Toynbee 2001). Others on the political right, who might ordinarily have opposed a Labour Prime Minister, found themselves agreeing with him (Osborne 2001, col. 654).

The mass street protests of 15 February 2003 pushed the government to make the moral case for war in Iraq. At the time, it was a significant shift. For most of the pre-invasion period Blair avoided talking about the moral arguments for action. But faced with "the moral case against war" he felt he had to offer "a moral answer" (Blair 2003c). He could hardly ignore over a million protestors marching in London and other cities while he spoke to Labour Party activists in Glasgow: that was the organizers' intent. It mattered, too, that those marching were not the "usual suspects" who could be relied upon to protest any use of force regardless of the merits (Cook 2003, 298; Kampfner 2003, 272–273). Instead, the media framed the crowds who rallied against war with Iraq in February 2003 as "quiet, decent people" (*Daily Mail* 2003), "the types who don't demonstrate" brought onto the streets by the scale of the government's folly (Parris 2003). As Michael White concluded in the *Guardian*, "when even the [traditionally reactionary] *Daily Mail* prints maps to show its readers how to join the march, and [traditionally pro-war] Tory MPs express sympathy, Mr Blair faces the greatest test of his premiership" (White 2003). Eyewitnesses described the typical marcher as "middle-class, middle-aged, politely-mannered and jolly angry" (Ellam 2003). Many of the large number of eye-witness despatches that appeared in the next few days' newspapers underlined the fact that the average protester was reasonably affluent, politically centrist, and often someone who voted Labour for the first time in its 1997 landslide victory. The marchers, then, were Tony Blair's most significant supporters, the people whose votes made him such an electoral force, who might otherwise for cultural or economic reasons have voted against Labour, were they not so personally impressed by him. Such was the penetration of anti-war feeling through the government's core constituencies that even within Downing Street most of Blair's closest colleagues had family members who marched against him (Campbell 2010, 54). He knew he was in difficulty. He told Campbell "even I am a bit worried about this one" (Campbell and Stott 2007, 667). Jack Straw similarly told Chilcot he was "profoundly concerned" by the march (Straw 2010a, 102).

Pushed into this tight spot, however, Blair chose to revise his rhetoric rather than his substantive stance (Blair 2010b, 424). Observers described his Glasgow speech as "the clearest sign yet that Mr Blair is rattled" (*Independent on Sunday* 2003). To a degree that was true. For all his private belief, Blair held back on making the moral case for war in Iraq until he was directly challenged in February 2003. He shifted tack only when arguments about the threat and the need to uphold international law failed to secure sufficient support. This was hardly the sort of conduct that legitimacy is made of. Nevertheless, it did deliver some short-term benefits. Waverers in Downing Street felt reassured (Seldon *et al.* 153). So, did some Labour MPs (George 2003). Even if they disagreed with the substance of what the Prime Minister was doing, they liked the fact that he remained seized of moral arguments. Some probably suspected he was right and that he knew better than they did on what was the right thing to do. Most media observers remained sceptical but some, like Polly Toynbee, accepted that Blair might yet win the wider argument (Toynbee 2003). Crucially, Blair's moral claims split natural opponents of war, with individuals such as Labour MP Ann Clwyd, along with the columnists Nick Cohen, David Aaronovitch and Johann Hari (writing in the left-wing *Observer*, *Guardian* and *Independent* respectively) resurrecting the 'hard liberal' line from Afghanistan and arguing that Britain should not shy from asserting its own convictions (Clwyd 2003; Cohen 2003; Aaronovitch 2003; Hari 2003). That proved at least a short-term benefit for the government.

In the end, the fact that Blair believed sincerely that invading Iraq was the morally right thing to do made his arguments more persuasive. It also strengthened his commitment to communicative action as his public statements came to reflect his private reasoning. Blair's certainty sustained him in the face of concerted opposition, and won over some of those on the left of the political spectrum who might otherwise have stood against a war launched by the Bush administration. It also, however, underlined how inflexible Blair was in responding to the ideas levied against him, for it epitomized the fact that much of the

British government's case for war in Iraq relied on the Prime Minister's gut instincts, and how little was derived from the exercise of reasoned judgment. Without reason, you cannot secure legitimacy through deliberation, since deliberation is the exercise of public reason. The moral dimension thus represents, in its purest form, the paradox of the Iraq debate. The arguments that did the most to win supporters in the short term did the most to undermine the conflict's normative legitimacy over the longer term.

Legality and morality

There was a fundamental conceptual problem at the heart of the Blair government's moral case for war in Iraq, though in this case not one of its own making. Having committed to acting only in line with international law, ministers were unable to place too great an emphasis on moral arguments without contradicting themselves. Legality and morality need not necessarily clash, but in matters of military intervention they fairly often do. This problem goes deeper than Tony Blair's personal emphasis on justifying his decision to use force in Iraq in moral terms. It speaks to the very nature of international law and how morality can best be incorporated into meaningful accounts of international legitimacy.

At a basic level, the difficulty emerges from the fact that international law predominantly applies to relations among states, ignoring individuals. It depends, in other words, on a pluralist rather than a solidarist, universal or cosmopolitan account of proper international behaviour, one likely to place far greater emphasis on the rights of individuals. As his moral arguments for war in Iraq make clear, Blair strongly identified with a cosmopolitan understanding of how international order should operate. He believed in universal human rights, in democracy and in the basic principle that states should not harm their subjects. Advocates of this sort of stance typically find dealing with international law unsettling because for the most part it quite deliberately makes no moral judgment on the existence or appropriateness of different political practices in different states (Hurd 1999, 381; Clark 2005, 208; Hurrell 2005, 21). In effect, international law and Blair's form of international morality placed different levels of emphasis on two distinct ways of thinking about morality. Where Blair preferred a "cosmopolitan" stance, international law was derived from the "morality of states" (Beitz 1979, 406).

To an extent, Blair's approach wound up reflecting the 'third way' logic captured by Nicholas Wheeler and Tim Dunne with the idea of "good international citizenship". Wheeler and Dunne argued persuasively that the notion, first developed by Australian foreign minister Gareth Evans between 1988 and 1996, offered a middle ground approach capable of balancing realism and idealism (Wheeler and Dunne 1998, 848). In the particular case of the British approach to Iraq in 2003, good international citizenship took on two forms. First, Blair claimed the right to act on behalf of the international community, even without its explicit consent. He argued repeatedly, as Chapter 6 discusses, that the UN could not be allowed to prevent the US and UK from acting to uphold

UN Security Council Resolutions in Iraq. This was problematic in itself. As Jason Ralph has argued, the "cynical" way that Blair used the notion of acting on behalf of the international community to try to legitimize the invasion ensured his claim to morality was "simply rhetorical ... a veil to disguise the selfish interests of the powerful" (Ralph 2011, 308). Second, Blair placed himself within a broader tradition of international moral thought that equates the legitimacy of a state with its participation in an international moral community (Price and Reus-Smit 1998, 287; Clark 2005, 176). In other words, he asserted the right to use force against Iraq because of Saddam Hussein's human rights abuses on the grounds that not only would external intervention prevent further abuse, but also because the fact that Saddam *was* abusing human rights meant he no longer deserved the protection of sovereignty. As Ralph further put it, this "neoliberal" interpretation of international law and international morality directly challenged the procedural norms embedded in the UN process (Ralph 2014, 4–5), which in turn is a prerequisite for the position discussed in Chapter 6 that certain international acts can be illegal but legitimate (Hurd 1999, 381; Hurrell 2005, 21; Clark 2005, 208). What was especially problematic about this stance was the very real difficulty Blair and his ministers had in justifying their stance to themselves. Dan Bulley argued persuasively that the real problem with the Iraq War in terms of the apparent clash between legality and morality was the fact the British government agonized over it. "One cannot credibly accept that a moral question is finely balanced", Bulley argues, "and simultaneously argue with complete conviction that one's own solution is unequivocally correct" (Bulley 2010, 454). That, however, was precisely what British decision-makers attempted to do.

In specific terms, the clash between legality and morality emerged in the Iraq debate over the question of so-called 'regime change', the removal of Saddam Hussein from power and his replacement with a less brutal and less dangerous regime. David Manning told the Chilcot Inquiry that the question of regime change raised particular difficulties. The British were willing to overthrow Saddam in order to achieve their objectives, if it was necessary. The US view, on the other hand, was "almost the opposite". Saddam had to be dealt with once and for all. Disarmament was a means to do that (Manning 2009, 24). This was a problem for Blair. British government lawyers made it quite clear that while "it could be that another lawful basis for force might lead to regime change ... wanting regime change was not of itself a lawful basis for the use of force" (Goldsmith 2010, 26; Grainger 2002). Jack Straw insists he thought "a foreign policy objective of regime change", the very objective being pursued by his American counterparts, to be "improper and self-evidently unlawful" (Straw 2010a, 17; 2010b, 2). Blair's position was more flexible, and one of the key themes running through the Chilcot Report is the way it took until early March 2003 for Blair and Straw to actually agree a clear set of objectives they both felt able to support. Though he continued to insist that Britain would comply with international law, and though Lord Goldsmith repeatedly advised that regime change was illegal (Goldsmith 2003), Blair held on to the view that if international law forbade action against a tyrant like Saddam, the law itself was wrong (Clark 2005, 179).

Blair's personal commitment to a cosmopolitan view of international morality need not have undermined the legitimacy of his case for war in Iraq. Cosmopolitan values offer valid grounds for international action. But Blair never really addressed, let alone resolved, the tension between following his moral arguments to their logical conclusion, and international law. This was not a challenge of his own making, for once. But it was one he failed to resolve.

Regime change

That Blair was personally committed to regime change in Iraq from an early stage in the Iraq debate seems fairly evident. He was not alone. In November 2001 Jonathan Powell wrote to the Prime Minister noting "that our over-riding objective is the removal of Saddam not the insertion of arms inspectors" (Powell 2001). In a follow-up memo, he "advocated a strategy for regime change based on a demand for the return of inspectors and the use of military force to support an internal uprising, with public lines explaining why Iraq was a threat" (Chilcot 2016b, 356). In February 2002 John Sawers, formerly Blair's personal foreign policy advisor and later Chief of SIS, but at that time Ambassador to Egypt, sent a widely-circulated telegram advocating a robust approach to Iraq. Describing "whether or not we actually express" a desire for regime change as "purely a matter of tactics", he urged that "the lawyers and peaceniks should not prevent us from saying what we really want in Iraq" (Sawers 2002). Powell and Manning ordered Sawers slapped down, though more to avoid his opinions leaking than because they thought him wrong (Chilcot 2016b, 404–405). That such arguments were circulating within the British foreign policy system is significant. Blair told President Bush in December 2001 that "he was not opposed to the removal of Saddam Hussein, but an extremely clever plan would be needed" (Chilcot 2016b, 357). The US and UK would "need a strategy for regime change that builds over time", he argued, but in principle it could be done (Blair 2001c). Chilcot concluded that Blair was not yet referring to a full-scale land invasion, suggesting instead that the US and UK foment rebellion then "back it militarily". He was unaware that Bush had already asked General Tommy Franks to look at more robust options (Chilcot 2016b, 378–382).

Reporting back to London from a preparatory visit ahead of the Crawford trip, Manning told Blair he advised Bush that "you would not budge in your support for regime change but that you had to manage a press, a Parliament and a public opinion that was very different from anything in the States" (Manning 2002). Blair's Foreign Office briefing for Crawford suggested that "Mr Blair should state that the UK supported the US objective of regime change in Iraq" (FCO 2002). Colin Powell reported as much to the President. He noted that "Blair knows he may have to pay a political price for supporting us on Iraq, and wants to minimize it. Nonetheless, he will stick with us on the big issues" (Powell 2002). Three days after receiving Manning's memo, Blair wrote to

Jonathan Powell, copying Manning in, to set out his position. Noting neither he nor Bush had "a proper worked-out strategy on how we would do it", he argued that "from a centre-left perspective, the case should be obvious ... a political philosophy that does care about other nations – e.g. Kosovo, Afghanistan, Sierra Leone – and is prepared to change regimes on the merits, should be gung-ho on Saddam" (Blair 2002a). Straw wrote to Blair on 25 March:

> suggesting the "case against Iraq and in favour (if necessary) of military action" might be made in the context of seeking regime change as an essential part of a strategy of eliminating Iraq's WMD, rather than an objective in its own right.
>
> (Chilcot 2016b, 468)

These private documents, later leaked or declassified, cast some doubt on the claim that Blair continues to advance, that his objective was never 'regime change' per se (Blair 2010a, 21–30). They suggest, rather, that he was at least thinking about it right from the very start of the public debate. Given what we know about the arguments Blair later advanced, this is unsurprising. He clearly did believe that removing Saddam Hussein from power was simply the right thing to do. He also believed, apparently, that admitting as much in public would cost him public support. If it meant also having to admit that invading Iraq might not be legal, which is at least an implication of the clash between morality and legality that has just been discussed, openness could well have been more damaging than reticence. The problem, again, is that reticence and communicative action do not mix. In a particularly damning paragraph, Chilcot notes that Blair "told Cabinet on 11 April that regime change in Iraq was greatly to be desired but no plans for achieving that had been tabled during his discussions with President Bush". At the same time, he "did not disclose that he had informed Vice President Cheney on 11 March that the UK would help the US to achieve its objective of regime change provided that there was a clever plan" (Chilcot 2016b, 508).

Christopher Meyer speculated at the Chilcot Inquiry that Blair and President Bush "signed in blood" a deal to go to war in Iraq during the Crawford meeting in April 2002. Meyer probably exaggerates. For one thing, he was not actually at Crawford. Manning and Powell accompanied the Prime Minister, while the Ambassador was consigned to a hotel in Waco, some 30 miles distant (Powell 2010a, 24). Blair did however deliver what he described as "a strong message" at a joint press conference with his host. At the same time, he maintains that "behind closed doors ... our talk was more nuanced", referring not only to the threat from Iraq, but the need to consider it as part of a wider strategy towards a "region in transition" (Blair 2010b, 401). More nuanced it may have been. But the underlying point was the same. Saddam Hussein was bad. Britain and the US would remove him from power, and both Blair and President Bush believed to do so would be an unquestionable moral good. Technically, it was true that "no decisions had been taken" (Chilcot 2016b, 449), in that no specific troop commitments were made.

Morality and regime change 131

But Blair knew which way his policy was developing, and he failed to admit as much publicly.

British journalists framed Blair's public statements in Crawford as the "clearest signal yet" that the allies intended action against Iraq. Articles filed by Joe Murphy and Francis Elliott in the right-leaning *Sunday Telegraph* and Kamal Ahmed in the left-leaning *Observer* both used the phrase (Murphy and Elliott 2002; Ahmed 2002). Oonagh Blackman of the *Sunday Mirror* reported that Blair "said that the British policy toward Iraq was clear – 'regime change'" (Blackman 2002). That was not quite how Blair put it. But having repeatedly claimed that 'no decisions have been taken' on how his earlier call to 're-order the world' might play out, Blair's statements in Texas did mark a clear rhetorical escalation. Echoing precisely one of the key points President Bush made in his State of the Union a few months earlier, Blair warned in his speech on 11 September that Western nations must "learn from our experience". If Britain and the US wanted security, he went on, "we must be prepared to act where terrorism or Weapons of Mass Destruction threaten us". He made no attempt to discuss whether there was an actual link between the two dangers. As Chapter 5 suggests, the evidence was slim. Instead he echoed Bush still further, declaring that "leaving Iraq to develop WMD, in flagrant breach of no less than nine separate UNSCRs, refusing still to allow weapons inspectors back to do their work properly, is not an option". By ruling out the *status quo* option, Blair made it quite clear that he intended to escalate the post-Gulf War standoff over Iraq's alleged WMD development. Crucially, he added, "if necessary the action should be military and again, if necessary and justified, it should involve regime change". Though the exchange of memos with Manning and Powell makes it clear that Blair spoke freely about regime change in private, this was the first time he used the phrase in public, as Meyer rightly noted (Meyer 2009, 29). He still insisted that "the moment for decision on how to act is not yet with us" (Blair 2002b). But the caveat looked hollow in light of what preceded it. Indeed, Blair's own later recollections of the Crawford meeting underline the point. He wrote he had, by this point, "resolved in my own mind that removing Saddam would do the world, and most particularly the Iraqi people, a service". Somewhat incongruously, though, he went on to say "though I knew regime change could not be our policy, I viewed a change with enthusiasm, not dismay". Even three years after leaving Downing Street, he continued to split verbal hairs. In the space of a single page he wrote of his "enthusiasm" for regime change, and dismissed as a "myth" the suggestion he agreed to support it at Crawford (Blair 2010b, 400). He may have been constrained by the conceptual difficulty of balancing a solidarist understanding of international morality with a pluralist model of international law. But, because he failed even to admit the difficulty, he remained in many ways the author of his own misfortunes.

Journalists were not the only actors convinced by Blair's public statements at Crawford that Britain would assist the US in bringing about 'regime change' in Iraq. Simon Webb, Policy Director at the Ministry of Defence, wrote an internal memo on 12 April noting that "the Prime Minister's speech in Texas contained a commitment to regime change" and discussing the implications for the MoD specifically and the country more generally (Webb 2002a). That many journalists *were* convinced, despite Blair's attempts to manage expectations, underscored the significance of the Crawford trip. A *Daily Telegraph* editorial concluded "it is now the agreed policy of the one superpower and its closest ally that Saddam Hussein be overthrown" (*Daily Telegraph* 2002). The *Guardian* described Blair as having "parroted Mr Bush's views on Iraqi 'regime change'" (*Guardian* 2002). Back in parliament he did little to shift such views. Conservative leader Iain Duncan Smith demanded confirmation "that getting rid of Saddam Hussein may now be an objective of the government" (Duncan Smith 2002, col. 12). Blair refused. But he did further cement what were already quite firm public expectations. "I have been involved in three regime changes", he told MPs, "Milosevic, the Taliban and the gangster group that took over Sierra Leone". This seemed unlikely to reassure critics that 'no decision' had been taken, as he kept insisting. But there was more. "I can honestly say", Blair went on, "that we should not regret any of them" (Blair 2002c, col. 37). Again, by denying that he planned to seek regime change in Iraq in one breath and praising it as an intrinsic good in the next, Blair caused some confusion.

How actors within government resolved the dilemma appears clearly in another memo from Simon Webb. "While regime change may not be an objective in its own right", he wrote to his Foreign Office counterpart, Peter Ricketts, in May, "we are all still working to the line in the Prime Minister's Crawford speech that it might become justified and necessary". The MoD, Webb went on, saw regime change "as a likely – though not certain – way point in a campaign to secure the strategic objective" of Iraqi disarmament (Webb 2002b). This position contrasted with Powell's November 2001 memo, highlighted above, which put the order of priorities the other way around. It was not necessary, in other words, for officials to share the Prime Minister's moral stance. Regime change was both intrinsically good, as a route to liberating the Iraqi people from Saddam's brutality, and strategically necessary in order to eliminate the WMD threat. This was essentially Straw's position, and Blair adopted it to some extent. In both the 17 March memo to Powell and Manning, and the 23 July Downing Street meeting, Blair expressed the view that "regime change and WMD were linked in the sense that it was the regime that was producing the WMD" (Rycroft 2002). This formulation helped with the legal issues to some extent, at least in the short term. Blair could praise the virtues of regime change all he wanted, provided he made clear that Britain would only use force against Iraq in line with international law, which in practice meant to uphold UN Security Council Resolutions.

This line raised a further problem, however. Blair made very clear that, whatever he personally believed, "the basis" for both the UN process and any military action that might follow had to be "the disarmament of Iraq" (Blair 2003d). He conflated his different goals, telling Downing Street aides in January 2003 "the truth is removing Saddam is right; he is a threat; and WMD has to be countered" (Blair 2003a). At the same time, he contradicted himself to some extent by insisting "I have never put the justification for action as regime change" before going on to justify invading Iraq by highlighting the "brutality of the repression" under the "barbaric" Saddam and concluding "if we do act, we should do so with a clear conscience and a strong heart". Regime change was good. But it still was not the British plan (even despite Iain Duncan Smith's best efforts to push the contrary). This sounded strange when Blair said it out loud. He argued eloquently, for example, that British inaction would "mean for the Iraqi people, whose only true hope lies in the removal of Saddam, the darkness will simply close back over" (Blair 2003f, cols. 772–773). He also conceded that Saddam would have to be left in power should he verifiably disarm through the UNMOVIC process. "I detest his regime – I hope most people do", he told MPs on 25 February 2003. "But even now, he could save it by complying with the UN's demand" for disarmament (Blair 2003e, col. 124). It was imperative that Britain rescue Iraq's benighted people from their oppression. They were suffering great brutality at Saddam Hussein's hands. But if Saddam complied with the UN weapons inspection process, Britain would leave them to their fate. This was more than just confusing. It was fundamentally inconsistent. And it contradicted the JIC's advice that Saddam would rather fight than back down (Chilcot 2016c, 187). Blair's moral case did not make sense, even on its own terms.

Conclusion

Like the arguments about the threat from WMD and the basis of the invasion in international law, the Blair government's efforts to 'sell' the Iraq war as an inherently moral act produced mixed results in terms of short-term public opinion. By effectively unleashing the Prime Minister's private rationale for pursuing regime change, the 'moral turn' in February 2003 helped dispel his critics' barbed complaints about how closely he appeared to be following President Bush. It was clear, from the moment he made his Glasgow speech, that Blair meant what he said. He believed invading Iraq was simply the right thing to do (Dumbrell 2009, 275). His conviction in turn proved convincing. Though he probably won few converts to the pro-war cause, he did make it easier for reluctant supporters, especially those within the Labour Party, to salve their consciences and follow him. His internal conviction also helps us understand how he was able to withstand the immense public pressure placed upon him, especially in the final weeks before the start of the invasion.

At the same time, the moral dimension of the case for war also shares with the 'threat' and 'legality' dimensions the fact it raised serious questions about the government's commitment to communicative action. Part of the problem lay in the clash between the cosmopolitan understanding of international morality that Blair held to, and the pluralist basis of international law. Unable to reconcile his twin commitments to legality and his own brand of morality, Blair decided to downplay the case for regime change. In the process, he withheld information about the basis for his belief that Britain should join military action in Iraq. By trying to take the moral high ground in the domestic debate, Blair furthermore placed pressure on those who opposed him to alter course. Indeed, the 'moral turn' itself represented the triumph of Foucauldian persuasion and "representational force" over Habermasian deliberation and reason (Bially Mattern 2005, 586). Few contemporary observers doubted that Blair approached the Iraq war "possessed of certainty" (Stothard 2003, 13). That very certainty, and the frequency and vehemence with which he expressed it publicly, made opposition difficult.

It also pointed towards the most fundamental issue that Blair's moral case for war in Iraq raised. Communicative action requires that every participant keeps at least a partly open mind (Risse 2000, 8; Bjola 2009, 76). Blair's mind was not open. He was not willing to reconsider his stance in response to critics' complaints. His response to senior church leaders condemning his policy as immoral, or to millions of ordinary citizens marching against him, underlines the point. This strength of purpose is why Britain went to war despite the breadth and depth of public opposition. Blair started off in a position of greater formal authority than his critics, and ultimately wanted to win the argument more. That helped him push his preferred policy through, and even won him some support from those unable to believe he would act so rashly and they were willing to give an experienced and successful leader the benefit of the doubt (Campbell 2010, 54; Powell 2010a, 137). But it also damaged the war's legitimacy in the longer term. The moral objections to the use of force in Iraq never went away. Fuelled by anger over the missing WMD and the controversy over the Attorney General's legal advice, they in fact grew stronger over time. A particular zenith arrived with Chilcot's conclusion that military action was "not a last resort", that it was not therefore a Just War (Chilcot 2016d, 573). Combined with the sense, quite reasonable in light of the evidence this chapter presents, that Blair never really sought the public's input in the first place, the legitimacy deficit surrounding Iraq makes sense after all.

References

Aaronovitch, David. 'We're not all peaceniks – but you wouldn't know it.' *Guardian*, 18 March 2003.

Ahmed, Kamal. 'Blair to back US war on Saddam: PM's grim warning on action against Saddam threatens Cabinet rift.' *Observer*, 7 April 2002.

Beitz, Charles. 'Bounded morality: justice and the state in world politics.' *International Organization* 33, no. 3 (1979): 405–424.

Bially Mattern, Janice. 'Why "soft power" isn't so soft: representational force and the sociolinguistic construction of attraction in world politics.' *Millennium: Journal of International Politics* 33, no. 3 (2005): 583–612.

Bjola, Corneliu. *Legitimising the Use of Force in International Politics: Kosovo, Iraq and the Ethics of Intervention*. London: Routledge, 2009.

Blackman, Oonagh. 'We'll get him out; Blair backs Bush plan for attack on Saddam.' *Sunday Mirror*, 7 April 2002.

Blair, Tony. 'The doctrine of international community.' 24 April 1999. http://webarchive.nationalarchives.gov.uk/+/www.number10.gov.uk/Page1297 (accessed 30 September 2015).

Blair, Tony. 'Speech to the Labour Party conference.' 2 October 2001a. www.british politicalspeech.org/speech-archive.htm?speech=186 (accessed 7 June 2016).

Blair, Tony. 'Speech to the Welsh Assembly.' 30 October 2001b. http://webarchive.nationalarchives.gov.uk/20040621031906/http://number10.gov.uk/page1636 (accessed 8 June 2016).

Blair, Tony. 'Letter to President Bush.' 4 December 2001c. www.iraqinquiry.org.uk/media/243731/2001-12-04-note-blair-to-bush-the-war-against-terrorism-the-second-phase.pdf (accessed 15 July 2016).

Blair, Tony. 'Memo to Jonathan Powell.' 17 March 2002a. www.iraqinquiry.org.uk/media/75831/2002-03-17-Minute-Blair-to-Powell-Iraq.pdf (accessed 17 August 2016).

Blair, Tony. 'Speech at the George H.W. Bush Presidential Library.' 7 April 2002b. www.theguardian.com/politics/2002/apr/08/foreignpolicy.iraq (accessed 10 June 2016).

Blair, Tony. *Hansard House of Commons Debates*, vol. 383, 10 April 2002c.

Blair, Tony. 'Prime Minister's monthly press conference.' 25 July 2002d. http://webarchive.nationalarchives.gov.uk/20061004051823/http://number10.gov.uk/page3000 (accessed 22 September 2015).

Blair, Tony. 'Memo to Downing Street staff.' 4 January 2003a. www.iraqinquiry.org.uk/media/233490/2003-01-04-note-tb-blair-iraq-extract.pdf (accessed 18 July 2016).

Blair, Tony. 'Prime Minister's monthly press conference.' 13 January 2003b. http://webarchive.nationalarchives.gov.uk/20061004051823/http://number10.gov.uk/output/Page3005.asp (accessed 12 October 2015).

Blair, Tony. 'Speech to the Labour Party spring conference, Glasgow.' 15 February 2003c. www.theguardian.com/politics/2003/feb/17/uk.iraq1 (accessed 8 June 2016).

Blair, Tony. 'Prime Minister's monthly press conference.' 18 February 2003d. http://webarchive.nationalarchives.gov.uk/20061023193551/http://number10.gov.uk/page3007 (accessed 28 June 2016).

Blair, Tony. *Hansard House of Commons Debates*, vol. 400, 25 February 2003e.

Blair, Tony. *Hansard House of Commons Debates*, vol. 401, 18 March 2003f.

Blair, Tony. 'Evidence to the Chilcot Inquiry.' 29 January 2010a. www.iraqinquiry.org.uk/media/229766/2010-01-29-transcript-blair-s1.pdf (accessed 17 August 2016).

Blair, Tony. *A Journey*. London: Hutchinson, 2010b.

Bromund, Ted. 'A just war: Prime Minister Tony Blair and the end of Saddam's Iraq.' In *The Blair Legacy: Politics, Policy, Governance, and Foreign Affairs*, by Terrence Casey, 260–272. Basingstoke: Palgrave Macmillan, 2009.

Bulley, Dan. 'The politics of ethical foreign policy: a responsibility to protect whom?' *European Journal of International Relations* 16 (2010): 441–454.

Bush, George W. 'Press conference with Prime Minister Blair.' 6 April 2002. https://georgewbush-whitehouse.archives.gov/news/releases/2002/04/20020406-3.html (accessed 7 June 2016).

Campbell, Alastair. 'Evidence to the Chilcot Inquiry, afternoon session.' 12 January 2010. www.iraqinquiry.org.uk/media/95146/2010-01-12-Transcript-Campbell-S1-pm.pdf (accessed 17 August 2016).

Campbell, Alastair, and Richard Stott. *The Blair Years: Extracts from the Alastair Campbell Diaries*. London: Arrow Books, 2007.

Chandler, David. 'Rhetoric without responsibility: the attraction of "ethical" foreign policy.' *British Journal of Politics and International Relations* 5, no. 3 (2003): 295–316.

Chilcot, John. *Report of the Iraq Inquiry: Executive Summary*. London: HMSO, 2016a.

Chilcot, John. *Report of the Iraq Inquiry: Volume 1.* London: HMSO, 2016b.
Chilcot, John. *Report of the Iraq Inquiry: Volume 3.* London: HMSO, 2016c.
Chilcot, John. *Report of the Iraq Inquiry: Volume 6.* London: HMSO, 2016d.
Clark, Ian. *Legitimacy in International Society.* Oxford: Oxford University Press, 2005.
Clwyd, Ann. *Hansard House of Commons Debates*, vol. 400, 26 February 2003.
Cohen, Nick. 'The only path to peace: anti-war campaigners believe there is another way to be rid of Saddam. There isn't.' *Observer*, 2 March 2003.
Cook, Robin. *The Point of Departure.* London: Simon & Schuster, 2003.
Cox, Michael. 'Beyond the West: terrors in Transatlantia.' *European Journal of International Relations* 11, no. 2 (2005): 203–233.
Crampton, Robert. 'Labour exchange.' *The Times*, 30 September 1995.
Daddow, Oliver. ' "Tony's war"? Blair, Kosovo and the interventionist impulse in British foreign policy.' *International Affairs* 85, no. 3 (2009): 547–560.
Daily Mail. 'Leading article', 15 February 2003.
Daily Telegraph. 'Leading article.' *Daily Telegraph*, 9 April 2002.
Dumbrell, John. 'US–UK relations: structure, agency and the special relationship.' In *The Blair Legacy: Politics, Policy, Governance, and Foreign Affairs*, edited by Terrence Casey, 273–284. Basingstoke: Palgrave Macmillan, 2009.
Duncan Smith, Iain. *Hansard House of Commons Debates*, vol. 383, 10 April 2002.
Dyson, Stephen Benedict. 'Personality and foreign policy: Tony Blair's Iraq decisions.' *Foreign Policy Analysis* 2, no. 3 (2006): 289–306.
Dyson, Stephen Benedict. 'Alliances, domestic politics, and leader psychology: why did Britain stay out of Vietnam and go into Iraq?' *Political Psychology* 28, no. 6 (2007): 647–666.
Dyson, Stephen Benedict. 'What difference did he make? Tony Blair and British foreign policy from 1997–2007.' In *The Blair Legacy: Politics, Policy, Governance and Foreign Affairs*, by Terrence. Casey, 235–246. Basingstoke: Palgrave Macmillan, 2009.
Dyson, Stephen Benedict. 'New Labour, leadership, and foreign policy-making after 1997.' In *British Foreign Policy: The New Labour Years*, by Oliver Daddow and Jamie Gaskarth, 63–83. Basingstoke: Palgrave Macmillan, 2011.
Ellam, Dennis. 'Protest virgins.' *Sunday Mirror*, 16 February 2003.
FCO. 'Visit of US Vice President Dick Cheney.' 8 March 2002. www.iraqinquiry.org.uk/media/211011/2002-03-08-briefing-fco-visit-of-us-vice-president-dick-cheney-11-march-as-attached-to-letter-mcdonald-to-rycroft-8-march-2002.pdf (accessed 15 July 2016).
Frost, David. 'BBC Breakfast with Frost.' 29 September 2002. http://news.bbc.co.uk/1/hi/programmes/breakfast_with_frost/2287239.stm (accessed 8 June 2016).
Gaskarth, Jamie. 'Discourses and ethics: the social construction of British foreign policy.' *Foreign Policy Analysis* 2, no. 4 (2006): 325–341.
George, Bruce. *Hansard House of Commons Debates*, vol. 400, 26 February 2003.
Goldsmith, Lord. 'Iraq: legal advice: memo to Tony Blair.' 7 March 2003. http://image.guardian.co.uk/sys-files/Guardian/documents/2005/04/28/legal.pdf (accessed 20 August 2015).
Goldsmith, Lord. 'Evidence to the Chilcot Inquiry.' 27 January 2010. www.iraqinquiry.org.uk/media/235686/2010-01-27-transcript-goldsmith-s1.pdf (accessed 17 August 2016).
Grainger, John. 'Iraq: regime change: memo to Simon MacDonald.' 21 March 2002. www.iraqinquiry.org.uk/media/75839/2002-03-21-Minute-Grainger-to-PS-Iraq-Regime-Change.pdf (accessed 17 August 2016).
Guardian. 'Leading article', 10 April 2002.

Morality and regime change 137

Hain, Peter. 'We cannot be effete: it's time to fight: people are scared, but that was true before the second world war.' *Guardian*, 24 September 2001.

Hari, Johann. 'If this war with Iraq is to be a moral war, it must be fought in a moral way.' *Independent*, 7 March 2003.

Hensher, Philip. 'Let's be honest: we need to impose our imperial rule on Afghanistan.' *Independent*, 17 October 2001.

Hermann, Margaret. 'Explaining foreign policy behavior using the personal characteristics of political leaders.' *International Studies Quarterly* 24, no. 1 (1980): 7–46.

Hitchens, Peter. 'We're not at war yet, but the Tories have already surrendered.' *Mail on Sunday*, 2 March 2003.

Hurd, Ian. 'Legitimacy and authority in international politics.' *International Organization* 53, no. 2 (1999): 379–408.

Hurrell, Andrew. 'Legitimacy and the use of force: can the circle be squared?' *Review of International Studies* 31, no. 1 (2005): 15–32.

Independent. 'Leading article', 2 November 2001.

Independent. 'Leading article', 21 February 2003a.

Independent. 'Leading article', 18 March 2003b.

Independent on Sunday. 'Leading article', 16 February 2003.

Kampfner, John. *Blair's Wars*. London: Free Press, 2003.

Kennedy-Pipe, Caroline, and Rhiannon Vickers. 'Blowback for Britain? Blair, Bush and the war in Iraq.' *Review of International Studies* 33, no. 2 (2007): 205–221.

Kramer, Steven P. 'Blair's Britain after Iraq.' *Foreign Affairs* 82, no. 4 (2003): 90–104.

Kratochwil, Friedrich. 'The embarrassment of changes: neo-realism as the science of realpolitik without politics.' *Review of International Studies* 19, no. 1 (1993): 63–80.

Maddox, Bronwen. 'Peacekeeping and face-saving at No 10.' *The Times*, 13 December 2001.

Manning, David. 'Memo to Tony Blair.' 14 March 2002. www.iraqinquiry.org.uk/media/211115/2002-03-14-minute-manning-to-prime-minister-your-trip-to-the-us.pdf (accessed 15 July 2016).

Manning, David. 'Evidence to the Chilcot Inquiry.' 30 November 2009. www.iraqinquiry.org.uk/media/94802/2009-11-30-Transcript-Manning-S1.pdf (accessed 17 August 2016).

Margolick, David. 'Blair's big gamble.' *Vanity Fair*. June 2003. www.vanityfair.com/news/2003/06/blair-200306 (accessed 8 June 2016).

Marr, Andrew. 'Blair's masochism makes great television, but is it a war strategy?' *Daily Telegraph*, 12 March 2003.

Mercer, Patrick. *Hansard House of Commons Debates*, vol. 372, 16 October 2001.

Meyer, Christopher. 'Evidence to the Chilcot Inquiry.' 26 November 2009. www.iraqinquiry.org.uk/media/94794/2009-11-26-Transcript-Meyer-S1.pdf (accessed 17 August 2016).

Mirror. 'Leading article', 20 February 2003.

Murphy, Joe, and Francis Elliott. 'Labour fury as Blair backs Bush plans for war in Iraq.' *Sunday Telegraph*, 7 April 2002.

Observer. 'Leading article', 16 March 2003.

Orr, Deborah. 'He has so few followers, yet Blair has never been a more believable leader.' *Independent*, 14 March 2003.

Osborne, George. *Hansard House of Commons Debates*, vol. 372, 14 September 2001.

Parris, Matthew. 'Forgotten, ignored, scared. And on the march today.' *The Times*, 15 February 2003.

Parris, Matthew. 'Slogans by the many, deeds by the few.' *The Times*, 8 October 2001.
Powell, Colin. 'Your meeting with UK Prime Minister Tony Blair: Memo to President Bush.' 28 March 2002. https://foia.state.gov/searchapp/DOCUMENTS/April2014/F-2012-33239/DOC_0C05446915/C05446915.pdf (accessed 10 June 2016).
Powell, Jonathan. 'Memo to Tony Blair.' 15 November 2001. www.iraqinquiry.org.uk/media/203220/2001-11-15-minute-powell-to-prime-minister-the-war-what-comes-next.pdf (accessed 15 July 2016).
Powell, Jonathan. 'Evidence to the Chilcot Inquiry.' 18 January 2010a. www.iraqinquiry.org.uk/media/95166/2010-01-18-Transcript-Powell-S1.pdf (accessed 17 August 2016).
Powell, Jonathan. *The New Machiavelli: How to Wield Power in the Modern World*. London: The Bodley Head, 2010b.
Price, Richard, and Christian Reus-Smit. 'Dangerous liaisons? Critical international theory and constructivism.' *European Journal of International Relations* 4, no. 3 (1998): 259–294.
Ralph, Jason. 'After Chilcot: the "doctrine of international community" and the UK decision to invade Iraq.' *British Journal of Politics and International Relations* 13, no. 3 (2011): 304–325.
Ralph, Jason. 'The liberal state in international society: interpreting recent British foreign policy.' *International Relations* 28, no. 1 (2014): 3–24.
Rawnsley, Andrew. 'Journey into the unknown.' *Observer*, 2 March 2003.
Riddell, Peter. 'The actor's mask slips to reveal true conviction.' *The Times*, 19 February 2003.
Risse, Thomas. 'Let's argue!: Communicative action in world politics.' *International Organization* 54, no. 1 (2000): 1–39.
Robinson, Nick. 'Nick Robinson's notebook.' *The Times*, 28 February 2003.
Rycroft, Matthew. 'Memo to David Manning: Iraq: Prime Minister's meeting.' 23 July 2002. www.iraqinquiry.org.uk/media/210955/2002-07-23-minute-rycroft-to-manning-iraq-prime-mi-nisters-meeting-23-july.pdf (accessed 6 August 2016).
Salmond, Alex. *Hansard House of Commons Debates*, vol. 372, 8 October 2001.
Sawers, John. 'Telegram to Michael Jay.' 21 February 2002. www.iraqinquiry.org.uk/media/210163/2002-02-21-teleletter-sawers-to-jay-iraq-policy.pdf (accessed 15 July 2016).
Seldon, Anthony, Peter Snowdon and Daniel Collings. *Blair Unbound*. London: Simon & Schuster, 2007.
Stothard, Peter. *30 Days: A Month at the Heart of Blair's War*. London: Harper Collins, 2003.
Straw, Jack. *Hansard House of Commons Debates*, vol. 372, 4 October 2001.
Straw, Jack. 'Evidence to the Chilcot Inquiry.' 21 January 2010a. www.iraqinquiry.org.uk/media/95186/2010-01-21-Transcript-Straw-S1.pdf (accessed 17 August 2016).
Straw, Jack. 'Evidence to the Chilcot Inquiry: written statement.' 8 February 2010b. www.iraqinquiry.org.uk/media/96018/2010-02-XX-Statement-Straw-2.pdf (accessed 17 August 2016).
Sunday Telegraph. 'Leading article', 7 October 2001.
The Times. 'Leading article', 7 March 2003.
Tonge, Jenny. *Hansard House of Commons Debates*, vol. 372, 16 October 2001.
Toynbee, Polly. 'Limp liberals fail to protect their most profound values.' *Guardian*, 10 October 2001.
Toynbee, Polly. 'Blair's unpopularity over Iraq could be used to progressive advantage.' *Guardian*, 19 February 2003.

Webb, Simon. 'Bush and the war on terrorism.' 12 April 2002a. www.iraqinquiry.org.uk/media/75879/2002-04-12-Minute-Webb-to-PS-SofS-Bush-and-the-war-on-terrorism.pdf (accessed 17 August 2016).

Webb, Simon. 'Memo to Peter Ricketts.' 10 May 2002b. www.iraqinquiry.org.uk/media/75891/2002-05-10-Letter-Webb-to-Ricketts-Iraq-Contingency-Planning.pdf (accessed 17 August 2016).

Wheeler, Nicholas, and Tim Dunne. 'Good international citizenship: a third way for British foreign policy.' *International Affairs* 74, no. 4 (1998): 847–870.

White, Michael. 'Blair's stance could make him war casualty.' *Guardian*, 15 February 2003.

8 Politics and authority

This chapter considers the relationship between diplomacy, domestic politics and legitimacy in Britain's Iraq debate. It highlights the difficult "two-level game" (Putnam 1988) the Blair government faced in seeking influence in Washington without losing authority at home. Authority and legitimacy are closely linked. To exercise authority, governments must wield legitimate power (Hurrell 2005, 29; Clark 2005, 20; Reus-Smit 2013, 236). As Martha Finnemore put it, "using power as more than a sledgehammer requires legitimation" (Finnemore 2009, 60). Though authority is more fragmented at the international than at the domestic level (Aron 1966, 6), the two are related. Just as discursive interactions shape domestic legitimacy, so too they matter among states (Mitzen 2005, 401). The two arenas feed back into each other. This was problematic for the Blair government. Its power was in doubt. It was clearly the junior partner in the transatlantic 'special relationship'. Domestic critics rightly questioned how far British ministers could influence Bush administration decision-making. Though Washington values and listens to its allies, it does not really need them and does not like the suggestion that it is beholden to them. The result was a difficult trade-off. The Blair government had to demonstrate its independent influence in order to assert its power and subsequent authority for audiences at home. At the same time, it needed to avoid offending the White House by pushing the point too far. If it did not try to exert influence, its authority would suffer. Its authority would also suffer, however, if it publicly asserted itself, and then failed to deliver (Buzan and Gonzalez-Pelaez 2005, 31). In the end, Britain did fail to resolve the "clear divergence" between Washington's timetable for military action in early 2003 and its own more gradual approach (Chilcot 2016e, 589).

A minor political crisis shortly before the invasion epitomized the situation British ministers found themselves in. Speaking in Washington on 11 March about the coming war, Secretary Rumsfeld told reporters that divisions in the Labour Party might prevent Britain taking part. There was no cause for concern, he argued. US forces could and would succeed alone. It was an off-the-cuff remark. It was also true. President Bush privately told Blair that if necessary "he would find another way to involve the UK" (Chilcot 2016, 408). Rumsfeld was hardly likely to yoke US strategic ambitions to a junior ally's domestic politics. He believed the mission should define the coalition, not the other way around

(Burke 2011, 48–49). His intervention nevertheless provoked uproar in Britain. Critics were already complaining about the government "scampering to give the Americans help they did not really need" (Kampfner 2003, 291; Waterhouse 2003). Rumsfeld seemed to prove the point. Others pointed to a "real and widening" divergence between US and UK priorities. The *Independent* dismissed the possibility "that Mr Rumsfeld was speaking rashly or out of turn" and argued instead that "he knew what he was saying and why he was saying it". Either he "was offering Tony Blair an escape route ... or firing a warning shot across an apparently 'wobbly' Britain's bows" (*Independent* 2003b). Either way, the message was clear. It was time for Britain to put up or shut up. Even within Downing Street, interpretations differed. Manning saw the incident as "a rather crude attempt to shaft us" (Chilcot 2016h, 449). Alastair Campbell called it a "f*ck-up", driven by the fact that Rumsfeld "didn't get other people's politics" (Campbell and Stott 2007, 676). Rumsfeld might have meant to pressure Blair, or he might have been offering a loyal ally a lifeboat. Either way, he apparently miscalculated how best to do it. He was hardly known for diplomatic sensitivity. He probably also underestimated how powerfully US leaders' public statements 'reverberate' in Britain (Strong 2017). As Campbell's anger shows, it did not matter *why* Rumsfeld failed to appreciate the damage his intervention might do. It only mattered *that* he intervened. The damage occurred all the same.

This chapter begins by considering how the British domestic politics of the 'special relationship' affected the Iraq debate. Next, it looks at how diplomatic disagreements at the Security Council helped the Blair government at home. Blaming France for preventing an international consensus was dishonest, but it worked. Interestingly, unlike other exaggerated claims ministers made during the pre-invasion debate, this one did not hurt them in the longer term. Finally, the chapter considers the parliamentary politics of Iraq. It is impossible to avoid domestic politics when making foreign policy. But the more overtly political a policy debate becomes, the more likely it is that power prevails rather than reason (Bially Mattern 2005, 586; Krebs and Jackson 2007, 42). Political debates boil down to contests over authority. Blair government ministers repeatedly asserted their own domestic authority. Communicative action, however, takes place only among equals (Habermas 1989, 25–57; 1981, 295). Ministers' assertions accordingly undermined their claim to legitimacy in a Habermasian sense. They also did not work. In theory Tony Blair possessed the personal authority as Prime Minister to direct the British armed forces, through the ancient royal prerogative (Joseph 2013). In practice, however, his critics felt his inability to constrain President Bush meant parliament had to have a say as well. Blair conceded the point (Strong 2015a). Involving parliament helped Blair signal to Washington the depth of the domestic difficulties he faced, by triggering domestic audience costs (Fearon 1994, 1997). The fact even Rumsfeld understood what was going on demonstrates as much. It also created a lasting "veto point" in the British foreign policy decision-making system (Edmunds 2010, 393). This, in turn, politicized questions about the use of force, undermining its legitimacy in the longer term (Kesgin and Kaarbo 2010; Edmunds *et al.* 2014, 506; Strong 2015b; Kaarbo and Kenealy 2016).

The 'special relationship'

That Britain enjoys a 'special relationship' with the US remains an enduring foreign policy trope. Though practitioners and observers disagree over how 'special' the transatlantic alliance actually is, everyone agrees that governments think it matters greatly. During the Iraq debate, however, the Blair government struggled to answer domestic critics who feared the Bush administration was dragging their country to war against its interests. These fears were not groundless. Britain's capacity to influence US decision-making is questionable. The Blair government considered Iraq less directly dangerous than Iran and less likely to proliferate WMD than North Korea. It targeted Iraq because, as David Manning told Chilcot, "the Americans were determined to focus on it. We weren't given a choice" (Chilcot 2016b, 515). A significant proportion of the opposition to British involvement stemmed from this simple point. Exacerbating the difficulty, the complex diplomatic balancing act that ministers pursued across European capitals, the UN Security Council, Washington DC and Baghdad, militated against full and frank public communication. The result was a fundamental clash between the government's diplomatic strategy and its commitment to communicative action. Not for the first time during the Iraq debate, the government thought too much transparency would be counter-productive.

Different views of the 'special relationship'

Underpinning all of this was a challenging clash between two different visions of how the 'special relationship' should work. Tony Blair instinctively supported the US, and, therefore, the Bush administration. He believed at an emotional level that Britain had a responsibility to stand by its traditional ally. Though his position also involved a rational calculation that bandwagoning with the superpower was in Britain's national interest, Blair's 'gut' stance ensured he never seriously thought alternative strategies through. This was problematic in both principle and practice. As Chilcot concluded, "influence should not be sought as an objective in itself. The exercise of influence is a means to an end" (Chilcot 2016e, 631). Most British people took a more instrumental view of the US alliance. Many felt alienated by the Bush administration's isolationist tendencies and unilateralist rhetoric. Blair initially caught the public mood with his emotional response to 11 September. But the public soon moved on. Where he saw an absolute British duty to support the US, his constituents preferred a more conditional approach. This clash raised questions about the Prime Minister's authority. Critics demanded to know what Britain gained in return for Blair's support. They saw Bush taking key decisions, and Blair merely implementing them. Authority matters, and appearing beholden to an unpopular President cost Blair authority at home.

Previous chapters found ministers at fault for the way the arguments they made failed to generate legitimacy. It is less clear that the government deserves exclusive blame for struggling to resolve this political paradox. Tony Blair made quite clear the extent of his support for the US. No one was under any real illusion that he believed very strongly that Britain should participate directly in any military response to the 11 September attacks. On 11 September itself, Blair announced that Britain would "stand shoulder to shoulder with our American friends" in facing up to terrorism (Blair 2001a). His message to Washington was expansive and deliberate; the US was not and would not be alone in fighting terrorism. He later wrote that he "chose the words ['shoulder to shoulder'] carefully", and acknowledged "this was a big commitment that would come to be measured not in words but in actions" (Blair 2010b, 352). Three days after the attacks he reminded MPs that more British citizens died in New York than in any previous terrorist attack. It was a striking point, given Britain's long experience of terrorism. For Blair, this was Britain's fight, too. But it was more than that. It was about more than 'just' the national interest. It was about identity. In a crisis, he argued, the British people "stand by their friends" (Blair 2001b, col. 604). Whether the people behind 11 September threatened Britain directly or not, Blair argued, the British were duty-bound to respond. Joining the 'coalition of the willing', fighting terrorism and ultimately invading Iraq all flowed from the position Blair stated explicitly and publicly from the start.

Blair was equally clear about the broader normative implications of this commitment for his policy approach. In his autobiography, he referred to "reasons both of principle and of national interest" in explaining his approach to the 'special relationship'. Tellingly, he went on, he "never believed the two are mutually exclusive" (Blair 2010b, 352). The problem with this was twofold. First, many British people believed they *were* mutually exclusive and that it was possible to support US power in principle while questioning its specific use in practice. That meant Blair and his critics agreed on the need to help the Bush administration respond to 11 September, and disagreed on what that help should properly entail. Second, Blair's public expressions of support challenged received wisdom about how the 'special relationship' ought to work, undermined his personal authority and prompted doubts about the more interest-based arguments he made. As the BBC's veteran interviewer John Humphrys put it in a *Sunday Times* article, "if Blair's main reason for sending troops to the Gulf is that Britain should be Washington's best friend, then let him say so" instead of trying to identify some sort of direct British interest (Humphrys 2003). Blair's position was complicated, however, and more developed than Humphrys realized. He told MPs he saw the 'special relationship' as an "article of faith", not just a political bargain (Blair 2002d, col. 21). He told journalists who criticised his failure to restrain the Bush administration "it's worse than you think. I believe in it" (Ashley and MacAskill 2003). He said exactly the same thing at the 23 July 2002 Downing Street meeting. Blair, Campbell recorded, "was acutely conscious of how difficult it would be both with the PLP [Parliamentary Labour Party] and the public, but ... he felt maximum closeness publicly was the best way to maximise influence privately" (Campbell and Stott 2007, 630).

Blair's approach to the 'special relationship' damaged his claim to legitimacy less because he failed to explain it publicly and more because he explained it perfectly clearly. In the process, he raised serious questions about the limits of his personal authority. Many observers feared Blair's "faith in the transatlantic alliance" left him "trapped" into war regardless of Britain's actual interests (Cornwell 2003a). In any event, this might have damaged him. It is problematic for an elected leader effectively to abrogate his responsibilities to the head of an allied state. But the Bush administration's unpopularity in Britain made things worse. Two key trends appear in how British public actors discussed the US response to 11 September, and the march to war in Iraq. First, many observers criticised the Bush administration's overt, quasi-religious bellicosity, and Blair's apparent accommodation with it. As one account of the Prime Minister's 2001 Labour Party conference speech noted, his "fervour" and "messianic" approach suited the US political culture much better than it did the traditionally staid British domestic arena (Buncombe 2001). US policymakers would pursue "a new isolationism" (D. Anderson 2001, col. 629) or "instant gratification for their anger" (George 2001, col. 636) in response to 11 September, warned MPs. The White House was "run by madmen" warned the *Mirror* (2003a). US public opinion was "ready for revenge", it demanded "a firework display" and it expected "blood in the sand", journalists cried (*Guardian* 2001; Maddox 2001; Raven 2001). Regardless of the real security threat, the Bush administration would use extraordinary measures to appease public anger. It was the only way "to keep up President Bush's poll results", wrote one *Independent on Sunday* columnist (Smith 2001a). Afghanistan represented a "something must be done, 'do my poll ratings look good in this?' war" (Cohen 2001). Britain shared the initial shock of 11 September, and backed the use of force against the Taliban. Doubts remained, however, about the character of the Bush administration, and the American public.

Second, different actors disagreed over the importance of multilateralism, in principle as well as in practice. Liberal Democrat MP Paul Keetch reflected one strand of argument, arguing in October 2001 that the long-term benefits of maintaining coalition unity far outweighed the short-term gains of any particular use of force (Keetch 2001, col. 845). Conservative leader Iain Duncan Smith expressed a second view, which was that working with allies might provide useful means to desirable ends but that sustaining an alliance was not a sufficient end in itself (Duncan Smith 2001, col. 677). A third argument emerged in the writings of right-leaning journalists, who echoed Rumsfeld's fears about the downsides of multilateralism. David Hart warned in the *Times* against allowing allies' fears to "diminish" vital war aims (Hart 2001). A *Daily Telegraph* editorial similarly cautioned that the coalition might wind up "inhibiting the core task of fighting terrorism" (*Daily Telegraph* 2001). So long as holding the coalition together was straightforward, the clash between these three distinct views made little practical difference. As the focus of the debate in the US shifted from Afghanistan to Iraq, however, it became more significant.

Doubts over British influence

It was bad enough that many British people did not trust the Bush administration. What really undermined the Blair government's authority, and so the legitimacy of the decision to go to war in Iraq, however, was the widely-shared belief that British ministers lacked real influence over plans decided in Washington. Chilcot's conclusion that Britain influenced the US decision to work through the UN, but little else, underlines this (Chilcot 2016a, 54). There is an established and contentious debate amongst practitioners and observers of British foreign policy over whether US allies must offer total loyalty in public to earn a fair hearing in private (Wallace 2005, 54). Many people assumed that British ministers would support the US vocally while perhaps seeking to restrain the administration's more aggressive tendencies in private. Many assumed, in other words, that ministers would withhold information about their views on US policy. This was a problematic starting point for a truly open public debate. But the assumption exacerbated a broader issue. Tony Blair believed in the Iraq War, and several of his senior ministers went along with it willingly enough (Kennedy-Pipe and Vickers 2007, 207). Those who expected Blair to restrain Bush felt doubly betrayed by his apparent unwillingness to do so, first because they felt he was letting them down, and second because they eventually realised that he actually agreed with Bush. Few spotted the wider implications of Blair's 'shoulder to shoulder' commitment in September 2001. Established anti-war and anti-US campaigner George Galloway MP warned the government not to grant the US a "blank cheque" for war (Galloway 2001, cols. 639–640). Most of his colleagues, however, echoed media commentators who praised the Prime Minister for forging a "genuine transatlantic bond" (Jones 2001), a "seamless alliance" and "pillar of world order" (Cornwell 2001). Blair basked in both the popular approval and, perhaps more importantly, the affection of the US. Declaring 'war on terrorism' before a special joint session of Congress on 20 September, President Bush drew attention to Blair, seated in the gallery as his special guest. "America has no truer friend than Great Britain", he declared (Bush 2001). Never had the 'special relationship', long a British foreign policy priority and one with widespread domestic legitimacy, looked so strong.

It did not take long, however, for the issue of what Britain gained in return for its support to arise. For ministers the answer was simple. Public support brought access, and access brought influence (Campbell and Stott 2007, 563). Some domestic observers accepted this argument. Andrew Rawnsley remarked that standing 'shoulder to shoulder' was "the only way to get a word in George Bush's ear" (Rawnsley 2001). A leading article in the *Independent* suggested Blair's professed backing for Bush meant "when in private he advises restraint, he will be taken seriously" (*Independent* 2001). Donald MacIntyre concluded that Britain's ability to shape US decisions might be limited, but that it could expect "no influence" at all without unquestioning public loyalty (MacIntyre 2001). Rawnsley (again) warned that "resentful sniping" might make Blair's task that much worse (Rawnsley 2002a). Others took a more sceptical view. Steve Richards remarked that the whole notion of standing 'shoulder to shoulder' made no sense given the power disparities between the US and UK. "A giant and a dwarf", he argued, "can never stand shoulder to shoulder" (Richards 2001). Peter Riddell warned against exaggerating Britain's influence while Bruce Anderson predicted allies would have "minimal" power to constrain US ambitions in the post-11 September world

(Riddell 2001; B. Anderson 2001). Some, like Hugo Young, thought a more critical approach from the Blair government might actually increase its leverage in Washington (Young 2002). That was not the government's view. A final group extended the logic of this argument still further, into outright cynicism. The *Mirror* complained that "the prime minister has done nothing but play lapdog to the Washington Red Neck" (*Mirror* 2002a). Its journalists dismissed him as a presidential "poodle" (Blackman 2002). This "poodle problem", as Campbell put it (Campbell and Stott 2007, 669), recurred repeatedly in the run-up to war.

Ironically, part of what drove this cynicism was Blair's open admission that he did not seek to prevent the Bush administration going to war. Had he not made so clear his commitment to the US stance, he might simply have appeared incapable of influencing his transatlantic counterparts, rather than actively unwilling. "I know people sometimes think it is my job to sit there restraining this or restraining that", he told a television interviewer days before visiting Bush in Texas. Over Afghanistan, he went on, it was not like that; "it wasn't a question of restraining the President, the discussion was what is the best way of doing it?" (Blair 2002b). Backed by a conservative press who were eager to praise his "commendable bravery" when he disagreed with his party (*The Times* 2002c) and determined to ensure he stayed "unwilling to compromise" (*The Times* 2002b), Blair stuck to this stance despite the fact it fuelled domestic criticism. In other words, his commitment to communicative action clashed with his claim to independent authority. By openly admitting that he agreed strongly with Bush, Blair equally confirmed that the decisions he advocated were not entirely his own.

As the Iraq debate continued to unfold, two specific questions emerged about the timing and the nature of British involvement. Together, these issues shaped discussions about the government's authority. The issue of when exactly ministers promised to support the use of force in Iraq upset several critics. Chilcot concluded that at Crawford, Blair "offered president Bush a partnership in dealing urgently with the threat posed by Saddam Hussein" (Chilcot 2016a, 112). The official Foreign Office telegram reporting the discussions made no mention of a commitment to go to war and instead focused on the need to engage the UN (Foreign and Commonwealth Office 2002). In his public statements, Blair took a hard line and talked about regime change, prompting a range of reactions at home. He "rolled over like a rather docile poodle", in the eyes of the *Mirror* (2002b). He adopted a "brave and right" stance, argued the *Daily Telegraph* (2002a). He made a "subtle and important" speech, according to a *Guardian* editorial (*Guardian* 2002a). His arguments were "unconvincing", concluded the *Independent* (2002a). Sceptical journalists assumed there would be war before the end of 2002 (Borger and MacAskill 2002). Their pro-war colleagues agreed, complaining that Blair was "too slow in preparing British opinion for the inevitable" (*The Times* 2002a).

Widespread discussions in the press about the growing inevitability of war angered MPs, who complained vociferously about being shut out. Labour's Harry Cohen observed that "the press is full of reports that the US plans a large-scale attack on Iraq", but MPs were not being kept informed (Cohen 2002, col. 364). Alice Mahon quoted the Borger and MacAskill story noted above when raising her own concerns (Mahon 2002). Ministers stuck to the line that "no decision has been taken", and criticised both MPs and the media for getting carried away with "speculation" (Blair 2002a, col. 32). Their efforts at reassurance failed. Tony Blair was "lying to parliament", wrote one regular critic, and "lying to his own MPs" (Routledge 2002a). "A decision has already been taken to send British troops into Iraq with the Americans" wrote the same columnist a few months later; "the invasion will take place in the autumn" (Routledge 2002b). The government's repeated denials did not matter. Nor, apparently, did the fact that autumn passed without a war. So certain were some observers that British ministers were simply obeying aggressive US instructions, they consistently expected the worst and distrusted everything the government said to the contrary. If Blair actually did deliberately use public expressions of loyalty to buy access to Bush administration decision-making, it seems, he both raised questions about his commitment to communicative action and undermined his own political authority. What made this point more damaging was the fact that Blair clearly *was* making promises to Bush in private which he failed to share in public. On 28 July 2002, for example, he opened a note to the President with: "I will be with you, whatever" (Blair 2002c). Manning tried to get the line excised on the grounds it was "too sweeping". Blair overruled him. The Cabinet neither discussed nor knew about this letter (Chilcot 2016c, 76, 89–90). Just as critics suspected, the Prime Minister was making major and potentially irreversible commitments entirely on his own.

Many domestic observers believed Blair when he pledged to uphold the authority of the Security Council. No one thought Bush shared that stance, and since they doubted Blair could restrain the President, they thought his assurances disingenuous. British commentators complained about the "internal American rationale" of the march to war (Dawkins 2003), and about "the Americans trying to impose their definition of regime change unilaterally and in defiance of the principles of international law" (Morgan 2003). Far from being the centrepiece of the British diplomatic effort to disarm Iraq, "the UN route was a detour intended to pick up supporters along the way", complained the *Independent* (2003a). Anatole Kaletsky of *The Times* identified "the contradiction between Washington's not-so-hidden agenda and its publicly stated objectives" as the primary force driving anti-war concerns (Kaletsky 2003). Benefitting from hindsight at the end of the debate, Simon Jenkins concluded that "knowing America's intent, the Government would have been more honest to leave the UN in the gutter from the start" (Jenkins 2003). Jenkins' observation raises an interesting question about whether the British government fully appreciated the extent of US unilateralism, whether it fell victim to wishful thinking and Tony Blair's faith in his own persuasive powers, or whether it simply downplayed its own private doubts. Regardless, the widely-shared belief that the UN process was merely "window-dressing" covering up the fact that Britain could not stop a determined US administration from going to war undermined the invasion's legitimacy (*Independent on Sunday* 2003).

A sense of inevitability permeated the latter stages of the debate. This raised difficulties for the government. Blair admitted publicly that the legitimacy of his approach depended on offering Iraq a plausible alternative route to disarmament other than war. "People want to know that war is not inevitable", he told journalists (Blair 2003a). He apparently told Bush "the public opinion problem stemmed from people feeling the US wanted a war" come what may, rather than from any real disagreement with US objectives (Campbell and Stott 2007, 674). To a degree, Blair was correct in his conclusion. Conservative MP Kenneth Clarke won plaudits for making exactly this point during the penultimate major parliamentary debate on Iraq. Clarke expressed considerable concern "that the course to war upon which we are now embarked was decided on many months ago, primarily in Washington, and there has been a fairly remorseless unfolding of events since that time" (Clarke 2003, col. 294). What mattered was less the substance of the specific policy proposed and more the procedural dimension: the fact that the British government seemed willing to cede its sovereign authority to another state. "Mr Clarke spoke for Britain", wrote the *Guardian* (2003a). Mr Blair, by contrast, appeared to many British people to speak for the United States. That damaged his authority.

Doubts about what exactly Britain's support for the US entailed also permeated public discourse in this period. Again, these doubts dated back to the private discussions between Bush and Blair at Crawford. Most second-hand accounts agree that Blair promised to support the US in confronting Saddam Hussein, while arguing also for parallel progress on the Middle East Peace Process, an effort to engage the UN and a concerted public communications campaign (Seldon *et al.* 2007, 89). Even within the Cabinet, however, different individuals understood these points in different ways. Blair's three arguments do not appear in the FCO note of the meeting (Chilcot 2016b, 493). David Manning described them as "conditions" for action in discussions with Condoleezza Rice in May 2002 (Chilcot 2016c, 14). Writing to Blair in the summer of 2002, Jack Straw expressed concern that US policymakers seemed to be forgetting about "your three conditions for UK involvement" in military action (Straw 2002a). Meyer similarly warned that "the 'buts' in our 'yes, but' approach" were being forgotten (Meyer 2002a). Manning, Meyer and Straw apparently thought Blair had set out clear criteria for British involvement in military action. He had not. Blair told the Chilcot Inquiry that the three 'conditions' represented simply his advice on how best to approach the question of military action (Chilcot 2016c, 23). Though Bush understood Blair's domestic circumstances, the Prime Minister never made his support conditional on any particular US approach (Blair 2010a, 45). Even the Foreign Secretary was confused about this critical point. No wonder others found it difficult to grasp.

As the Rumsfeld incident in March 2003 suggests, the notion that the US did not need Britain, militarily, added to the confusion about what unequivocal support actually entailed. Internal documents suggest that officials saw British involvement as vitally important, but equally that many thought Britain's real contribution lay on the diplomatic side. Jeremy Greenstock, for example, recalled at the Chilcot Inquiry that Britain "often raises fewer hackles" in highlighting issues of joint US–UK concern at UN meetings, even when the US position is well known (Greenstock 2009a). In the final weeks before the invasion of Iraq Tony Brenton, acting ambassador to Washington following Christopher Meyer's retirement, cabled London to report his latest discussions with Bush administration officials. The US was "pulling out all the stops in the UN", he noted. At such a late stage, "the only event which might significantly affect [the US] timetable would be problems for the UK" (Brenton 2003). One report described the US trying to act without the UK as "huge – like trying to play football without the quarterback" (Chilcot 2016a, 29). The form of 'football' described suggests this was a direct Bush administration quote. Manning told Blair in March 2002 that "Bush wants to hear your views on Iraq ... he also wants your support.... This gives you real influence" (Manning 2002). Jonathan Powell noted in a December 2002 meeting that "it was unlikely the US would proceed" to war without British involvement (Brummell 2002). Britain was important enough to alter US policy, in sum. Unfortunately for the government, however, making this importance visible publicly would mean embarrassing the White House. The logic of diplomacy clashed with the requirements of communicative action.

Diplomatic logic raised further challenges during the course of the Iraq debate. The fact the British government faced considerable domestic political dissent should have helped ministers bargain with their US counterparts, by making clear they faced significant domestic "audience costs" should they fail to achieve their goals (Fearon 1994, 1997). A major rebellion by Labour Party MPs on 26 February 2003 led the *Guardian*'s Polly Toynbee to highlight the "paradox" that "100 or more No votes might just strengthen Tony Blair's restraining hand on the US president" (Toynbee 2003a). Some MPs even suggested that ministers helped arrange the rebellion to drive home to Washington the difficulties they faced (White and Wintour 2003). There is no independent evidence that this was in fact the case. It does appear, however, that knowledge of the British domestic situation helped persuade the Bush administration to go along with attempts to secure a 'second' UN Security Council Resolution in early 2003 (Chilcot 2016d, 163). At the same time, the leverage secured through this route remained limited by the fact the Blair government shared most of the Bush administration's policies, and that Blair was unwilling to appear 'wobbly' by playing up his domestic difficulties to Bush (Chilcot 2016c, 132). Meyer advised in October 2002 that "Mega-hawk Scooter Libby, Cheney's chief of staff, told me once that the UK was the only indispensable ally for an attack on Iraq". This meant "what the UK decides to do in these circumstances could be the decisive factor for the White House" (Meyer 2002b). Straw argued a few days later that Blair should "tell [Bush] that you have politics too" (Straw 2002b). Differences between Blair and Straw in terms of their emphasis on the need for a 'second' SCR concerned Colin Powell as late as March 2003 (Chilcot 2016d, 435). None of it affected Blair. To a non-trivial extent, he was "trapped by the logic" of his earlier pronouncements (Coates and Krieger 2009, 248–249).

150 *Legitimacy*

Observers noted that the Prime Minister risked undermining his own personal authority should he change his course, even though many of his domestic opponents would welcome such a shift (MacIntyre 2003a). Chilcot concluded it was "very difficult for the UK subsequently to withdraw its support for the US" given Blair's statements to Bush, especially in his note of 28 July 2002 (Chilcot 2016a, 112). Doing so would arguably have been worse than refusing to support the US at all. Domestic commentators recognized as much. Blair had "painted himself into a corner" (Alexander 2003) and "surrendered his ability to control policy completely" (Finkelstein 2003). Changing course would entail a "disastrous loss of face", "humiliation" and "political suicide", observers warned (*Mail on Sunday* 2003; Guardian 2003b). Saddam Hussein would have to go (Clark 2003). It would also be problematic for President Bush who, unlike Blair, enjoyed clear domestic support for confronting Iraq. He had no interest, observed British commentators, in inviting comparison with the "Grand Old Duke of York" by marching his troops back down the Iraqi hill without achieving their objectives (Sunday Mirror 2003; Howard 2003).

Authority and legitimacy

Whether a particular policy appears legitimate depends in part on whether policymakers possess authority (Franck 1988, 725; Clark 2005, 4). Part of the problem the Blair government faced when trying to legitimize the invasion of Iraq stemmed from its inability (or perhaps unwillingness) to assert its independence from the Bush administration. Doubts about British ministers' ability to influence their US counterparts fed doubts about their authority, and in turn about the legitimacy of the actions they took. No one questioned the Prime Minister's personal right to decide when Britain went to war. They did question, however, whether Tony Blair was really making the decisions he professed to support. Blair's openness about his faith in the 'special relationship' and his vocal support for President Bush exacerbated these concerns. In the immediate aftermath of the 11 September attacks domestic commentators largely accepted that supporting the US in public gave British leaders greater scope to influence it in private. Over time they grew more sceptical, and so more doubtful about the government's authority. By early 2003 more sophisticated analysts recognized that Blair was trapped (Rawnsley 2003). Having committed to supporting Bush, he had to follow through or risk losing authority. But he faced losing authority in any event if people at home thought he was unable to affect decisions in Washington. Ultimately two elements together undermined the legitimacy of the Blair government's Iraq stance. First, the power discrepancy between the US and the UK and, second, Tony Blair's personal commitment to confronting Saddam Hussein. Together these factors raised questions about ministers' authority that brought the legitimacy of their policies into doubt.

Blaming France

If diplomacy undermined the Blair government's attempt to secure domestic legitimacy for its decision to go to war, it also offered it a way to roll back commitments it could not keep. Specifically, France's vocal rejection of a 'second' UN Security Council Resolution and concerted effort to prevent the US cutting short the UNMOVIC inspection process helped British ministers justify giving up the 'UN route'. Having long trailed the possibility that an 'unreasonable' veto might prevent the Security Council reaching agreement, the government ultimately blamed French obstructionism for its decision to circumvent the UN process. This effort largely worked.

Though the form it takes is often more jocular than serious, antipathy to France is deeply embedded in British public debate. British domestic audiences were primed to accept images of French recklessness, selfishness and perfidy. When ministers accused their cross-channel counterparts of wrecking a nascent UN consensus, many commentators believed them. This is interesting because of the effect it had on the Blair government's ability to secure sufficient domestic backing to take Britain to war in Iraq, which was otherwise in doubt. It is interesting, also, because this dimension of the official case for war failed to meet the standard for communicative action to a greater extent than most. French President Jacques Chirac and Foreign Minister Dominique de Villepin exacerbated the stand-off at the UN to project authority to their own domestic audiences, gaining improved poll ratings as a result (Chilcot 2016c, 320). They also genuinely disagreed with Britain's approach to managing the unilateralist US, which made compromise difficult. But they never intended to shut down the UN process entirely, something French officials communicated clearly to London. Indeed, France consistently stated its concerns and the conditions it thought necessary for any confrontation with Iraq to work, while reserving the right to participate under the right circumstances (Chilcot 2016b, 399, 2016c, 154). The Blair government took a deliberate decision to exploit the French position to justify its own failure to secure a 'second' SCR, despite knowing that France remained open to compromise. Not only did this decision work in the short term, it became one of the few aspects of the official case for war not to subsequently cause the government trouble. The claim that France destroyed the UN process contributed to the invasion's political legitimacy despite undermining its normative legitimacy. Sometimes the two dimensions *are* in fact opposed.

Underlying antipathy

It is to some extent fair to frame the Blair government's Iraq approach as the product of a deliberate decision to prioritize relations with the US over those with France (Gamble and Kearns 2007, 121). Indeed, that British ministers took this route should not appear surprising. Though anti-Americanism, as the previous section suggested, plays an important part in public debates over international politics, antipathy to France runs deeper still. That is especially true amongst white working-class voters and in the right-wing press. Though France supported SCR 1441 in November 2002, and remained officially willing to join the 'coalition of the willing' right up until the final days before the war, in practice it sided with Russia against the US–UK alliance. This made reaching a compromise difficult. It also offered the Blair government a potential way out. Even before the final confrontation developed at the Security Council, British commentators began to mutter darkly about the French approach. In the *Daily Mail*, Harold Evans labelled President Chirac "Saddam's pimp" and complained that France lacked the wider perspective motivating British policy (Evans 2003). A *Times* editorial meanwhile called Russia, Germany and France "chancers" for daring to challenge the US-led course (*The Times* 2003a). Writing in the same publication, William Rees-Mogg described France and Germany as "Saddam's useful idiots", while reflecting "that these sophisticated governments knew what they were doing" in preventing consensus (Rees-Mogg 2003).

As France grew more vocal in its doubts about the wisdom of military action and the US willingness to cut short the UN route, right-wing British commentators increasingly questioned the reasoning behind the French approach. The *Sun* attributed Chirac's "hypocrisy" to "his country's lucrative trade deals" with Baghdad (*Sun* 2003b). The *News of the World* predicted the removal of Saddam Hussein would reveal extensive "French financial links" with his regime (*News of the World* 2003a). Attacking France's "reckless indulgence of debased Gaullism", the *Daily Telegraph* similarly attributed Chirac's sceptical stance to "his historic links with Saddam" (*Daily Telegraph* 2003a). This was heady stuff. Though only the *Sun* regularly descended into outright abuse, at one point labelling France and Germany "the worms in our midst" (*Sun* 2003a). This wider willingness to treat France as the enemy ensured a significant proportion of the media accepted ministers' efforts to blame Paris for their own shortcomings in New York.

The Blair government genuinely felt frustrated at the way France approached the Iraq issue. Two particular moments stood out. First, on 14 February 2003 Dominique de Villepin 'ambushed' Colin Powell by using a press conference following a Security Council meeting to attack the US approach. De Villepin drew applause from many of those present, perhaps emboldening Chirac to strike a more intransigent tone (Marfleet and Miller 2005, 339). Then, on 9 March, Chirac gave a television interview in which he promised that France would veto any SCR that authorised the use of force. France and Russia had already promised to "assume all their responsibilities on this point" in an earlier joint declaration (Ehrenberg *et al.* 2010, 143). Chirac's statement did not, at least in theory, mark a change of policy. It reflected known disagreements, and left some room for a future compromise once UNMOVIC concluded its work. But on this occasion he went further. France would vote "non", he insisted, "quelques soit les circonstances" (Chirac 2003). Whatever the circumstances.

This more absolute statement changed the diplomatic calculus. Jack Straw told the Chilcot Inquiry that the moment Chirac spoke, the "situation" with regard to the second resolution "became terminal" (Straw 2010, 19). Smaller states were hardly going to risk standing out in a hopeless cause. Chilcot noted that Chirac referred specifically to two scenarios based on the draft text immediately on the table, not to any possible circumstances in which the US and UK might propose to use force. At the same time, the report also observed that Chirac's statement earned favourable coverage on the front page of *Le Monde* (Chilcot 2016d, 423–425). Even the otherwise anti-war *Independent* ran an editorial suggesting Chirac and de Villepin had "overplayed their hand" (*Independent* 2003c). The British Ambassador to Paris, John Holmes agreed that Chirac "may have played this card too soon", suggesting his goal was to make "it as hard as possible for the Russians and Chinese not to follow, and as easy as possible for the swing six to abstain, as an obvious middle course between the two opposing blocs" (Holmes 2003a). When de Villepin followed up on Chirac's statement by denouncing a compromise motion put forward by Britain in conjunction with Hans Blix, without even waiting for Iraq to respond, it allowed the Blair government, in Alastair Campbell's words, "to go to an aggressive position re French intransigence" (Campbell and Stott 2007, 677). On 11 March 2003 Blair told Bush that Chirac's remarks "gave some cover" for terminating efforts to get agreement at the Security Council (Chilcot 2016a, 35).

Attributing responsibility

Thanks in part to the underlying distrust of France, which is prevalent at least in parts of British public debate, the Blair government found attributing responsibility for its own failure to secure a consensus at the Security Council to French obstructionism relatively straightforward. Its claims on this point were not, however, entirely honest. Indeed, Clare Short later called the argument "one of the big deceits" of the government's case for war (Short 2010, 104). To begin with, it did not actually matter whether France vetoed a new SCR or not. The US and UK never secured the necessary minimum of nine Security Council votes for their draft 'second' resolution. Greenstock told Chilcot as much (Greenstock 2009b, 72). Veto powers only come into play once a majority of Council members back a motion. That was not the case in early 2003 over Iraq. More broadly, it became clear during the course of the Chilcot Inquiry that French officials made frantic efforts in the aftermath of Chirac's 9 March statement to keep open the possibility of a future compromise. Britain refused to take "maybe" for an answer. Instead the Blair government deliberately and knowingly exploited the ambiguity in Chirac's statement to paint the French stance as more absolute than it apparently was.

On 12 March Matthew Rycroft emailed Powell, Manning, Campbell and others in No. 10 to report a conversation with Gerard Errera, the French Ambassador to London, in which the latter insisted Chirac's remarks had been taken out of context, and "it is not the case that he said that he would vote no against any resolution" (Rycroft 2003). The following day, Holmes cabled London to report a:

complaint from the Élysée about our beginning to criticise France more openly, particularly Chirac's remarks about the veto ... [and] our repeated taking out of context of the President's remarks on the veto in all circumstances. We must be well aware that he had been talking about the particular position that evening, with the draft then on the table.

Holmes records having responded that:

our position can hardly surprise the French, nor the fact that we are using Chirac's words against him when the stakes are so high – he did say them, even if he may not have meant to express quite what we have chosen to interpret.

(Holmes 2003b)

Further evidence that British officials knew they were playing a game, and felt comfortable playing it, comes from a response to Holmes sent by Peter Ricketts, describing an exchange with Errera that closely mirrored Holmes's report:

he began with some remonstrating ... I brandished *Le Monde* at him with the quotation prominent on the front page. The French should not be surprised if Ministers were contrasting this with the constant efforts we were making to build common ground in the Security Council.

(Ricketts 2003)

Jeremy Greenstock claimed at Chilcot that he was "acting under instructions" when he denounced France at the UN, but Jack Straw disputes this, and other officials clearly accepted the approach (Chilcot 2016d, 532).

Straw told De Villepin directly:

that Chirac's statement ... had caused great difficulties. It was clear that France would veto. Villepin said that Chirac had never said that. Chirac had not meant that France would not try to find common ground. He had not meant that, whatever happened, France would vote no.

In a telling phrase, the meeting note records that Straw "said that he read the comments differently" (Straw 2003a). When the time came for Britain to abandon its efforts to secure a 'second' SCR, on 17 March, Straw went out of his way to blame France. "President Chirac's unequivocal announcement last Monday that France would veto a second resolution", he told MPs, "inevitably created a sense of paralysis in our negotiations ... France has thereby put a Security Council consensus beyond reach" (Straw 2003b, col. 703). Two elements are visible in these exchanges. First is the genuine frustration on the British side about the French approach, which is particularly evident in Straw's account. Second is a willingness to make use of Chirac's words to reinforce the British argument. Holmes's comment about the importance of the British interpretation placed on what the French President actually said underlines this point. Straw urged France to accept SCR 1441 in November 2002 by arguing that the phrase "to consider" in OP12 implied a Council decision, not just a discussion, and insisting it meant more in English than the equivalent concept did in French (Chilcot 2016c, 305–306). He wound up arguing exactly the opposite, and criticizing the French for holding the position he previously insisted they accept. So much for consistency.

These efforts to blame the stalemate at the Security Council on France raise questions about the Blair government's commitment to communicative action. For one thing, they underline ministers' limited interest in international-level deliberation. Within policymaking circles, no one suggested taking France's objections seriously, or considered accepting its calls for military action to be delayed. This betrayed a lack of flexibility. More significantly, however, the repeated British insistence that France was unwilling to compromise contradicted what French officials said privately. British diplomats and officials knowingly privileged a particularly hard-line interpretation of Chirac's public pronouncements over the softer stance other French figures employed. This indicates a lack of truthfulness. Even the implication, widely taken up in the pro-war press, that France somehow did not deserve a voice in such an important debate points away from a truly communicative approach. It suggests a lack of openness, an unwillingness to countenance contrary views. Together these shortcomings brought the normative legitimacy of the British case for war into question. What is interesting about this specific argument, however, is that it did not also damage the invasion's political legitimacy. Though not every domestic actor accepted the government line uncritically, many did. Above all, blaming France offered conflicted centrists, especially those who wanted to trust Tony Blair but instinctively disliked President Bush, a way out. It helped salve consciences otherwise inflamed by the prospect of Britain ignoring the Security Council and abandoning a truly multilateral approach.

There were critics of the Blair government's approach. Attacking the French stance was "unjustified and distasteful", not to mention "not in Britain's interests", warned the *Guardian* (2003d, 2003c). France was nothing more than a "convenient scapegoat" for "a breathtaking failure of American diplomacy" at the UN, wrote Rupert Cornwell (2003b). An editorial in the *Mirror* accused ministers of "hypocrisy run riot and double-think of scandalous proportions" (*Mirror* 2003b). These complaints encountered powerful rebuttals. With its attacks on France now enjoying a degree of official endorsement, the *Sun* unleashed a wave of scorn. Chirac was "like a cheap tart who puts price before principle, money before honour" thundered one editorial (*Sun* 2003c). While the French President displayed only "arrogance and greed", Tony Blair embodied "the highest moral principles", continued a second (*Sun* 2003d). The very prospect of war itself owed more to Chirac's "stupidity and personal vanity" than to Iraq's conduct or US attitudes (*Sun* 2003e). *Sun* columnist Trevor Kavanagh labelled Chirac a "grandstanding egomaniac", a "worm" whose conduct had "inflicted irreparable damage on some of the most important yet fragile structures of international order" (Kavanagh 2003). If the UN process was failing, in other words, it was emphatically Chirac's fault. *The Times*, News Corporation stable mate of the *Sun*, shared these assessments. One editorial blamed "French intransigence and Iraqi belligerence" for the prospect of war (*The Times* 2003c). Another attacked France for treating the threat of "serious consequences" contained within SCR 1441 as nothing more than "rhetorical window-dressing" (*The Times* 2003d). The *Sunday Times* attributed Chirac's behaviour to "naked national interest" (*Sunday Times* 2003b). Together this battery of criticism and abuse presented a simple, powerful image. France was to blame for the impasse at the Security Council. It could, and should, legitimately be bypassed.

As some commentators noted at the time, this narrative both offered the Blair government a way to justify its own failings and presented critics of military action with a way to get themselves "off the hook" (Sieghart 2003). It went down particularly well in parliament. Donald Anderson complained that "so long as 'immediate' is not defined as 'immediate', and 'final' not defined as 'final', the Security Council will lose credibility for its own resolutions" (Anderson 2003, col. 175). This line exactly echoed the government's established argument that Security Council members owed their counterparts certain obligations, including the obligation to apply agreed resolutions consistently. If a permanent member preferred to use an "unreasonable" veto, those states willing to uphold earlier judgements could legitimately proceed regardless. Media reports suggested a number of Anderson's fellow MPs shared his frustration with France and accepted the government line (Grice 2003b). Poll results pointed towards similar views amongst the mass public (*News of the World* 2003b). YouGov found 22 per cent of respondents agreed with Chirac's approach, while 70 per cent disagreed. Support for war without a second resolution was growing, as it continued to grow until the fighting began (Smith and Speed 2003). Blaming France helped the Blair government win the political argument, gaining support and so political legitimacy. It also undermined its claim to legitimacy in normative terms.

Domestic politics

Iraq transformed how domestic politics affects British foreign policymaking. Over the course of the pre-invasion debate public pressure forced the Blair government to concede MPs the right to veto the final decision to go to war – a significant shift in the balance of power between Downing Street and parliament (Strong 2015a). No longer would the Prime Minister make such critical judgements alone, relying on the authority vested in the historic Royal Prerogative (Joseph 2013). In future, the House of Commons would have to be involved. Bringing MPs into the decision-making process changed its nature. In particular, it brought party-political concerns to the fore (Strong 2015b). That actually helped ministers pushing for war in Iraq. Their Conservative opponents supported the invasion more vociferously even than did Tony Blair. Blair was able to frame the choice in front of Labour MPs as one between his continued leadership and

Saddam. Most MPs voted along party lines, in the end. There were too few leaders for critics to follow.

That the Blair government worked hard to delay, or outright avoid, public debate on aspects of its Iraq policy undermined its claim to legitimacy. It also prompted opposition, especially amongst MPs. An important early moment in the path towards parliament's involvement in the final deployment decision arose in September 2002, when parliamentary pressure forced the government to recall the House of Commons to debate the WMD dossier. Tam Dalyell's initial attempt to secure a debate in late July failed. As Mary Dejevsky put it, despite "for the umpteenth time this year, informed opinion ... working itself into a panic", there was still no immediate prospect of Britain actually going to war (Dejevsky 2002). On 4 September, however, Labour MP Graham Allen announced he planned to hold an 'unofficial' sitting of the Commons to debate the dossier. In the process, he directly challenged the government's authority to decide when parliament should consider foreign policy. In contrast to Dalyell's earlier abortive effort, Allen's proposal gained press support. The *Guardian* warned that "the storm of war is clearly gathering". The *Daily Mail* pointed that Blair had promised "to pay 'the blood price' for supporting America against Iraq", and agreed that parliament should have its say at once (*Daily Mail* 2002a). These complaints grew both bolder and broader the longer the government delayed. Editorials in the *Independent*, for example, began to demand that MPs have a formal vote to approve or reject the government's approach. "It ought to be a basic rule of democracy" that such votes took place, argued one (*Independent* 2002c). That the Prime Minister could still wield such absolute powers was a "standing affront", commented another (*Independent* 2002c). These arguments won wider support. Leader of the House of Commons Robin Cook articulated similar demands on behalf of MPs. But the rest of the Cabinet stood firm (Grice 2002). There would be a debate, but not yet a formal vote.

Two things changed between September 2002 and March 2003. First, the prospect of war in Iraq went from hypothetical and remote to immediate, without any positive shift in public support. Divisions between Labour ministers and their own MPs threated to bring the government down. Second, the UN Security Council process failed. Ministers used France as a scapegoat to justify abandoning the UN route. But they still needed approval of some sort from a political body, to reassure nervous citizens that they were on the correct course (Voeten 2005, 527). They chose parliament. It was a risky step. Numerous Labour MPs opposed the use of force in Iraq. Going the UN route helped, though even then 30 Labour MPs voted against a motion endorsing SCR 1441 on 25 November 2002. On 26 February 2003, 121 voted against the government on 26 February 2003 and 139 ultimately rebelled in the final vote on 18 March. British political party leaders often find themselves agreeing with their nominal opponents while fighting their own backbench MPs (Wallace 1977, 93; King 1976, 12). But Iraq was an extreme example. Allowing MPs a formal vote meant recruiting parliament's authority to help legitimize a decision to go to war. It also raised the possibility that they might vote no.

Opposition

Though a wide range of public actors criticised the Blair government's Iraq policy, they never coalesced around a coherent opposition voice. Some submitted to disciplining moves by the pro-war press, such as the *Sun*'s naming and shaming of supposed "traitors" (*Sun* 2002; Robinson *et al.* 2009, 537). Others misdirected their criticism. Too many of the arguments deployed focused on process rather than substance. A number of newspapers dismissed the September recall because they felt one day of discussion was not long enough (*Daily Mail* 2002b; *Guardian* 2002b). There was nothing wrong with the sentiment, but the more critics expended energy on procedural matters, the less time and space they had to challenge the government's substantive claims. Finally, a decent number of erstwhile opponents resigned themselves to Iraq's fate. After a gesture of defiance, reflected above all in the 15 February 2003 marches, came "a great national shrug" (Ashley 2002).

That the Conservative Party supported the invasion helped the government in parliament, if not necessarily in the eyes of Labour supporters or the wider public. Daniel Finkelstein observed in the aftermath of the Crawford visit that "the last thing Mr Blair wants is Tory support" (Finkelstein 2002). The more Iain Duncan Smith praised Blair's strategy, the more his Labour base grew restless. Duncan Smith's support, however, also left the official opposition effectively "neutered" and "irrelevant" (Richards 2002; Collins 2003). He was struggling to challenge Blair effectively anyway. Journalists routinely dismissed him as "Mr Thing", "baldilocks" or simply "a disaster" (Carr 2003; Routledge 2003a; Steven 2003). His Iraq stance exacerbated the problem. By early 2003, one poll found 71 per cent of respondents thought "there is no real political opposition in this country" (*Sunday Times* 2003a). Cautious Labour MPs saw the weakness of the Conservatives as a sign of Blair's good leadership, and kept whatever doubts they had about Iraq quiet (Riddell 2003a). Their more rebellious colleagues felt emboldened by the absence of a credible electoral threat, and spoke out. Journalists, meanwhile, responded to Britain's development into "an elective one-party state" by attempting "to function as a synthetic opposition" (Rawnsley 2002b). Part of the hostility the government faced from the press, in other words, stemmed from its parliamentary dominance.

Cabinet divisions represented a greater threat. Both Clare Short and Robin Cook expressed doubts about the prospect of war in Iraq. They agreed, however, on little else. Short, for example, dismissed the Cabinet's discussions on Iraq as "little chats" devoid of substance (Short 2010, 3). Cook, however, reported a "real discussion" on 7 March 2002, and added that "over the next six months we were to discuss Iraq more than any other topic". For Cook, the problem was not so much that Blair sidelined his senior colleagues, but rather that "only Clare Short and I ever expressed frank doubts about the trajectory" of his Iraq policy (Cook 2003, 115–116). That said, it was true that Blair regularly failed to update Cabinet as he made increasingly firm commitments to the US. For example, in October 2002 he offered full UK involvement in a land invasion without consulting colleagues (Chilcot 2016a, 121). By March 2003 it was clear that

Blair planned to take Britain to war. Short and Cook reacted to this quite differently, but neither really threatened the Prime Minister's position.

Short moved first. On 9 March, she gave a radio interview attacking Blair for being "reckless". She threatened to resign in the event of war (Short 2003). It was an extraordinary move. Cabinet ministers are supposed to observe the principle of collective responsibility. Those who wish to disagree with government policy in public are expected to resign. Blair might have sacked Short for her outburst. In the end, however, he concluded she was simply "being her usual self". He persuaded her to stay on (Blair 2010b, 428). At first observers thought this a sign of a desire on Blair's part to avoid "having her outside the Cabinet as a standard bearer of opposition to the war" (Glover 2003) and of "just how weak his position is" (Routledge 2003b; *The Times* 2003b). Despite her "blatant act of ministerial insubordination" he was worried a sacking might wind up "triggering more resignations", wrote one columnist (Jones 2003a). Others, however, put a more Machiavellian spin on Blair's conduct, pointing out that removing Short might have made her a "martyr" to the anti-war cause (White 2003; Jones 2003c). Blair enjoyed the last laugh. Short resigned anyway, six weeks after the invasion, her reputation shot. She became a "laughing stock" (Wilson 2003), pilloried for being "self-indulgent" (Riddell 2003b), too obsessed with "creating headlines" to focus on her job (Lee-Potter 2003), and "self-serving" (*News of the World* 2003c). Even the *Guardian*'s Polly Toynbee, who sympathised with Short's concerns, criticised her "delusions of sainthood" (Toynbee 2003b). Very few individuals possessed sufficient personal authority to allow them potentially to challenge the Prime Minister. Short's threat to resign, failure to resign and ultimate resignation underlined that she was not one of them.

Cook followed quite a different strategy. Though he made his views publicly known, often through intermediary 'friends', he managed to do so without damaging his reputation. One columnist noted the "pointed contrast" between Cook and Short, with Cook avoiding controversy despite being "at least as dangerous" to Blair (MacIntyre 2003b). At Cabinet on 13 March, Cook strongly hinted he would leave the government in the event Britain went to war (Stothard 2003, 38). On 14 March, he met Alastair Campbell to agree the "rules of engagement" for his resignation. The two men agreed the text of both Cook's resignation letter and the Prime Minister's response (Cook 2003b, 322; Campbell and Stott 2007, 677). Downing Street released the letters on 17 March, and Cook gave a personal statement explaining his decision in the House of Commons later that day. It was an explosive moment, but also one that offered some comfort for his former colleagues in government. Though Cook systematically attacked the official case for war, he made clear also that he had "no sympathy with" critics looking to overthrow Blair (Cook 2003a, col. 726). He could have spoken directly after Blair in the main war debate the following day, and might have done more damage that way. But he pulled his punches. When it came to it, Cook was not willing to sacrifice Blair to prevent war in Iraq.

Cook may not have wanted to challenge Blair's leadership, but he did offer the clearest, most coherent and most damaging attack on the Prime Minister's arguments to appear during the entire pre-war debate. On the supposed threat posed by Iraq, he maintained that Saddam Hussein "probably has no weapons of mass destruction in the commonly understood sense of the term". It was a powerful point coming from an individual with access to raw intelligence reports. In any event, Cook went on, "we cannot base our military strategy on the assumption that Saddam is weak and at the same time justify pre-emptive action on the claim that he is a threat". On international law, he applauded the "heroic efforts" made to reach consensus at the Security Council but insisted "the very intensity of those attempts underlines how important it was to succeed". Echoing the concerns of many who had not sat around the Cabinet table in the months leading up to war, Cook argued that the US went to the UN only to make "the case for war", hence "why any evidence that inspections may be showing progress is greeted in Washington not with satisfaction but with consternation". On whether France was to blame for preventing agreement at the Security Council, Cook pointed out that:

> it is not France alone that wants more time for inspections. Germany wants more time for inspections; Russia wants more time for inspections; indeed, at no time have we signed up even the minimum necessary to carry a second resolution.
>
> (Cook 2003a, cols. 726–728)

Iraq was not really a threat; the invasion was not really legal and the diplomatic impasse was not France's fault. It was a powerful argument, delivered effectively by a master orator. Cook was heard in attentive silence, a stark contrast to the chamber's normal raucous atmosphere. He received a standing ovation from the assembled MPs. Media commentators described the speech as "electrifying" (Waugh and Woolf 2003). Benedict Brogan of the *Telegraph*, a critic of Cook, nevertheless described his speech as a "masterclass in foreign policy analysis" (Brogan 2003). Quentin Letts of the *Daily Mail*, again far from a natural bedfellow for Cook, called it "a dynamite blast of dissent done without self-pity" (Letts 2003a). Only the *Sun* disagreed, dedicating its leading article on 18 March to attacking the "enemy within", meaning both Cook and Short (*Sun* 2003f). Had Cook chosen to attack Blair directly, he might have made some headway. Had he chosen to contradict the Prime Minister's statement during the following day's debate, he might have swayed wavering MPs. But he did not want to bring the government down. For all the quality of his contribution, Cook was not willing to stop Blair at all costs. Alastair Campbell rightly labelled Cook's speech "the high point of the rebellion" (Campbell and Stott 2007, 681). From the moment, he sat down, the die was largely cast.

Politics wins the vote

Though Cook, in particular, challenged the government's case for war head on, in the end political calculation won out over rational deliberation. Labour MPs proved unwilling to risk losing Blair over his Iraq policy. He was willing to sacrifice himself. Blair's efforts to delay the debate, though problematic in normative terms, ensured that by the time MPs actually came to vote, few felt in a position to affect events positively. That Blair was a powerful and persuasive speaker helped, too. But ultimately politics won the Iraq vote. Within the political class the very fact MPs approved the decision to invade granted it extra legitimacy. It is less clear whether the veneer of authority long survived contact with the wider public. Certainly, the mere fact that a vote took place seems to have had little impact on whether people consider the invasion legitimate in hindsight. Parliament does not grant legitimacy. Parliamentary oversight has become, instead, a check on executive power that only really does its job when it prevents the use of force. Even then, politics still seems to matter more than the specific action proposed to deciding how MPs vote (Strong 2015b).

A significant Labour rebellion on 26 February 2003, against a motion endorsing the government's efforts to enforce SCR 1441, presaged the challenge ministers faced on 18 March. Even in this earlier vote, however, Labour MPs held back. Lord Hattersley, Labour's former deputy leader, wrote in the *Observer* that the rebels "meant to make a gesture, not a difference ... to rock the boat, not scuttle it" (Hattersley 2003). The same pressures that helped protect Tony Blair from senior rivals within the Cabinet also helped him with the parliamentary party. In early March, the Campaign Group of left-wing Labour MPs began to agitate for an emergency party conference to replace Blair as leader (Kampfner 2003, 294). In response, a number of junior members of the government withdrew threats to resign in the event of war. Much as they disliked the idea of going to war, they feared losing Blair more (Watt and Perkins 2003). Whatever he might have done to provoke them, they were "not yet ready to ditch him as their leader", as one commentator put it (Jones 2003b). With the very real prospect of military action advancing, the fatalism that undermined public opposition affected MPs, too. The author and Blair confidante Robert Harris argued that "a Labour MP with an ounce of courage" should have voted against the government in February, but that "a Labour MP with an ounce of common sense" should support Blair in the final vote (Harris 2003).

During the final few days immediately preceding the invasion, similar sentiments percolated through the Parliamentary Labour Party. A meeting on 13 March saw extraordinary scenes. Government critics made "passionate" speeches in Blair's favour. "Colleague after colleague" spoke up to defend the leader. Tam Dalyell stormed out in disgust (Sieghart 2003). Most of those present apparently realised that "the most successful Labour prime minister ever" faced genuine peril (Carr-Brown *et al.* 2003). Calling the rebels, a "bunch of deadbeats, crypto-Trots, bearded headbangers, ale-soaked has-beens, failed poly lecturers, and professional whingers", Matthew D'Ancona summed up a belief many of those same individuals ultimately (if reluctantly) shared, which was that "the public did not vote for Labour in 1997 and 2001: it voted for Blair" (D'Ancona 2003). On 15 March a meeting at Downing Street between Blair and Labour Party Chairman John Reid produced an agreement. MPs were sent back to their constituencies for the weekend, where "local Labour leaders, chairmen of constituency parties, may remind them why they were elected in the first place" (Stothard 2003, 52).

Alongside this political calculation sat the more pragmatic realisation that the US was probably going to invade Iraq regardless of what parliament did. Tony Brenton reported from Washington on 6 March that "problems for the UK" might yet slow the timetable for military action down (Brenton 2003). Slowing the timetable was not, however, the same as stopping the war entirely. Despite "grave doubts", former general Patrick Cordingley wrote in the *Daily Mail*, "we have to confront reality" (Cordingley 2003). There was going to be a war. As the *Daily Mail* itself put it, "the die has been cast" (*Daily Mail* 2003). There was no point voting to stop an unstoppable war, warned the *Telegraph*. Such a vote would no longer be an "expression of principle", but rather an "act of defeatism" (*Daily Telegraph* 2003b). Several critics publicly pledged to "bow to the inevitable" (Woods 2003). Others consoled themselves that the invasion would at least "not be in their name" (Keane 2003). It was "too late to be worth damaging the government" (Toynbee 2003b).

Blair did his best to smooth the way for reluctant supporters to swallow their doubts. He could still have avoided the risks of an actual vote. But, Chief Whip Hilary Armstrong recalled, "in the end he just thought it was the right thing to do" (Seldon *et al.* 2007, 159). Opening the debate, he stated that he knew he was making "the most important speech" he had ever made (Blair 2010b, 436). For an orator of his calibre, this was significant. His speech's peroration is worth quoting extensively, to underline the strength of the claims Blair made at the end of 15 months of contentious argument:

> in this dilemma, no choice is perfect, no choice is ideal, but on this decision hangs the fate of many things.... To retreat now, I believe, would put at hazard all that we hold dearest. To turn the United Nations back into a talking shop; to stifle the first steps of progress in the middle east; to leave the Iraqi people to the mercy of events over which we would have relinquished all power to influence for the better; to tell our allies that at the very moment of action, at the very moment when they need our determination, Britain faltered: I will not be party to such a course. This is not the time to falter. This is the time not just for this Government – or, indeed, for this Prime Minister – but for this House to give a lead: to show that we will stand up for what we know to be right; to show that we will confront the tyrannies and dictatorships and terrorists who put our way of life at risk; to show, at the moment of decision, that we have the courage to do the right thing.
>
> (Blair 2003b, cols. 773–774)

Commentators observed that the Prime Minister's performance elevated him above the mass of ordinary parliamentarians. He was "furious with intent, fizzing with conviction, at times imploring, at others raging against the recklessness of inaction", wrote one observer (Letts 2003b). Blair "was roaring, alive, quivering with ferocious tension, like a sub-lieutenant about to lead a battalion into battle", observed another (Hoggart 2003). His speech was "raw, simple, dignified, and bleak: a promise, a plea, and a warning" (MacIntyre 2003). Even long-term critics, like the *Independent* newspaper, described it as "the most persuasive case yet made" (*Independent* 2003d). More supportive press voices concluded that "it was not only the vote that Tony Blair won in the House of Commons last night. It was the argument, too" (*Daily Telegraph* 2003c). No one doubted that "the Prime Minister was in complete command of the chamber" (*The Times* 2003e). So much for deliberation. When the final debate came, Blair set out explicitly, powerfully and successfully to persuade.

It helped that he implicitly threatened to resign, raising the prospect of not only his own retirement, but also a bruising general election. Making policy debates into questions of confidence in government represents a powerful tool that parliamentary leaders wield to coerce their own backbenchers (Huber 1996; Diermeir and Feddersen 1998). Blair deployed the threat expertly, forcing MPs to back him or vote to bring him down. In the end, of the 55 backbench members who spoke in the debate, a majority supported the government, citing French obstructionism and the Prime Minister's leadership as decisive factors. Several, like Geraint Davies, recognized that "the choice tonight is not whether to prevent war ... the choice is either to go in alongside the Americans to topple Saddam Hussein, or to let the Americans go in on their own" (Davies 2003, col. 867). Both a sense of resignation and a fear of one specific resignation affected parliament's conduct. With Conservative support and a notably weak anti-war amendment to the government's motion on the agenda, ministers won the final vote by the comfortable margin of 412 to 149. Within 36 hours the first bombs fell.

Conclusion

The political dimension of the pre-invasion Iraq debate in Britain looked quite different to those around the necessity, legality and morality of war. While the arguments discussed in the previous three chapters concerned questions of principle above all else, the points highlighted in this chapter were much more practical. That is not to say that principle did not matter. Authority remains an important component of legitimacy, and the way public debate discussed the relative power of British and US policymakers, the diplomatic manoeuvres under way at the Security Council and the role of parliament highlighted how central it can be. Part of the problem the Blair government faced, as it sought to make the case for war, stemmed from the widespread belief that the Prime Minister was simply following orders issued to him from Washington. By surrendering his power to decide the right course on their behalf, Blair had in the eyes of critics given up his authority to tell them what to do. That undermined his personal legitimacy, and cast doubt on his actions in turn. At the same time, the political debate revealed the difference between political consent and political legitimacy. Ministers secured sufficient support to enable them to take Britain into the Iraq

War. Despite the attitude adopted by several pro-war newspapers, however, the government never really persuaded the majority of the British public that using force was the right thing to do. Instead, it benefitted from the weakness of its opponents, and, in particular, the fact that most critics proved less willing to risk overthrowing Tony Blair than Blair was to risk being overthrown.

As a domestic political bargaining gambit, Blair's efforts to delay proper discussions of the prospect of Britain going to war in Iraq without explicit UN Security Council approval worked. By the time MPs actually debated this possibility, most felt it was too late for their vote to stop the war. Instead the only option available to Labour Party critics was damaging their most successful leader ever. Despite their broader antipathy to Blair, the Conservatives supported him because they agreed with what he was trying to do. But as a route to securing legitimacy, both political and normative, actively limiting the opportunities you offer your critics for a full and frank debate has considerable shortcomings. In the end, part of what helped Blair win the Iraq vote was an approach that also undermined the invasion's legitimacy.

Underpinning all of this was an inescapable fact. Britain remained clearly the junior partner in the transatlantic partnership. The Blair government repeatedly deferred to the Bush administration over Iraq because it feared the damage that appearing uncooperative might do and because it saw public loyalty as the best route to private influence (Chilcot 2016h, 618). US officials wanted British support, but not at any costs. They were willing to make concessions to ensure allied support, chief among them President Bush's decision to confront Iraq through the UN route. But when it came to it, US military planners would decide the time for war (Chilcot 2016e, 572). That put the Blair government's authority in question, and undermined its claim to legitimacy in turn.

References

Alexander, Andrew. 'Too late to kill Blair's hunger for battle?' *Daily Mail*, 28 February 2003.
Anderson, Bruce. 'A confident America is choosing its next targets.' *Independent*, 10 December 2001.
Anderson, Donald. *Hansard House of Commons Debates*, vol. 372, 14 September 2001.
Anderson, Donald. *Hansard House of Commons Debates*, vol. 401, 11 March 2003.
Aron, Raymond. *Peace and War: A Theory of International Relations*. New Brunswick, NJ: Transaction Publishers, 1966.
Ashley, Jackie. 'Instead of a debate over war, there's been a national shrug.' *Guardian*, 23 December 2002.
Ashley, Jackie, and Ewen MacAskill. 'History will be my judge.' *Guardian*, 1 March 2003.
Bially Mattern, Janice. 'Why "soft power" isn't so soft: representational force and the sociolinguistic construction of attraction in world politics.' *Millennium: Journal of International Studies* 33, no. 3 (2005): 583–612.
Blackman, Oonagh. 'Blair backs Bush plan for attack on Saddam.' *Sunday Mirror*, 7 April 2002.

Blair, Tony. 'Statement on the terrorist attacks in the United States.' 11 September 2001a. http://news.bbc.co.uk/1/hi/uk_politics/1538551.stm (accessed 19 May 2016).
Blair, Tony. *Hansard House of Commons Debates*, vol. 372, 14 September 2001b.
Blair, Tony. *Hansard House of Commons Debates*, vol. 382, 18 March 2002a.
Blair, Tony. 'Interview with NBC.' 4 April 2002b. http://webarchive.nationalarchives.gov.uk/+/www.number10.gov.uk/Page1709 (accessed 27 May 2010).
Blair, Tony. 'Letter to President Bush.' 28 July 2002c. www.iraqinquiry.org.uk/media/243761/2002-07-28-note-blair-to-bush-note-on-iraq.pdf (accessed 15 July 2016).
Blair, Tony. *Hansard House of Commons Debates*, vol. 390, 24 September 2002d.
Blair, Tony. 'Prime Minister's monthly press conference.' 18 February 2003a. http://webarchive.nationalarchives.gov.uk/20061101012618/http://number10.gov.uk/page3006 (accessed 28 June 2016).
Blair, Tony. *Hansard House of Commons Debates*, vol. 401, 18 March 2003b.
Blair, Tony. 'Evidence to the Chilcot Inquiry.' 29 January 2010a. www.iraqinquiry.org.uk/media/229766/2010-01-29-transcript-blair-s1.pdf (accessed 6 August 2016).
Blair, Tony. *A Journey*. London: Hutchinson, 2010b.
Borger, Julian, and Ewen MacAskill. 'US targets Saddam: Pentagon and CIA making plans for war against Iraq this year.' *Guardian*, 14 February 2002.
Brenton, Tony. 'Iraq: UN endgame: cable to the FCO.' 6 March 2003. www.iraqinquiry.org.uk/media/242721/2003-03-06-telegram-294-washington-to-fco-london-iraq-un-endgame.pdf (accessed 17 August 2016).
Brogan, Benedict. 'Final burst of glory for falling star who craves attention.' *Daily Telegraph*, 18 March 2003.
Brummell, David. 'Iraq: note of meeting at No. 10 Downing Street.' 19 December 2002. www.iraqinquiry.org.uk/media/242591/2002-12-19-minute-brummell-ago-note-of-meeting-at-no-10-downing-street-400-pm-19-december-2002.pdf (accessed 17 August 2016).
Buncombe, Andrew. 'Blair praised by US pundits for talking tougher than the President.' *Independent*, 4 October 2001.
Burke, Jason. *The 9/11 Wars*. London: Allen Lane, 2011.
Bush, George W. 'Address to a joint session of Congress and the American people.' 20 September 2001. http://georgewbush-whitehouse.archives.gov/news/releases/2001/09/20010920-8.html (accessed 23 June 2016).
Buzan, Barry, and Ana Gonzalez-Pelaez. 'International community after Iraq.' *International Affairs* 81, no. 1 (2005): 31–52.
Campbell, Alastair, and Richard Stott. *The Blair Years: Extracts from the Alastair Campbell Diaries*. London: Arrow Books, 2007.
Carr, Simon. 'Fools! It's the perfect time to have a leadership contest.' *Independent*, 6 March 2003.
Carr-Brown, Jonathan, Nick Speed, Eben Black, and Tony Allen-Mills. 'The eve of war.' *Sunday Times*, 16 March 2003.
Chilcot, John. *Report of the Iraq Inquiry: Executive Summary*. London: HMSO, 2016a.
Chilcot, John. *Report of the Iraq Inquiry: Volume 1*. London: HMSO, 2016b.
Chilcot, John. *Report of the Iraq Inquiry: Volume 2*. London: HMSO, 2016c.
Chilcot, John. *Report of the Iraq Inquiry: Volume 3*. London: HMSO, 2016d.
Chilcot, John. *Report of the Iraq Inquiry: Volume 6*. London: HMSO, 2016e.
Chirac, Jacques. 'Interview with TF1 and France 2.' 9 March 2003. www.lemonde.fr/international/article/2003/03/11/quelles-que-soient-les-circonstances-la-france-votera-non_312437_3210.html (accessed 17 August 2016).

Clark, David. 'Mr Blair is in a state of confusion over this war.' *Independent*, 18 February 2003.

Clark, Ian. *Legitimacy in International Society.* Oxford: Oxford University Press, 2005.

Clarke, Kenneth. *Hansard House of Commons Debates*, vol. 400, 26 February 2003.

Coates, David, and Joel Krieger. 'The mistake heard round the world; Iraq and the Blair legacy.' In *The Blair Legacy: Politics, Policy, Governance, and Foreign Affairs*, by Terrence Casey, 247–259. Basingstoke: Palgrave Macmillan, 2009.

Cohen, Harry. *Hansard House of Commons Debates*, vol. 380, 14 February 2002.

Cohen, Nick. 'The West goes on bombing, the Taliban keep resisting and the Afghans face a catastrophic famine.' *Observer*, 28 October 2001.

Collins, Patrick. 'People of Britain vote for peace.' *Mail on Sunday*, 16 February 2003.

Cook, Robin. *Hansard House of Commons Debates*, vol. 401, 17 March 2003a.

Cook, Robin. *The Point of Departure.* London: Simon & Schuster, 2003b.

Cordingley, Patrick. 'This bickering is a betrayal of Britain's troops.' *Daily Mail*, 11 March 2003.

Cornwell, Rupert. 'War is almost upon us – but how did it come to this?' *Independent*, 6 March 2003a.

Cornwell, Rupert. 'Diplomatic shambles augurs badly for summit of last resort.' *Independent*, 15 March 2003b.

Cornwell, Rupert. 'Special relationship bound by a military two-step.' *Independent*, 8 October 2001.

Daily Mail. 'Leading article', 6 September 2002a.

Daily Mail. 'Leading article', 13 September 2002b.

Daily Mail. 'Leading article', 17 March 2003.

Daily Telegraph. 'Leading article', 13 October 2001.

Daily Telegraph. 'Leading article', 8 April 2002a.

Daily Telegraph. 'Leading article', 14 March 2003a.

Daily Telegraph. 'Leading article', 18 March 2003b.

Daily Telegraph. 'Leading article', 19 March 2003c.

D'Ancona, Matthew. 'Brown's message to plotters: not in my name.' *Sunday Telegraph*, 16 March 2003.

Davies, Geraint. *Hansard House of Commons Debates*, vol. 401, 18 March 2003.

Dawkins, Richard. 'Why should we in Britain help Bush to get re-elected.' *Independent*, 1 March 2003.

Dejevsky, Mary. 'America's plan to invade Iraq is just a giant bluff.' *Independent*, 31 July 2002.

Diermeir, Daniel, and Timothy Feddersen. 'Cohesion in legislatures and the vote of confidence procedure.' *American Political Science Review* 92, no. 3 (1998): 611–621.

Duncan Smith, Iain. *Hansard House of Commons Debates*, vol. 372, 4 October 2001.

Edmunds, Timothy. 'The defence dilemma in Britain.' *International Affairs* 86, no. 2 (2010): 377–394.

Edmunds, Timothy, Jamie Gaskarth, and Robin Porter. 'Introduction: British foreign policy and the national interest.' *International Affairs* 90, no. 3 (2014): 503–508.

Ehrenberg, John, J. Patrice McSherry, Jose Ramon Sanchez, and Caroleen Marji Sayej. *The Iraq Papers.* Oxford: Oxford University Press, 2010.

Evans, Harold. 'Saddam's pimp.' *Daily Mail*, 15 February 2003.

Fearon, James. 'Domestic political audiences and the escalation of international disputes.' *American Political Science Review* 88, no. 3 (1994): 577–592.

Fearon, James. 'Signaling foreign policy interests: tying hands versus sinking costs.' *Journal of Conflict Resolution* 41, no. 1 (1997): 68–90.
Finkelstein, Daniel. 'Question time briefing.' *The Times*, 11 April 2002.
Finkelstein, Daniel. 'Questions go on but the course is set.' *The Times*, 27 February 2003.
Finnemore, Martha. 'Legitimacy, hypocrisy, and the social structure of unipolarity: why being a unipole isn't all it's cracked up to be.' *World Politics* 61, no. 1 (2009): 58–85.
Foreign and Commonwealth Office. 'The Prime Minister's meeting with President Bush, 5–7 April 2002.' 10 April 2002. www.iraqinquiry.org.uk/media/224443/2002-04-10-telegram-73-fco-london-to-madrid-prime-ministers-meeting-with-president-bush-extract.pdf (accessed 17 August 2016).
Franck, Thomas. 'Legitimacy in the international system.' *American Journal of International Law* 82, no. 4 (1988): 705–759.
Galloway, George. *Hansard House of Commons Debates*, vol. 372, 14 September 2001.
Gamble, Andrew, and Ian Kearns. 'Recasting the special relationship.' In *Progressive Foreign Policy*, by David Held and David Mepham. Cambridge: Polity, 2007.
George, Bruce. *Hansard House of Commons Debates*, vol. 372, 14 September 2001.
Glover, Stephen. 'Will the pound be the ultimate victim of war?' *Daily Mail*, 11 March 2003.
Greenstock, Jeremy. 'Evidence to the Chilcot Inquiry: written statement.' 27 November 2009a. www.iraqinquiry.org.uk/media/242305/2009-11-xx-statement-greenstock.pdf (accessed 17 August 2016).
Greenstock, Jeremy. 'Evidence to the Chilcot Inquiry.' 27 November 2009b. www.iraqinquiry.org.uk/media/94798/2009-11-27-Transcript-Greenstock-S1.pdf (accessed 17 August 2016).
Grice, Andrew. 'Parliament: Commons recall will be announced today.' *Independent*, 12 September 2002.
Grice, Andrew. 'Short prepares to withdraw her threat to resign over Iraq.' *Independent*, 15 March 2003.
Guardian. 'Leading article', 29 November 2001.
Guardian. 'Leading article', 8 April 2002a.
Guardian. 'Leading article', 6 September 2002b.
Guardian. 'Leading article', 27 February 2003a.
Guardian. 'Leading article', 1 March 2003b.
Guardian. 'Leading article', 13 March 2003c.
Guardian. 'Leading article', 15 March 2003d.
Habermas, Jurgen. *The Theory of Communicative Action: Volume 1: Reason and the Rationalisation of Society*. Translated by Thomas McCarthy. London: Heinemann Educational Books Ltd, 1981.
Habermas, Jurgen. *The Structural Transformation of the Public Sphere*. Translated by Thomas Burger. Cambridge: Polity, 1989.
Harris, Robert. 'Despite everything, we must dare to back Blair and this war.' *Daily Telegraph*, 18 March 2003.
Hart, David. 'Narrow war aims will produce only slim pickings.' *The Times*, 12 October 2001.
Hattersley, Roy. 'The days of obedience are over.' *Observer*, 2 March 2003.
Hoggart, Simon. 'PM goes over the top and survives skirmish in no man's land.' *Guardian*, 19 March 2003.
Holmes, John. 'Telegram to David Manning.' 11 March 2003a. www.iraqinquiry.org.uk/media/244116/2003-03-11-telegram-124-paris-to-fco-london-iraq-chiracs-tv-interview-frances-veto.pdf (accessed 18 July 2016).

Holmes, John. 'France: Iraq: memo to Manning and Rycroft.' 13 March 2003b. www.iraqinquiry.org.uk/media/242761/2003-03-13-telegram-127-paris-to-fco-london-france-iraq.pdf (accessed 17 August 2016).

Howard, Anthony. 'War is going to happen, if only to avoid the loss of face involved in re-calling the military mass.' *The Times*, 18 March 2003.

Huber, John. 'The vote of confidence in parliamentary democracies.' *American Political Science Review* 90, no. 2 (1996): 269–282.

Humphrys, John. 'Can you face the pitiless test of global politics?' *Sunday Times*, 23 February 2003.

Hurrell, Andrew. 'Legitimacy and the use of force: can the circle be squared?' *Review of International Studies* 31, no. 1 (2005): 15–32.

Independent. 'Leading article', 17 September 2001.

Independent. 'Leading article', 8 April 2002a.

Independent. 'Leading article', 6 September 2002b.

Independent. 'Leading article', 14 September 2002c.

Independent. 'Leading article', 17 February 2003a.

Independent. 'Leading article', 13 March 2003b.

Independent. 'Leading article', 18 March 2003c.

Independent. 'Leading article', 19 March 2003d.

Independent on Sunday. 'Leading article', 16 March 2003.

Jenkins, Simon. 'Bin Laden's laughter echoes across the West.' *The Times*, 19 March 2003.

Jones, George. 'Blair visit strengthens the "special relationship".' *Daily Telegraph*, 22 September 2001.

Jones, George. 'Clare Short is cast into limbo.' *Daily Telegraph*, 11 March 2003a.

Jones, George. 'Crowded commons sees embattled leader stand his ground.' *Daily Telegraph*, 13 March 2003b.

Jones, George. '"Road map" offers Blair a way out of his troubles.' *Daily Telegraph*, 15 March 2003c.

Joseph, Rosara. *The War Prerogative: History, Reform and Constitutional Design*. Oxford: Oxford University Press, 2013.

Kaarbo, Juliet, and Daniel Kenealy. 'No, prime minister: Explaining the House of Commons' vote on intervention in Syria.' *European Security* 25, no. 1 (2016): 28–48.

Kaletsky, Anatole. 'Oil, intimidation, rage – why we are really at war.' *The Times*, 20 March 2003.

Kampfner, John. *Blair's Wars*. London: Free Press, 2003.

Kavanagh, Trevor. 'Le worm sold out his nation.' *Sun*, 14 March 2003.

Keane, Fergal. 'This is not just the end of Saddam, but the creation of a new world order.' *Independent*, 8 March 2003.

Keetch, Paul. *Hansard House of Commons Debates*, vol. 372, 8 October 2001.

Kennedy-Pipe, Caroline, and Rhiannon Vickers. 'Blowback for Britain?: Blair, Bush, and the war in Iraq.' *Review of International Studies* 33, no. 2 (2007): 205–221.

Kesgin, Baris, and Juliet Kaarbo. 'When and how parliaments influence foreign policy: the case of Turkey's Iraq decision.' *International Studies Perspectives* 11, no. 1 (2010): 19–36.

King, Anthony. 'Modes of executive-legislative rleations: Great Britain, France and West Germany.' *Legislative Studies Quarterly* 1, no. 1 (1976): 11–36.

Krebs, Ronald, and Patrick Thaddeus Jackson. 'Twisting tongues and twisting arms: the power of political rhetoric.' *European Journal of International Relations* 13, no. 1 (2007): 35–66.

Lee-Potter, Linda. 'She's selfish, arrogant and vain but Clare can't fool me.' *Daily Mail*, 12 March 2003.
Letts, Quentin. 'A dynamite blast of dissent done without self-pity.' *Daily Mail*, 18 March 2003a.
Letts, Quentin. 'Another dab-dab and a ladylike parp from Beckett.' *Daily Mail*, 19 March 2003b.
MacIntyre, Ben. 'Blair plays to the gallery but not the heart.' *The Times*, 19 March 2003.
MacIntyre, Donald. 'Ultimately, America will do what America wants to do.' *Independent*, 20 September 2001.
MacIntyre, Donald. 'He may have won the vote, but how will he be judged by history?' *Independent*, 27 February 2003a.
MacIntyre, Donald. 'A second UN resolution is more important than a dissident minister.' *Independent*, 11 March 2003b.
Maddox, Bronwen. 'Missions impossible and unlikely.' *The Times*, 22 September 2001.
Mahon, Alice. *Hansard House of Commons Debates*, vol. 380, 14 February 2002.
Mail on Sunday. 'Leading article', 16 February 2003.
Manning, David. 'Memo to Tony Blair.' 14 March 2002. www.iraqinquiry.org.uk/media/211115/2002-03-14-minute-manning-to-prime-minister-your-trip-to-the-us.pdf (accessed 15 July 2016).
Marfleet, B. Gregory, and Colleen Miller. 'Failure after 1441: Bush and Chirac in the UN Security Council.' *Foreign Policy Analysis* 1, no. 3 (2005): 333–360.
Meyer, Christopher. 'Letter to David Manning.' 24 July 2002a. www.iraqinquiry.org.uk/media/210959/2002-07-24-letter-meyer-to-manning-iraq.pdf#search=meyer (accessed 15 July 2016).
Meyer, Christopher. 'Telegram to David Manning.' 11 October 2002b. www.iraqinquiry.org.uk/media/210455/2002-10-11-telegram-1326-washington-to-fco-london-us-iraq-will-the-president-go-to-war.pdf (accessed 15 July 2016).
Mirror. 'Voice of the Mirror', 5 April 2002a.
Mirror. 'Voice of the Mirror', 8 April 2002b.
Mirror. 'Voice of the Mirror', 15 February 2003a.
Mirror. 'Voice of the Mirror', 17 March 2003b.
Mitzen, Jennifer. 'Reading Habermas in anarchy: multilateral diplomacy and global public spaces.' *American Political Science Review* 99, no. 3 (2005): 401–417.
Morgan, Lord. 'Him and us: the spinners have spun, the plagiarists plagiarised: we are still opposed to Blairs war.' *Guardian*, 1 March 2003.
News of the World. 'Leading article', 23 February 2003a.
News of the World. 'Jacques is pure poison', 16 March 2003b.
News of the World. 'Leading article', 16 March 2003c.
Putnam, Robert. 'Diplomacy and domestic politics: the logic of two-level games.' *International Organization* 42, no. 3 (1988): 427–460.
Raven, Charlotte. 'They said this war would be different…' *Guardian*, 9 October 2001.
Rawnsley, Andrew. 'His greatest gamble.' *Observer*, 4 November 2001.
Rawnsley, Andrew. 'How to deal with the goliath.' *Observer*, 24 February 2002a.
Rawnsley, Andrew. 'Tony Blair's midlife crises.' *Observer*, 29 December 2002b.
Rawnsley, Andrew. 'Journey into the unknown.' *Observer*, 2 March 2003.
Rees-Mogg, William. 'In all honesty, they were still Saddam's useful idiots.' *The Times*, 17 February 2003.
Reus-Smit, Christian. 'Constructivism.' In *Theories of International Relations*, by Scott Burchill and Andrew Linklater, 217–240. Basingstoke: Palgrave Macmillan, 2013.

Richards, Steve. 'A giant and a dwarf can never stand shoulder to shoulder.' *Independent on Sunday*, 28 October 2001.

Richards, Steve. '2003: Good year, bad year.' *Independent on Sunday*, 29 December 2002.

Ricketts, Peter. 'France and Iraq: letter to John Holmes.' 13 March 2003. www.iraqinquiry.org.uk/media/76291/2003-03-13-Letter-Ricketts-to-Holmes-France-And-Iraq.pdf (accessed 17 August 2016).

Riddell, Peter. 'Britain keeps its walk-on part on the world stage.' *The Times*, 22 October 2001.

Riddell, Peter. 'Ministers and MPs are not at risk in Blair's war.' *The Times*, 4 March 2003a.

Riddell, Peter. 'Prime Minister must show he cares for tiresome MPs.' *The Times*, 11 March 2003b.

Robinson, Piers, Peter Goddard, Katy Parry and Craig Murray. 'Testing models of media performance in wartime: UK TV news and the 2003 invasion of Iraq.' *Journal of Communication* 59 (2009): 534–563.

Routledge, Paul. 'Truth or dare time for MPs: nail the PM's lies on Iraq.' *Mirror*, 12 April 2002a.

Routledge, Paul. 'Please sir, can I have some war?' *Mirror*, 19 July 2002b.

Routledge, Paul. 'Will IDS finally croak?' *Mirror*, 28 February 2003a.

Routledge, Paul. 'Short and Blair in deadlock: PM failure to fire her shows he is weak.' *Mirror*, 11 March 2003b.

Rycroft, Matthew. 'French veto: urgent'. 12 March 2003. www.iraqinquiry.org.uk/media/76275/2003-03-12-Email-Rycroft-to-Powell-Manning-Campbell-Pruce-and-Wall-French-Veto-Urgent.pdf (accessed 17 August 2016).

Seldon, Anthony, Peter Snowdon, and Daniel Collings. *Blair Unbound*. London: Simon & Schuster, 2007.

Short, Clare. 'Interview with BBC Parliament.' *BBC Paliament*. (9 March 2003).

Short, Clare. 'Evidence to the Chilcot Inquiry.' 2 February 2010. www.iraqinquiry.org.uk/media/95246/2010-02-02-Transcript-Short-S1.pdf (accessed 17 August 2016).

Sieghart, Mary-Ann. 'How Chirac and the Left saved the PM's skin.' *Times*, 14 March 2003.

Smith, David, and Nick Speed. 'French stance tilts voters towards war.' *Sunday Times*, 16 March 2003.

Smith, Joan. 'The spoils of war.' *Independent on Sunday*, 28 October 2001.

Steven, Stewart. 'IDS can offer nothing, except his resignation.' *Mail on Sunday*, 2 March 2003.

Stothard, Peter. *30 Days: A Month at the Heart of Blair's War*. London: Harper Collins, 2003.

Straw, Jack. 'Iraq: contingency planning: memo to Tony Blair.' 8 July 2002a. www.iraqinquiry.org.uk/media/75915/2002-07-08-Letter-Straw-to-Blair-Iraq-contingency-planning.pdf (accessed 17 August 2016).

Straw, Jack. 'Memo to Tony Blair.' 16 October 2002b. www.iraqinquiry.org.uk/media/210187/2002-10-16-letter-straw-to-prime-minister-iraq-us.pdf (accessed 18 July 2016).

Straw, Jack. 'Foreign Secretary's conversation with the French Foreign Minister.' 13 March 2003a. www.iraqinquiry.org.uk/media/242756/2003-03-13-telegram-53-fco-london-to-paris-iraq-foreign-secretarys-conversation-with-french-foreign-minister.pdf (accessed 17 August 2016).

Straw, Jack. *Hansard House of Commons Debates*, vol. 401, 17 March 2003b.
Straw, Jack. 'Evidence to the Chilcot Inquiry: written statement.' 21 January 2010. www.iraqinquiry.org.uk/media/194013/2010-01-xx-statement-straw-1.pdf (accessed 16 August 2016).
Strong, James. 'Why parliament now decides on war: tracing the growth of the parliamentary prerogative through Syria, Libya and Iraq.' *British Journal of Politics and International Relations* 17, no. 4 (2015a): 604–622.
Strong, James. 'Interpreting the Syria vote: Parliament and British foreign policy.' *International Affairs* 91, no. 5 (2015b): 1123–1139.
Strong, James. 'Two-level games beyond the United States: international indexing in Britain during the wars in Afghanistan, Iraq and Libya.' *Global Society*, forthcoming 2017.
Sun. 'The Sun says', 15 February 2002.
Sun. 'The Sun says', 19 February 2003a.
Sun. 'The Sun says', 6 March 2003b.
Sun. 'The Sun says', 12 March 2003c.
Sun. 'The Sun says', 13 March 2003d.
Sun. 'The Sun says', 14 March 2003e.
Sun. 'The Sun Says', 18 March 2003f.
Sunday Mirror. 'Voice of the Sunday Mirror', 9 March 2003.
Sunday Times. 'Leading article', 23 February 2003a.
Sunday Times. 'Leading article', 16 March 2003b.
The Times. 'Leading article', 15 February 2002a.
The Times. 'Leading article', 29 March 2002b.
The Times. 'Leading article', 8 April 2002c.
The Times. 'Leading article', 6 March 2003a.
The Times. 'Leading article', 11 March 2003b.
The Times. 'Leading article', 14 March 2003c.
The Times. 'Leading article', 18 March 2003d.
The Times. 'Leading article', 19 March 2003e.
Toynbee, Polly. 'Is today the day to say no? (And if not now, when).' *Guardian*, 26 February 2003a.
Toynbee, Polly. 'How this war could end up being Blair's LBJ moment.' *Guardian*, 19 March 2003b.
Voeten, Erik. 'The political origins of the UN Security Council's ability to legitimize the use of force.' *International Organization* 59, no. 4 (2005): 527–557.
Wallace, William. *The Foreign Policy Process in Britain*. London: Royal Institute of International Affairs, 1977.
Wallace, William. 'The collapse of British foreign policy.' *International Affairs* 81, no. 1 (2005): 53–68.
Waterhouse, Keith. 'Requiem for the fall of a sparrow.' *Daily Mail*, 13 March 2003.
Watt, Nicholas, and Anne Perkins. Parliamentary aides split over threat to resign: some private secretaries would stay in post if France used unreasonable veto.' *Guardian*, 12 March 2003.
Waugh, Paul, and Marie Woolf. 'Cook quits Cabinet and urges MPs to oppose invasion.' *Independent*, 18 March 2003.
White, Michael. 'Blair decides against the push – believing Short will jump.' *Guardian*, 11 March 2003.

White, Michael, and Patrick Wintour. 'Threat of war: what Blair needs now: that second UN resolution: diplomacy: PM calculates that another vote will subdue rebels.' *Guardian*, 28 February 2003.

Wilson, Graeme. 'Short's "still reflecting".' *Daily Mail*, 18 March 2003.

Woods, Vicki. 'War will happen anyway, so what does Clare Short think she will achieve?' *Daily Telegraph*, 11 March 2003.

Young, Hugo. 'If Blair persists in speaking for Bush, his voice will get smaller and smaller.' *Guardian*, 18 February 2002.

Part III
Tony Blair's war in Iraq

9 Aftermath

Long before the Chilcot Report demolished the Blair government's case for war, the 2003 invasion of Iraq lacked legitimacy in Britain. As the preceding chapters show, this legitimacy deficit derived from two related failings in the way ministers 'sold' the decision to use force. They failed repeatedly to meet the criteria of truthfulness, openness and flexibility required to secure legitimacy through communicative action. They also failed to make clear, coherent and consistent arguments. They did not convince a sufficient share of British public opinion that overthrowing Saddam Hussein was a necessary, legal and moral act, nor one that they possessed the right authority to decide upon; that the invasion was, in fact, a just war. Though the government won the crucial House of Commons vote, adequate legal cover and reluctant approval from a majority of poll respondents, it never won the argument. Despite exploiting every advantage its privileged position allowed, sacrificing its normative claim to legitimacy in the process, it still failed to persuade the British people that it was right. Worse still, in trying to convince critics to support the invasion, it made commitments it later failed to keep. In claiming that Iraq possessed WMD, that regime change would be good for the Iraqi people or that a full-scale land invasion was a proportionate response to Iraq's failure to meet obligations imposed by the UN Security Council, ministers gave hostages to fortune. Fortune, as this chapter describes, soon put them to the sword.

Understanding the consequences of Britain's decision to go to war requires more than two book chapters. Part III's purpose is narrower. Chapter 9 looks to say something about how the debate over using force against Iraq echoed in the invasion's aftermath. It investigates three key dimensions of the British domestic discourse as it played out in the years after 2003, namely the consequences of strategic failure, the death of Dr David Kelly and the 2005 election campaign. Adopting this focus means bracketing the invasion's most serious consequences: those the Iraqi people felt. Others are better placed and more qualified to comment on these vital matters, and better able to do so at sufficient length.

This chapter looks first at the influence of what Baum and Groeling termed the "elasticity of reality" (Baum and Groeling 2010, 474). It is one thing to make inflated claims to 'sell' a war, but sustaining those claims in the face of contradictory information from the battlefield grows increasingly difficult as time goes on. Though Tony Blair continues to assert his belief that invading Iraq was the right thing to do, even he acknowledges a great deal went wrong (Blair 2016). Chilcot dismissed his claim that the risks of removing Saddam loom large only with hindsight; "we do not believe hindsight is required" (Chilcot 2016b, 83). Britain suffered a strategic defeat in Iraq. Crucially for the invasion's legitimacy, the British public knew it, too.

Second, this chapter considers a defining moment in post-invasion arguments about Iraq's missing WMD. In May 2003, the BBC reported claims allegedly sourced from within the British intelligence community that Downing Street deliberately "sexed up" their advice to sell the case for war through the 'dossier' published in September 2002 (Gilligan 2003). It was an explosive claim, and it caused a public furore. A biological warfare expert at the Ministry of Defence named David Kelly confessed to being the story's source, but denied using the words attributed to him. After days at the centre of a media firestorm and faced with losing his job, Dr Kelly killed himself. The media blamed the government. Blair felt compelled to establish an independent inquiry under Lord Hutton, to try to clear the air. Hutton's report, however, exonerated the government and blamed the BBC. 'Whitewash!', cried the media. If the government did nothing wrong, where were Iraq's supposed WMD? Within months Blair was forced to order a second inquiry, into Britain's intelligence on Iraqi WMD. It, too, failed to calm critics down. In the end, Blair's successor, Gordon Brown, commissioned what became the Chilcot Report. Blair did not expect Chilcot to be the final Iraq inquiry. He thought there would always "be calls for more" (Blair 2010b, 407). In fact, so well-received was the Chilcot Report, Blair's pessimism looks likely to be proven wrong.

Finally, this chapter looks at the 2005 general election campaign. Thanks to the Conservative Party's support for the invasion, the fact that many Labour voters rallied behind their leader's stance and the sheer size of the Blair government's majority it comfortably survived its first post-invasion electoral test. But lingering questions about the public's trust in ministers, and especially in the Prime Minister, undermined the Labour vote. In particular, controversy surrounding Lord Goldsmith's legal advice of 7 March 2003, leaked during the campaign, affected the debate and partially shaped the outcome. Though Goldsmith concluded a "reasonable case" existed for the use of force, his private advice admitted much more nuance than the public statement which was released on the eve of war (Goldsmith 2003). Set against an undercurrent of distrust, the discrepancy between the two documents raised further the salience of doubts about how the Blair government made its case for war.

In terms of its impact on British politics, the public debate over the invasion of Iraq mattered (and matters) above all because it undermined the public's trust in government in general and Tony Blair, in particular. As the House of Commons vote against the use of force in Syria in 2013 showed, Iraq cast lasting doubt over the legitimacy of military intervention. Much of the damage was done during the pre-war debate through 2002 and early 2003. That has implications for how FPA accounts think about the relationship between public opinion,

Reality asserts itself

Many Americans continued to believe long after the invasion of Iraq that the coalition actually uncovered hidden WMD. One study found between 15 and 30 per cent of poll respondents believed as much until well into 2004 (Everts and Isernia 2005, 266). In Britain, the picture looked different. To begin with, the Baghdad regime fell without firing a single chemical shell. That immediately seemed odd. If Iraq was sitting on an arsenal of threatening weapons, it made sense for it to use them. Given that the Joint Intelligence Committee repeatedly assessed that Saddam would resort to WMD if his regime's survival was threatened, the fact he failed to do so naturally raised eyebrows. British ministers continued to expect a significant weapons find well into 2003 (Campbell and Stott 2007, 693, 731). Thanks in part to this belief, but also to a wider failure of imagination, they "underestimated the need for sustained communication of key strategic messages to inform public opinion about the objectives and progress of the military campaign" (Chilcot 2016b, 123). To a degree, they were trapped by how they framed the Iraqi threat before the invasion. Having failed to emphasize the role uncertainty played in their decision-making, British ministers proved unable to accommodate the missing WMD into a coherent narrative about why Britain was fighting in Iraq. The result was a gradual decline in public support for the war. An ICM poll on 23 May 2004 found 44 per cent of respondents agreed the decision to go to war was "justified", compared to 43 per cent who thought it "unjustified". It was the last time a British opinion poll showed more respondents in favour of the war than opposed to it (UK Polling Report 2007). As Figure 9.1 shows, the government's position in opinion polls grew progressively more precarious as the months dragged on.

From an FPA perspective this shift is unsurprising. To begin with, regardless of how persuasive it was (and, as Chapter 5 suggests, it was far from persuasive), the Blair government heavily based its case for war on the claim that Iraq posed a threat to UK national security as a consequence of its development of WMD. Once it became clear that Iraq did not in fact possess and was not developing WMD, this key plank of the pre-invasion argument for the use of force collapsed. Led by elites primed to distrust ministers by the shortcomings of the government's deliberative approach, the British public quickly accepted that Iraq did not pose a threat to Britain after all. "Once it was clear that this particular emperor had had no clothes, not even old ones", one retrospective study concluded, "perceptions of the legitimacy of the action against Iraq, already imbued with significant amounts of scepticism, became critically damaging" (Michalski and Gow 2007, 145). Iraq's missing WMD may not have threatened British security, but they did have a devastating impact on British politics. In the words of the Chilcot Report, their absence "challenged the credibility of the Government and the intelligence community, and the legitimacy of the war" (Chilcot

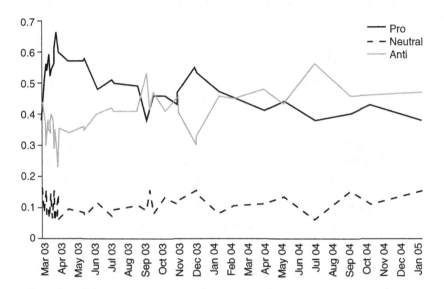

Figure 9.1 Opinion poll data showing approval of the decision to invade Iraq, March 2003–January 2005.

Source: ICM/YouGov.

2016b, 77). Claiming a state is a threat to justify military action usually works. It usually helps shore up public support, and win opponents over. Having to admit subsequently, as the Blair government was forced to do, that an invaded country did not actually pose a threat, inevitably has consequences.

Compounding the damage done by the missing WMD was the fact that Iraq quickly deteriorated into chaos after the invasion. Far more British service personnel (not to mention Iraqi civilians) died in the ensuing years of violence than in the initial invasion. Britain withdrew its forces from Basra in 2009 having failed to meet its original objectives. It was a humiliating defeat, made worse because it reflected both tactical and strategic weakness (Chilcot 2016a). As the chaos and the military casualty rates rose in tandem, critics' complaints about unsubstantiated pre-invasion claims grew more pointed (Daddow 2011, 230). Blair himself recalls the double blow he suffered, as the absence of WMD "seemed to disintegrate the *casus belli*" while the ongoing violence "served to keep the fact and consequence of it constantly in our thoughts" (Blair 2010b, 374). Every military casualty became a news story, and every news story highlighted the missing WMD. It was a perfect storm. Democratic publics do not like casualties. But their dislike is tempered by context. Studies in the US suggest that the concern raised by military fatalities depends on "beliefs about the rightness or wrongness of the war, and beliefs about a war's likely success" (Gelpi *et al.* 2005, 8). Body bags coming home force the public to take the reasons behind a conflict seriously, as indeed do ranks of wounded soldiers, struggling bravely

Aftermath 179

to overcome injuries that would in earlier wars have simply left them dead. Public opinion understands and accepts sacrifice, but it demands that sacrifice be justified.

Similarly, most voters are willing to accept even costly military action as a necessary evil provided they regard it as the best mechanism to stave off even greater anticipated future losses. A counter-trend emerges if arguments about the dangers of inaction turn out to be unfounded (Wolfe 2008, 76). Between the missing WMD and the continued inability of coalition forces to bring stability and security to Iraq, the British public lost faith in the project, as a whole. Increasingly they believed the invasion was wrong and that the continued prosecution of the occupation was unlikely to end successfully. Importantly, these pressures affected even those who believed strongly in the invasion before it took place. Post-invasion developments "do not change the facts about the war, but they can alter how the public recalls and evaluates it", as one study of the Vietnam War concluded (Mueller 1973, 168). It remains logically possible to distinguish between the flawed strategic decision to overthrow Saddam Hussein and its incompetent execution. Though invading Iraq was a bad strategic call, a better-prepared occupation force and a smarter political strategy might have brought stability (Dodge 2010, 2012). Politically, the two are intertwined. Poor implementation casts doubt on decision-making, too.

Blair later complained that:

> the problem with a military campaign to which a large part of opinion – public and most important media – is opposed is that this part continues to have a point to prove ... they approach the conflict with a strong desire, conscious and subconscious, to see it fail.
>
> (Blair 2010b, 441)

That may be true. Blair's critics did occasionally take their desire to attack the government too far. In a notorious incident, the *Mirror* published images of British troops abusing Iraqi detainees later proven to be forgeries. By associating Britain with a narrative already emerging around US forces following the revelations of prisoner maltreatment at Abu Ghraib, these claims did real damage, even when retracted. But Piers Morgan, the *Mirror*'s editor, ultimately resigned over the fake abuse photos incident. Tony Blair neither resigned nor properly apologised for the missing WMD. Indeed, he remains unapologetic. Given an opportunity at the Chilcot Inquiry, he expressed "responsibility but not a regret for removing Saddam", a stance he somehow stuck to in the face of Chilcot's Report (Blair 2010a, 246; 2016). In the process, Blair denied his critics the victory they crave, and sidestepped the opportunity to draw a line under events. Robin Cook thought "the public is mature enough to know that in the real world governments make mistakes", and suggested that the real problems over WMD stemmed from "subsequent attempts to deny that anything was wrong and to cover up any evidence to the contrary" (Cook 2003, 336). Blair did not. He thought:

it was never enough, in today's media, for there to have been a mistake ... it leads to a headline that doesn't satisfy today's craving for scandal ... so the search goes on for a lie, a deception, an act not of error but of malfeasance. And the problem is, if one can't be found, one is contrived or even invented.

(Blair 2010b, 454)

Given what we have seen of Blair's character and conduct during the Iraq debate, these lines seem to make one point clear: he wrote his autobiography himself.

Chilcot found that "the UK Government, including the intelligence community, was reluctant to admit, and to recognise publicly, the mounting evidence that there had been failings in the UK's pre-conflict collection, validation, analysis and presentation of intelligence on Iraq's WMD" (Chilcot 2016d, 605). As Cook pointed out, this reluctance exacerbated the public's distrust. It was bad enough that Britain got it wrong over WMD, and the resulting conflict went badly. Failing to admit promptly that they *had* got things wrong left ministers looking even more dishonest. It ultimately did not matter that the Blair government was genuinely surprised at the Iraq Survey Group's inability to turn up anything to indicate WMD production (Coates and Krieger 2004, 4; Scott and Ambler 2007, 84). The legitimacy of the invasion was already undermined. Even as he left office years later observers still felt it necessary to consider whether the Prime Minister could be trusted (Kennedy-Pipe and Vickers 2007, 212).

It was damaging enough that Iraq lacked WMD. But the Blair government did not begin the Iraq debate unblemished. After six years in office it had a record that critics held against it. Even before the invasion there were doubts about ministers' trustworthiness. Critics rightly doubted Blair's promises during the Iraq debate, especially about the extent to which he was committed to military action from early 2002. Their distrust pre-dated the Iraq debate itself, and lingered after the invasion. Polls found 49 per cent of respondents thought Tony Blair was untrustworthy (Ipsos MORI 2003). Others showed 63 per cent of likely voters thought ministers had not "on balance, been honest" (YouGov 2005). Iraq, in many ways, fitted neatly into a broader narrative, already well-established by 2003, that framed Blair himself, and his government more generally, as dishonest, too beholden to the 'dark arts' of media manipulation and too ready to twist facts to generate supportive headlines. That perception of dishonesty both fuelled and drew strength from arguments about Iraq.

David Kelly

As Dr Kelly was leaving I said to him: what will happen if Iraq is invaded? And his reply was, which I took at the time to be a throwaway remark – he said: I will probably be found dead in the woods.

(Hutton 2004, 101, quoting a British diplomat named Peter Broucher)

Controversy struck the Blair government's case for war in Iraq even before most British people recognized there were no hidden WMD. On 29 May 2003 BBC

Radio 4's flagship *Today* programme broadcast a report by investigative journalist Andrew Gilligan alleging that Downing Street manipulated the intelligence picture presented in the September 'dossier' to make the threat from Iraq appear more serious than it was. At the heart of the issue was the statement, discussed in Chapter 5, that "the Iraqi military are able to deploy chemical and biological weapons within 45 minutes of an order to do so" (British Government 2002, 19). Prompted by presenter John Humphrys, Gilligan reported having:

> been told by one of the senior officials in charge of drawing up that dossier ... that, actually the government probably erm, knew that the forty-five minute figure was wrong, even before it decided to put it in ... Downing Street ... a week before publication, ordered it to be sexed up.
> (Gilligan 2003)

In a subsequent *Mail on Sunday* piece, Gilligan blamed Alastair Campbell for this manipulation. Relations between No. 10 and the BBC were tense already, thanks to what many in government considered the BBC's "one-sided and negative" approach to covering Iraq (Seldon *et al.* 2007, 194). By 2003, everyone knew New Labour hated media criticism. But its response to Gilligan's report took the mutual animosity between Downing Street and journalists to an entirely new level (Robinson *et al.* 2009, 535). Campbell was furious. The BBC was "twisting" the facts, "trying to move the goalposts", and unreasonably refusing to accept even the possibility of an error in the original story. His psychological state was poor by this point. He admitted to Blair in February that he was struggling with stress, probably clinically depressed, and seeking to leave Downing Street (Campbell and Stott 2007, 703, 711, 606). Responding to Gilligan became an obsession. Campbell gave a combative live interview to *Channel 4 News* to argue his side (Channel 4 News 2003). In the process, he violated 'Whelan's law', a term he coined himself at the expense of one of Gordon Brown's former press advisors. Spin doctors must never let themselves become the story. Those who violate this injunction are finished. The time to stand aside had come.

What happened next raised a number of difficult questions about the conduct of both Downing Street and the BBC. To begin with, the BBC stood by Gilligan's report in the face of official denials and a direct complaint from Campbell. BBC executives felt under pressure to fulfil their commitment to neutrality, and felt unable to back down when challenged directly by a government still benefitting from the relative absence of coherent opposition in the pre-invasion period (Hollis 2010, 66–67). Jonathan Powell later even suggested that the fact both BBC Chairman Gavyn Davies and Director-General Greg Dyke had Labour Party connections exacerbated the situation, making them self-conscious and causing them to fight their corner too hard (Powell 2010, 205). Clearly the stakes were high. Before the Iraq Survey Group report emerged in early 2004, the government lacked a coherent explanation of why it was unable to show evidence of Iraqi WMD production. Gilligan's report offered just such a narrative, albeit in a form designed to undermine rather than reinforce ministers' credibility.

Audiences primed to expect perfidy from Downing Street, and increasingly aware that Iraq did in fact lack WMD, received his accusations favourably. For the first time since the invasion, opinion polls recorded a drop in support for war.

On 4 July Dr David Kelly, a relatively junior MoD official, informed his line manager that he had spoken to Gilligan shortly before the *Today* broadcast, and so could conceivably be the journalist's source. Kelly was one of the British government's top biological warfare experts. He served as a UN inspector in Iraq during the 1990s and wrote a history of UNSCOM's efforts that formed part of the September dossier, though (and this later proved crucial) he was not directly involved in the drafting process. Lord Hutton found evidence that he was under consideration for a knighthood in recognition of his work at the time of these events, and had a single lapse in judgement not tarnished his reputation, he might have enjoyed a dignified retirement in due course (Hutton 2004, 5). Though Kelly occasionally briefed journalists (off the record) about areas within his professional competence, he neither sought nor received approval to speak to Gilligan, something he was formally required to do and ordinarily would have done. Crucially, Kelly insisted the comments Gilligan attributed to his source went well beyond the statements he actually made. He waited so long before coming forward because he assumed Gilligan must also have spoken to someone else. Campbell wrote in his diary, with evident glee, that "it would fuck Gilligan if that was his source" (Campbell and Stott 2007, 713). Set alongside the Foreign Affairs Committee's (2003) conclusion the previous day that Downing Street did not influence the dossier improperly, the government seemed likely to recover from Gilligan's initial blow.

Keen to ensure a "clear win" (Campbell and Stott 2007, 714), No. 10 announced that Gilligan's source had come forward, and that he denied making the comments attributed to him. Speculation immediately spiked about the source's identity. Leery of being accused of lying to the press, and thus turning an apparent victory into another PR defeat, Downing Street ordered government press officers not to deny that Kelly was the source, if asked directly. Though not quite tantamount to 'outing' him directly, this decision essentially had the same effect. It highlights, also, how the Blair government's general reticence when it came to publishing information declined once getting that information out in public might benefit its position – the essence of news management, of course. Britain possessed a finite store of WMD experts, a minority of whom ever interacted with the media. Kelly, crucially, was part of that minority. Informed journalists simply called up the MoD press office and reeled off names until they got a hit. On 9 July, an MoD spokesperson confirmed the government believed David Kelly was Gilligan's source. With his name splashed across newspaper front pages, Kelly was summoned the following week to give evidence before the Foreign Affairs Committee. In a gruelling session on a sweltering day during which he frequently struggled to be heard over the background noise of a crowded press gallery, the soft-spoken official repeated what he told his line manager. He spoke to Gilligan without authorisation, but he did not make the statements attributed to him. Although the BBC continued to stick by the original story, not least because Gilligan refused to confirm or deny whether he had another source, the furore might have passed. Other than Campbell, no one in Downing Street really wanted the battle. Then David Kelly killed himself.

Uproar followed. the *Daily Mail* ran the headline "Proud of yourselves?" over pictures of Campbell, Hoon and Blair, alleging that they had driven "a decent, shy civil servant who had been savagely chewed up and spat out by a malign, amoral Downing Street machine" to a "tormented and tragic end" (*Daily Mail* 2003). Anthony Seldon described Kelly's death as "an event that would shake Blair to his core ... one of the most shocking reversals of the premiership" (Seldon *et al.* 2007, 201). Campbell considered resigning immediately, though he was talked out of it. He complained that the media should have asked what exactly an experienced civil servant working with the highest security clearance in a sensitive area during wartime was doing talking to a journalist about secret intelligence, rather than criticizing ministers for asking that question (Campbell and Stott 2007, 723, 727). It was, however, too late for that. Jonathan Powell recalls having "felt physically sick" watching the coverage. Against Powell's instincts, Blair "felt that he had little choice but to set up an inquiry" (Powell 2010, 222). Lord Hutton began work at once.

By the time the Hutton Report appeared in January 2004, Alastair Campbell was no longer in Downing Street. He resigned quietly shortly after giving evidence, fulfilling the ultimate requirement of Whelan's law. Hutton vindicated Campbell entirely, systematically clearing the government of wrongdoing in relation to Dr Kelly's treatment. He complained about "uncertainties" arising from Gilligan's evidence and observed that the journalist presented two different sets of notes purported to be from the same conversation (Hutton 2004, 144–145, 152, 172). Though Downing Street did indeed seek to make the strongest case possible with the dossier, the ultimate responsibility for its contents rested with the Joint Intelligence Committee. No. 10 did not exert undue influence over its contents. Though there were considerable problems with the document, later laid out comprehensively by the Chilcot Report (2016d), Gilligan's core accusation – that the government knowingly inserted false claims into the dossier in the face of objections from the intelligence community – simply was not accurate. Crucially, Hutton confirmed that Kelly was not personally involved in drafting the dossier. Given the BBC had by this point confirmed he was the sole source for the original story, that undermined its position considerably. Hutton was unable to determine what exactly the weapons expert actually said (Hutton 2004, 163). He did note that members of the Defence Intelligence Staff, to whom Kelly had unrestricted and regular access, raised concerns during September 2002 about the phrasing of the '45-minute claim', a point highlighted by Gilligan as having been 'sexed up'. Though MI6 withdrew the intelligence reports underpinning the claim in September 2004 (Chilcot 2016d, 379), it derived from JIC analysis and not from Downing Street. In keeping with established procedures, Chief of Defence Intelligence Air Marshal French considered the DIS concerns and concluded they did not require discussion at the JIC (Chilcot 2016d, 281). Hutton implied, therefore, that Kelly may have told Gilligan about qualms within

DIS about the inclusion of the '45-minute claim', without himself being aware that they were considered and addressed in the proper manner further up the hierarchy (Hutton 2004, 112–126). Gilligan then drew, and broadcast, his own conclusions about the role of Downing Street.

Hutton hit the BBC hard. Whatever the dossier's problems were, Alastair Campbell did not insert the 45-minute claim against the wishes of the intelligence community. Gilligan's report was wrong and, Hutton implied, possibly dishonest. Both Davies and Dyke resigned. Unfortunately for the government, the public trusted the BBC much more than Downing Street. One Ipsos MORI poll found just 14 per cent of respondents thought Alastair Campbell to be reliable, compared to the 59 per cent who trusted the BBC (Ipsos MORI 2003). The *Independent*'s front page focused on a single word, "whitewash". Though insiders continue to complain about the fact, this sceptical attitude stuck (Blair 2010b, 463; Powell 2010, 223; Campbell 2010, 119). Campbell later observed that the media divided into two camps: those who opposed the Iraq war, and the traditionally right-wing publications eager to see a Labour government take a kicking. Both wanted Hutton to rule against the government (Burrell 2013). Powell concluded that "the lesson from Hutton is that, no matter how clean a bill of health a prime minister is given, an inquiry is not going to vindicate them in the eyes of the media and therefore of the people" (Powell 2010, 223). With Hutton having failed to calm public anger, and with President Bush having announced his own inquiry (Chilcot 2016d, 608), Blair followed Hutton's Report by establishing a further investigation into British intelligence on Iraq's WMD under Lord Butler. Again, Butler largely exonerated ministers (and their advisers) of wrongdoing. At the same time, however, he criticised the dossier exercise itself, concluding it conflated intelligence assessment and policy advocacy in a manner that undermined both (Butler 2004, 76–127). Chilcot echoed and expanded upon this concern, observing that:

> the widespread perception that the September 2002 dossier overstated the firmness of the evidence about Iraq's capabilities and intentions in order to influence opinion and "make the case" for action to disarm Iraq has produced a damaging legacy ... undermining trust and confidence in Government statements, particularly those which rely on intelligence which cannot be independently verified.
>
> (Chilcot 2016d, 284)

As Chilcot's conclusion implied, the sorry story of David Kelly underlines both the damage done by shortcomings in the Blair government's communications efforts and the broader atmosphere of distrust surrounding its decision to go to war in Iraq. Gilligan's *Today* broadcast and subsequent *Mail on Sunday* story built upon existing narratives about excessive 'spin' surrounding Blair's Downing Street. His claims found favour in public debate because something clearly was wrong with the government's case for war. Iraq did not have WMD. Even if the specific broadcast proved incorrect, which it did, the fact remained that ministers claimed Iraq posed a threat to Britain, when in reality it did not. Gilligan sowed his seeds of doubt on ready, fertile ground. Dr Kelly's death counted against the government even after it was cleared of having helped facilitate it. There would have been no point killing him. He did not have first-hand knowledge of the dossier's genesis. He could not have known anything worth covering up. At the same time, his decision to end his life in the face of public criticism underlined Blair's relative refusal to accept responsibility.

The 2005 general election

That Iraq did not cost the Blair government the 2005 general election despite the distrust it generated and the questions it raised over ministers' competence is not in fact as surprising as it might at first appear. To begin with, it remains far from clear whether foreign policy influences voting behaviour at all. For every suggestion that "policymakers are held accountable by the electorate if their policies, foreign as well as domestic, fail" (Sobel 2001, 24) there exists an equally categorical counter-claim. Given that the fear of electoral punishment supposedly underpins policymakers' willingness to listen to the public's foreign policy views, this is important (Knecht and Weatherford 2006, 705). Evidence available as early as 2003 suggested that most British voters were more concerned about immigration than about the war (Stothard 2003, 197–198). At the same time, there was no room to be complacent. Blair's ally, Jose Maria Aznar lost the 2004 Spanish election at least partially on the back of public opposition to Spain's involvement in the 'coalition of the willing' (Buzan and Gonzalez-Pelaez 2005, 45). Although President Bush was re-elected later that year, lingering dissatisfaction with his foreign policy stance hampered his campaign (Eichenberg 2005, 28; Gelpi et al. 2007, 151, 158; Karol and Miguel 2007, 633). Public opinion can be fickle, and policymakers generally cannot control what voters choose to care about.

We should be cautious, however, about comparing the circumstances faced by Aznar's Partido Popular with Blair's New Labour, or (in a very different electoral system) with President Bush. To begin with, Aznar faced far greater public opposition to war in Iraq than either Bush or Blair. Polls taken before the invasion showed just 4 per cent of Spanish voters in favour of action without explicit UN support, and only 23 per cent even with the UN fully on board. As Blair put it, 4 per cent "was roughly the number you could get in a poll for people who believed Elvis was alive, so he had a struggle!" (Campbell and Stott 2007, 670). Aznar also had to contend with political rivals, in the shape of PSOE, who actively opposed the decision to use force from the start. Neither Bush nor Blair faced rivals credibly able to claim that they thought military action a mistake prior to March 2003. When both the sitting government and any plausible alternatives support the same policy, it is effectively neutralized as an electoral issue (Leblang and Chan 2003, 387; Hollis 2006, 45; Aldrich et al. 2006, 478; Chan and Safran 2006, 149; Kreps 2010, 199). In situations like that faced by Blair, gaining opposition support represents a win-win outcome. Not only did Conservative votes help limit the impact of rebellions in the Labour Party in early 2003, politicians who offer too much support to their rivals tend also to be punished for it (Colaresi 2004, 556). Iain Duncan Smith lost the confidence of his parliamentary colleagues and resigned as Leader of the Opposition in late 2003. With a (relatively) fresh face at the helm in the shape of Michael Howard, and mounting evidence of both official failings and public disquiet over Iraq, the change created space for the Conservative Party to shift its stance (Adams *et al.* 2004, 590). But it could not change the fact it voted for war in the first place.

Just as the Democrats in the US criticized President Bush for his handling of the invasion, despite mostly having supported the decision, so too the Conservatives seized upon shortcomings in the Blair government's communicative approach to challenge it over Iraq. It may not have been possible to second-guess the Prime Minister's judgement, having supported him at the time, but it was both possible and electorally profitable for the Conservatives to question his probity and competence. This helps explain why the issue of trust became so central. Iain Duncan Smith introduced the refrain, "you can't believe a word he says" into his public portrayals of Blair before the end of 2003 (Kampfner 2003, 336). During the 2005 campaign, Conservative billboards warned of Blair "if he's prepared to lie to take us to war, he's prepared to lie to win an election" (Conservative Party 2005). This was the Party's best line of attack. But doubts about the government's trustworthiness, driven primarily but not exclusively by Iraq, proved insufficient to alter the overall outcome of the vote. An ICM poll conducted for the *Guardian* on 3 May 2005 estimated that just 4 per cent of probable voters considered Iraq likely to sway their decision. By contrast, 21 per cent of respondents mentioned the health service, 15 per cent the economy, 15 per cent education and 13 per cent law and order as the most important issue to them. These were all areas where Labour's approval ratings outstripped those of the Conservatives (ICM Research Limited 2005b). An earlier poll for the *News of the World* found 48 per cent of probable voters thought Iraq to be at least somewhat significant as they tried to decide who to vote for. Again, though, a higher proportion of respondents selected almost all of the other options available. Critically, though 62 per cent of respondents thought Tony Blair was less honest than other politicians, and 57 per cent thought he was untrustworthy, 30 per cent nevertheless thought he made a better prime minister than would his rivals. Only 21 per cent thought the same of Michael Howard (ICM Research Limited 2005a). Trust matters, in other words, as does foreign policy competence. Just not enough to swing an election, at least not as far as the 2005 British election had to be swung.

Ministers even survived a particularly damaging incident relating to Iraq that occurred at the height of the election campaign. On 27 April 2005 *Channel 4 News* published a leaked version of Lord Goldsmith's full legal advice to the Prime Minister, which was previously given such restricted circulation that some Cabinet ministers did not know it existed. In contrast to the published parliamentary answer from Goldsmith, which simply stated the government's position that it possessed sufficient legal authority to invade Iraq without a further SCR, the earlier document admitted the considerable weakness of this stance. Both the media and MPs interpreted the discrepancy between the two versions as further evidence of official perfidy. Critics speculated about Campbell's role – of course, it would be Campbell, the perennial Blairite bogeyman – in pressuring Goldsmith to change his stance. Though Downing Street thought the level of attention paid to the issue was unwarranted (Powell 2010, 195; Blair 2010b, 522), the Goldsmith revelation clearly merited widespread coverage and attracted public interest. There was, as we have seen in Chapter 6, some truth to the accusation that ministers sought to influence the content, timing and form taken by Goldsmith's advice. And the fact it did not reach even the full Cabinet, let alone parliament, looked especially damning.

Labour's post-election voting analysis, also later leaked, identified a big surge of support for the anti-war Liberal Democrats in certain marginal seats during the final week or so before the election. This surge accounted for as much as a quarter of all the seats lost by Labour. It was driven primarily by the controversy over Iraq (Greenberg and Rosner 2005). Given the lateness of the surge, the campaign itself must have had an impact. Either the Conservative Party's efforts to raise the salience of the trust issue, or the media's focus on the Goldsmith leak evidently mattered. It was likely it was a combination of the two. A second internal analysis agreed with the first. It estimated that some 4 per cent of the overall vote swung from Labour to the Liberal Democrats as a direct result of Iraq, and in particular because the Goldsmith leak convinced voters the government had done something wrong (Penn, Schoen & Berland Associates, Inc 2005a). Despite these losses, the election never looked likely to be particularly close. Labour's massive majority cushioned it against losses to the Liberal Democrats, while the Conservatives did not profit from Iraq-related controversies to anything like the same degree. Though Baroness Morgan later recalled finding Blair on his own in the dark, wandering around the garden at his constituency home "muttering things like 'it's all my fault' and 'Iraq'", in the end the government won a reduced but still respectable majority of 66 (Seldon *et al.* 2007, 343–344). Foreign policy can affect electoral behaviour, especially when it raises doubts in voters' minds about more salient aspects of government performance like honesty and competence. But domestic policy matters more, and in 2005 the British electorate preferred a Labour government to the alternatives.

Looking at the detailed breakdown of voter attitudes contained in the leaked Labour analysis throws up some interesting trends, not least because the study gets around some of the shortcomings of survey methods set out in Chapter 2 by explaining actual voter behaviour in retrospect rather than trying to predict prospective behaviour. To begin with, the electorate remained visibly divided over whether invading Iraq was the right thing to do. Of the respondents 47 per cent said it was right that Britain joined the 'coalition of the willing' in 2003, and 47 per cent that it was wrong. Many were concerned by Tony Blair's handling of the post-invasion chaos, with a slim plurality of 42 per cent thinking the situation in Iraq was getting worse compared to 38 per cent who thought it was getting better. There was some positive news for ministers. A majority of respondents, some 55 per cent, thought the Iraqi people were glad to be rid of Saddam Hussein, compared to just 22 per cent who thought Iraq would rather have been left alone. Of the respondents, 76 per cent agreed that the Iraqis deserved British support in rebuilding their country. There were 70 per cent who accepted the official narrative that 'terrorists', rather than disaffected 'ordinary' Iraqis, were causing the continued instability, and believed Britain had a duty to resist. It was agreed by 68 per cent that invading Iraq showed rogue leaders the dangers of violating international norms and international law, while 60 per cent thought it proved the international community possessed sufficient resolve to tackle rogue states. The percentage that believed Britain should be proud of its part in bringing democracy to Iraq was 69 per cent and 64 per cent believed that British troops were fighting *al-Qaeda* in Iraq in order to avoid fighting it at home. Overall, a comfortable 67 per cent believed Britain should "stay the course" (Penn, Schoen & Berland Associates, Inc 2005a).

Ministers fared less well when voters talked about the pre-invasion debate. Crucially, some 50 per cent of poll respondents thought "the political campaign provided plenty of debate about the war and whether the country was misled or not, and we should now just get on with the business of calming and rebuilding Iraq". On one level, this was a helpful figure for the government, suggesting that even though the media and the political elite wanted to rerun the pre-invasion debate constantly, there was decreasing appetite amongst voters as a whole. On another, however, this result highlighted a problem. By focusing on "whether the country was misled or not" the question both echoed and reinforced a dynamic of the post-invasion debate that counted heavily against the government. Even the Labour Party's own private polling focused on the pre-invasion communication of the decision to go to war at least as much as on its implementation, and admitted that many people thought ministers lied to take Britain to war. Though some respondents seemed reasonably supportive of Britain's continued presence in Iraq, 60 per cent agreed with the statement that "the issue is not whether we were right to go to Iraq or not. The issue is that the people and the Parliament were lied to about the reasons for going". Some 53 per cent thought the invasion was illegal, 59 per cent believed that it turned the Muslim world against the West, and 47 per cent held the view that Saddam Hussein was never a real threat to the region and so "we had no real reason to go in". In other words, though the chaos, violence and British casualties that followed the invasion did damage public support for both the Blair government and its decision to go to war in Iraq, the real driver of later dissatisfaction was concern about the content of the pre-invasion public debate, and related doubts about the war's legitimacy. Though voters recognized that things were not going exactly to plan in Iraq, they remained willing (in 2005) to give British forces time to turn things around. They were unhappy because they believed the government lied in making the case for war. Rhetoric matters.

An additional point of detail worth reflecting upon here emerges from the way the analysis breaks down attitudes according to which party respondents voted for in 2005. At the time of the invasion, Conservative voters backed the use

Aftermath 189

of force, while Labour voters were more ambivalent. By 2005 these roles were reversed. Some 63 per cent of Labour voters maintained that Britain was right to take military action against Saddam Hussein, compared to just 38 per cent of Conservatives and 33 per cent of Liberal Democrats who agreed. The 54 per cent of voters who disapproved of Tony Blair's handling of the overall conflict included 24 per cent of Labour supporters, 73 per cent of Conservatives and 75 per cent of Liberal Democrats. The 54 per cent who did not trust Blair to handle Iraq policy in the future included just 15 per cent of Labour voters, compared to 84 per cent of Conservatives and 77 per cent of Liberal Democrats. Despite the Conservative Party's initial support for the decision to go to war, by 2005 its supporters held wildly different views about Iraq compared to Labour voters.

What is particularly interesting about these figures from an FPA perspective is the unresolved question of whether party identification drove poll responses or established attitudes on Iraq drove party choice. It may be the case that individuals who supported the conduct of the war voted Labour because the Labour government was conducting the war, while those who opposed it voted Conservative or Liberal Democrat instead. It may equally be the case that voters chose among the parties for reasons unrelated to Iraq, as the figures on issue salience discussed earlier suggest, and then used party identification as a heuristic approach to answer questions on the war. As Mueller put it, "many people use their party identification as a shortcut method for arriving at a position on an issue" (Mueller 1973, 116). It is possible that voters who chose Labour because they trusted it on the health service or the economy then responded more positively to questions about Iraq simply because invading Iraq was a Labour policy and Labour ministers were in charge of making it work. Those questions that asked respondents to make prospective judgements were especially likely to illustrate this effect, since voters were in effect being asked to consider whether or not their (only recently made) choice for prime minister was the right one. Just as party politics forms an intervening variable between public attitudes and policymaking behaviour, so too can it shape how policy outcomes feed back into public debate (Shapiro and Jacobs 2000, 228; Sobel 2001, 23–24; Ramsay 2004, 460; Schuster and Maier 2006, 223; Kreps 2010, 199). Blair's domestic popularity mitigated the political cost of failure in Iraq.

One final contrast is worth noting between the Blair government's electoral prospects in 2005 and Aznar's in 2004. On 10 February 2003, the Joint Intelligence Committee reiterated earlier warnings that "Al Qaida and associated networks would remain the greatest terrorist threat to the UK and its activity would increase at the onset of any military action against Iraq" (Chilcot 2016c, 212). In other words, the advice given to the British government before the invasion of Iraq was that military action was likely to exacerbate rather than reduce the existing terrorist threat. This advice proved prescient in both Britain and Spain. Both suffered large-scale *al-Qaeda*-inspired terror attacks directly linked by the perpetrators to the presence of their troops in Iraq. Crucially, however, the Spanish attacks took place three days before the 2004 election. Ten near-simultaneous explosions took place on four packed commuter trains entering the Spanish capital Madrid on 11 March 2004, killing 192 and wounding nearly 2,000. Mass street protests and an electoral victory for the anti-war PSOE followed. Spain withdrew its troops from Iraq shortly afterwards, though there is no consensus amongst terrorism scholars on whether this was solely a consequence of the bombings (Rose *et al.* 2007).

Britain suffered a similar attack, but not until two months after Blair's re-election. On 7 July 2005 four British men carried out suicide bombings on the London transport network, killing 52 people as well as themselves. *Al-Jazeera* subsequently broadcast video messages recorded prior to the attacks by Mohamed Siddique Khan, from Leeds, and Shehzad Tanweer, from Bradford. Khan, who spoke chillingly in a broad Yorkshire accent, justifying his action by telling the British people, "your democratically-elected governments continuously perpetrate atrocities against my people all over the world. And your support of them makes you directly responsible" (BBC News 2005). Tanweer linked the attacks more explicitly to the presence of British troops in the Middle East, declaring that "what you have witnessed now is only the beginning of a string of attacks that will continue and become stronger until you pull your forces out of Afghanistan and Iraq" (BBC News 2006). Blair later reflected on the challenge these claims posed, noting:

> it's a nightmare of an argument to deal with because, on one level, if you don't fight these people it's possible you don't feature so much on their hate list ... [but] if you give even a sliver of credence to the argument, then suddenly it's our fault, not theirs.
>
> (Blair 2010b, 570)

Further survey research found more respondents (38 per cent) blamed the attacks on "the hatred of certain Islamist groups for the West" than on British foreign policy (30 per cent). Ultimately, 68 per cent agreed that "if we let these attacks force us out of Iraq, it will send the wrong message to the terrorists", while the proportion who thought invading Iraq was the wrong thing to do temporarily fell from 47 per cent to 42 per cent (Penn, Schoen & Berland Associates, Inc 2005b). It is impossible to say for certain what impact the London bombings might have had on the 2005 election had they occurred immediately before rather than shortly after the vote took place. These figures suggest that voters might have rallied to the government, not least because unlike in Spain there was no easy anti-war choice on the ballot.

Conclusion

Britain's involvement in the 2003 invasion of Iraq lacked both political and normative legitimacy thanks to shortcomings in how the Blair government made its case for war. Events after the fighting started exacerbated this initial deficit, and ensured the pre-invasion debate mattered in the post-invasion period. Missing WMD and leaked legal advice cast doubt on ministers' honesty, and highlighted their unwillingness to allow an open public debate. Chaos on the ground and terrorism at home raised substantive questions about whether the war was actually a good idea, as well as more procedural issues with official arguments. David Kelly's death and the first major public inquiries into what went wrong underlined existing public concerns over official 'spin'. Though Labour won the 2005 election, it lost over 100 parliamentary seats. It survived in office thanks to the massive size of its 2001 victory, and to the fact that voters still trusted it more on domestic matters than its Conservative rivals. That the Conservatives supported the invasion of Iraq appears not to have hurt their prospects. With a new leader in place and a new narrative based on official perfidy and incompetence, they were able to damage the government's support. Only the overtly anti-war Liberal Democrats actually seem to have won seats from Labour because of Iraq, however, and the numbers involved were small.

What we learn from looking at the aftermath of the decision to go to war in Iraq is the way the government's conduct in the pre-invasion public debate continued to matter for years afterwards. Its failure to meet the standards required for true communicative action damaged its normative position, but also fuelled public concerns about its honesty that affected judgements beyond the narrow foreign policy arena. Its reliance on flawed or exaggerated arguments, especially about the necessity and legality of war, led many voters to reconsider their 2003 stance on whether invading Iraq was the right thing to do. Iraq was not developing WMD, and the legal case was "far from satisfactory" (Chilcot 2016b, 62). Both became clear in the initial aftermath. They mattered so much because the government chose to make them matter, but also because of how the post-invasion debate played out. The interactions discussed throughout this book laid the groundwork for later controversies, making it possible for Britain to wind up fighting an illegitimate war. What happened next depended on the controversies that followed in the invasion's aftermath.

References

Adams, James, Michael Clark, Lawrence Ezrow, and Garrett Glasgow. 'Understanding change and stability in party ideologies: do parties respond to public opinion or to past election results?' *British Journal of Political Science* 34 (2004): 589–610.

Aldrich, John, Christopher Gelpi, Peter Feaver, Jason Reifler, and Kristin Thomson Sharp. 'Foreign policy and the electoral connection.' *Annual Review of Political Science* 9 (2006): 477–502.

Baum, Matthew, and Tim Groeling. 'Reality asserts itself: Public opinion on Iraq and the elasticity of reality.' *International Organization* 64 (2010): 443–479.

BBC News. 'London bomber: Text in full.' 1 September 2005. http://news.bbc.co.uk/1/hi/uk/4206800.stm (accessed 20 July 2016).

BBC News. 'Video of 7 July bomber released.' 6 July 2006. http://news.bbc.co.uk/1/hi/uk/5154714.stm (accessed 20 July 2016).

Blair, Tony. 'Evidence to the Chilcot Inquiry.' 29 January 2010a. www.iraqinquiry.org.uk/media/229766/2010-01-29-transcript-blair-s1.pdf (accessed 6 August 2016).

Blair, Tony. *A Journey*. London: Hutchinson, 2010b.

Blair, Tony. 'Statement on the Chilcot Report.' 6 July 2016. www.tonyblairoffice.org/news/entry/statement-from-tony-blair-on-chilcot-report/ (accessed 19 July 2016).
British Government. *Iraq's Weapons of Mass Destruction: The Assessment of the British Government.* London: HMSO, 2002.
Burrell, Ian. 'Hutton Inquiry: Alastair Campbell, Andrew Gilligan and Greg Dyke look back ten years on.' *Independent*, 26 April 2013.
Butler, Lord. *The Butler Report.* London: HMSO, 2004.
Buzan, Barry, and Ana Gonzalez-Pelaez. 'International community after Iraq.' *International Affairs* 81, no. 1 (2005): 31–52.
Campbell, Alastair. 'Evidence to the Chilcot Inquiry, morning session.' 12 January 2010. www.iraqinquiry.org.uk/media/95142/2010-01-12-Transcript-Campbell-S1-am.pdf (accessed 6 August 2016).
Campbell, Alastair, and Richard Stott. *The Blair Years: Extracts from the Alastair Campbell Diaries.* London: Arrow Books, 2007.
Chan, Steve, and William Safran. 'Public opinion as a constraint against war: democracies' responses to Operation Iraqi Freedom.' *Foreign Policy Analysis* 2, no. 2 (2006): 137–156.
Channel 4 News. 'Jon Snow interviews Alastair Campbell.' 27 June 2003. www.youtube.com/watch?v=GBWE7QzADe8 (accessed 19 July 2016).
Chilcot, John. 'Statement by Sir John Chilcot.' 6 July 2016a. www.iraqinquiry.org.uk/media/247010/2016-09-06-sir-john-chilcots-public-statement.pdf (accessed 15 July 2016).
Chilcot, John. *Report of the Iraq Inquiry: Executive Summary.* London: HMSO, 2016b.
Chilcot, John. *Report of the Iraq Inquiry: Volume 3.* London: HMSO, 2016c.
Chilcot, John. *Report of the Iraq Inquiry: Volume 4.* London: HMSO, 2016d.
Coates, David, and Joel Krieger. *Blair's War.* Cambridge: Polity, 2004.
Colaresi, Michael. 'When doves cry: International rivalry, unreciprocated cooperation, and leadership turnover.' *American Journal of Political Science* 48, no. 3 (2004): 555–570.
Conservative Party. 'Election billboard.' 2005. www.theage.com.au/ffximage/2005/04/27/28TORIES_wideweb__430x213.jpg (accessed 19 July 2016).
Cook, Robin. *The Point of Departure.* London: Simon & Schuster, 2003.
Daddow, Oliver. 'Conclusion.' In *British Foreign Policy: The New Labour Years*, by Oliver Daddow and Jamie Gaskarth, 221–235. Basingstoke: Palgrave Macmillan, 2011.
Daily Mail. 'Proud of yourselves?' 19 July 2003.
Dodge, Toby. 'The ideological roots of failure: the application of kinetic neo-liberalism to Iraq.' *International Affairs* 86, no. 6 (2010): 1269–1286.
Dodge, Toby. 'Enemy images, coercive socio-engineering and civil war in Iraq.' *International Peacekeeping* 19, no. 4 (2012): 461–477.
Eichenberg, Richard. 'Victory has many friends: US public opinion and the use of military force 1981–2005.' *International Security* 30, no. 1 (2005): 140–177.
Everts, Philip, and Pierangelo Isernia. 'The polls – trends: the war in Iraq.' *Public Opinion Quarterly* 69, no. 2 (2005): 264–323.
Foreign Affairs Committee. *The Decision to go to War in Iraq.* London: HMSO, 2003.
Gelpi, Christopher, Jason Reifler and Peter Feaver. 'Success matters: casualty sensitivity and the war in Iraq.' *International Security* 30, no. 3 (2005): 7–46.
Gelpi, Christopher, Jason Reifler and Peter Feaver. 'Iraq the vote: retrospective and prospective judgements on candidate choice and casualty tolerance.' *Political Behavior* 29 (2007): 151–174.
Gilligan, Andrew. *Today.* London: BBC Radio 4, 29 May 2003.

Goldsmith, Lord. 'Iraq: interpretation of Resolution 1441.' 12 February 2003. www.iraqinquiry.org.uk/media/76187/2003-02-12-Paper-Attorney-General-Iraq-Interpretation-Of-Resolution-1441.pdf (accessed 17 August 2016).

Greenberg, Stan, and Jeremy Rosner. 'Looking at the 2005 vote and Labour's diminished standing.' 16 May 2005. http://s.telegraph.co.uk/graphics/viewer.html?doc=202570-doc4 (accessed 19 July 2016).

Hollis, Rosemary. 'Fateful decision, divided nation.' In *The Iraq War: Causes and Consequences*, by Rick Fawn and Raymond Hinnebusch, 37–47. London: Lynne Reinner, 2006.

Hollis, Rosemary. *Britain and the Middle East in the 9/11 Era.* London: Chatham House, 2010.

Hutton, Lord. *The Hutton Report.* London: HMSO, 2004.

ICM Research Limited. 'News of the World election issues survey.' London: ICM Research Limited, 10 March 2005a.

ICM Research Limited. 'Guardian opinion poll.' London, 3 May 2005b.

Ipsos MORI. 'Iraq opinion poll.' 27 July 2003.

Kampfner, John. *Blair's Wars.* London: Free Press, 2003.

Karol, David, and Edward Miguel. 'The electoral cost of war: Iraq casualties and the 2004 US presidential election.' *The Journal of Politics* 69, no. 3 (2007): 633–648.

Kennedy-Pipe, Caroline, and Rhiannon Vickers. 'Blowback for Britain?: Blair, Bush, and the war in Iraq.' *Review of International Studies* 33, no. 2 (2007): 205–221.

Knecht, Thomas, and Stephen Weatherford. 'Public opinion and foreign policy: the stages of presidential decision making.' *International Studies Quarterly* 50 (2006): 705–727.

Kreps, Sarah. 'Elite consensus as a determinant of alliance cohesion: why public opinion hardly matters for NATO-led operations in Afghanistan.' *Foreign Policy Analysis* 6 (2010): 191–215.

Leblang, David, and Steve Chan. 'Explaining wars fought by established democracies: Do institutional constraints matter?' *Political Research Quarterly* 56, no. 4 (2003): 385–400.

Michalski, Milena, and James Gow. *War, Image and Legitimacy: Viewing Contemporary Conflict.* Abingdon: Routledge, 2007.

Mueller, John. *War, Presidents and Public Opinion.* New York: Wiley, 1973.

Penn, Schoen & Berland Associates, Inc. 'Survey of likely voters and strategy discussion.' 8 June 2005a. http://s.telegraph.co.uk/graphics/viewer.html?doc=202568-doc2 (accessed 19 July 2016).

Penn, Schoen & Berland Associates, Inc. 'Survey of likely voters and strategy discussion.' 13 July 2005b. http://s.telegraph.co.uk/graphics/viewer.html?doc=202608-doc1 (accessed 20 July 2016).

Powell, Jonathan. *The New Machiavelli: How to Wield Power in the Modern World.* London: The Bodley Head, 2010b.

Ramsay, Kristopher. 'Politics at the water's edge: crisis bargaining and electoral competition.' *Journal of Conflict Resolution* 48, no. 4 (2004): 459–486.

Robinson, Piers, Peter Goddard, Katy Parry and Craig Murray. 'Testing models of media performance in wartime: UK TV News and the 2003 invasion of Iraq.' *Journal of Communication* 59 (2009): 534–563.

Rose, Wiliam, Rysia Murphy and Max Abrahms. 'Does terrorism ever work? The 2004 Madrid train bombings.' *International Security* 32, no. 1 (2007): 185–192.

Schuster, Jurgen, and Herbert Maier. 'The rift: explaining Europe's divergent Iraq policies in the run-up of the American-led war on Iraq.' *Foreign Policy Analysis* 2, no. 3 (2006): 223–244.

Scott, Shirley, and Olivia Ambler. 'Does legality really matter? Accounting for the decline in US foreign policy legitimacy following the 2003 invasion of Iraq.' *European Journal of International Relations* 13, no. 1 (2007): 67–87.

Seldon, Anthony, Peter Snowdon and Daniel Collings. *Blair Unbound*. London: Simon & Schuster, 2007.

Shapiro, Robert, and Lawrence Jacobs. 'Who leads and who follows? US presidents, public opinion, and foreign policy.' In *Decision Making in a Glass House: Mass Media, Public Opinion, and American and European Foreign Policy in the 21st Century*, by Brigitte Nacos, Robert Shapiro and Pierangelo Isernia, 223–245. Lanham, Maryland: Rowman & Littlefield, 2000.

Sobel, Richard. *The Impact of Public Opinion on US Foreign Policy Since Vietnam: Constraining the Colossus*. New York: Oxford University Press, 2001.

Stothard, Peter. *30 Days: A Month at the Heart of Blair's War*. London: HarperCollins, 2003.

UK Polling Report. 'Iraq.' 2007. http://ukpollingreport.co.uk/iraq (accessed 19 July 2016).

Wolfe, Wotjek. *Winning the War of Words: Selling the War on Terror from Afghanistan to Iraq*. Westport, CT: Praeger Security International, 2008.

YouGov. 'Current political issues poll.' London: YouGov, 29 March 2005.

10 Implications

This chapter identifies wider implications emerging from the preceding analysis. It offers a combination of specific empirical insights and broader conceptual suggestions. At an empirical level, this study's first conclusion seems inescapable. The Blair government was the author of its own misfortune in Iraq. The way ministers and officials engaged with the pre-invasion public debate made possible, even likely, the legitimacy deficit that subsequently surrounded their decision to go to war. Both the specific arguments they made and the manner in which they made them contributed to this failure. Official communications downplayed weaknesses in the government's evidence base. Ministers worked hard to avoid debating policy developments. Only Goldsmith showed any flexibility in the face of disagreement, and his change of heart only harmed the war's reputation, not least because the public only found out about it two years later. Having failed to meet the criteria for communicative action – truthfulness, openness and flexibility – the government struggled both to win audiences over and to claim normative legitimacy for its decision to go to war.

The study's second implication arises at a more conceptual level. Adopting a holistic approach to the relationship between public opinion and foreign policy works. It gets us around the ontological and epistemological shortcomings of a purely survey-based approach. It underlines the distinction between the direction and the intensity of opinions, adds an additional qualitative layer of insight and nuance to traditional FPA accounts and better reflects what policymakers actually do. It allows us to appreciate the iterative relationship between what public actors say and think and how policymakers respond, and to identify how important public communication efforts can be for substantive decision-making. If governments want to influence public attitudes, they have to shape the claims they make to fit what public actors want to hear. That in turn creates indirect feedback between what the public wants and substantive policymaking.

Finally, the study's third implication involves adding a constructivist twist to more traditional FPA theories of how the interaction between domestic and international political pressures can affect decision-making. In keeping with Robert Putnam's 'two-level game' theory, it shows the Blair government struggling to reconcile different demands arising from the two arenas. Moving slightly away from Putnam's rational choice epistemology while maintaining his underlying logic, it frames the 'game' in discursive terms. British promises to work through the UN reassured domestic critics but annoyed Bush administration hawks. Tony Blair's unequivocal support for the US approach won him access to and some influence over White House decision-making, but saw him attacked as a presidential 'poodle' at home. Foreign policy legitimacy emerges from domestic public debate. Domestic public debate both shapes and is shaped by international diplomacy. How governments seek to 'sell' policy decisions affects how legitimate those decisions are. To really understand this process, however, we have to appreciate both its material underpinnings, and the crucial international dimension. International pressures limit the domestic-level claims decision-makers can sustain, while domestic-level rhetoric can constrain substantive action abroad. That was the situation the Blair government faced, and the test it failed to pass.

Selling the Iraq war

The Blair government was the author of its own misfortune in Iraq. The way it presented the decision to go to war generated the legitimacy deficit that subsequently surrounded it. Ministers and officials said things that were untrue, dishonest or simply incorrect. Sometimes their claims were inconsistent. Tony Blair never addressed, let alone resolved, the clash between his commitment to international law and his cosmopolitan understanding of international morality. As Robin Cook pointed out, it made no sense to invade Iraq because it posed a threat while assuming it was too weak to resist. Blair warned that inaction would leave the Iraqi people suffering under Saddam, and promised to leave them suffering provided Saddam stopped threatening the West. Government spokesmen repeatedly insisted 'no decisions have been taken' in the face of questions about Iraq. They refused to engage with critics looking to debate hypotheticals. That was damaging enough, given that communicative action requires every interested actor be allowed to participate in a policy deliberation. What made matters worse was the fact that key decisions clearly *had* already been taken. British troops were in Kuwait. Tony Blair was committed to military action. Washington expected Britain's support. Commentators saw military preparations under way. They correctly guessed that Blair was making promises to Bush in private. They concluded they were being lied to. That undermined public support.

It is difficult to persuade sceptical audiences with arguments that fail on their own terms. Even without the later controversies discussed in Chapter 9, the inconsistencies and inaccuracies within the Blair government's case for war would have been problematic in terms of longer-term public approval, and so the invasion's political legitimacy. A more substantive conceptual failure underlay these deficiencies. The Blair government claimed it sought an open public deliberation around the prospect of military action against Saddam Hussein, one built on communicative action. It did not. Instead it deployed its considerable advantages in terms of information and institutional authority in a concerted effort to persuade. In Habermasian terms, legitimacy derives not only from consensus, but from consensus secured in the right way, through communicative action rather than strategic persuasion. Though persuasion can generate consensus, a consensus that is achieved strategically lacks normative force.

Truthfulness

The Blair government's "perceived record of distortion and manipulation" ensured it faced an uphill task trying to gain public confidence as it made its case for war in Iraq (Baum and Groeling 2010a, 475; Chandler 2003, 299; Heffernan 2006, 588). New Labour did not invent 'spin' (McNair 2000, 123). But it was, by 2003, inextricably linked in the public imagination with aggressive news management. After years in which a hostile right-leaning media relentlessly targeted the Labour Party, Tony Blair came to power determined to make changes. He appointed Alastair Campbell to run a professional, centralized communications operation (Moloney 2000, 127). He told Lord Leveson's Inquiry into British media ethics that it would be an "act of insanity" for any British political leader not to appoint a "world-class media head" (Blair 2012, 9). Blair was far from the first foreign policy decision-maker to identify a link between short-term headlines and long-term political and policy success (Knecht and Weatherford 2006, 710). US officials of a certain vintage regularly blame media criticism for their country's defeat in Vietnam, though this perception does not necessarily hold up under scrutiny and Britain experienced Vietnam differently (Mueller 1973; Hallin 1986, 211; Taylor 1992, 270). FPA accounts often frame news management as illegitimate "manipulation" (Page and Shapiro 1992, 283, 355; Jacobs 1992, 199; Nincic 1992, 17; Kaufmann 2004, 7–8). In principle, however, it is possible for governments to present the case for a given course of action without resorting to dishonesty (McNair 2000, 127; Louw 2005, 143; Gaber 2007, 225).

As the Chilcot Report made clear, the Blair government systematically suppressed shortcomings in the evidence supporting its case for war. SIS downplayed doubts about key sources that informed the WMD dossier. It failed to share its internal concerns until after the invasion. Chief of Defence Intelligence French looked at but did not act on qualms within the Defence Intelligence Staff about the dossier that David Kelly later apparently shared with Andrew Gilligan. The Joint Intelligence Committee offered assessments of Iraq's WMD capabilities that extrapolated from past Iraqi behaviour to an unacknowledged degree. It signed off on public statements issued with its blessing or in its name that went beyond the assessments it made. Ministers, principally Blair and Straw, then described those statements in terms that exaggerated their underlying certainty and downplayed important caveats, not least about the lack of direct information Britain possessed about developments in Iraq. This was dishonest, and deliberate. Ministers leveraged the information advantage that all governments enjoy when matters of foreign policy and secret intelligence are concerned to coerce critics towards supporting a decision to use force. As Chapter 4 makes clear, this sort of 'Foucauldian', power-driven approach can 'work' in political terms, generating a consensus around the idea that a particular policy is the right thing to do. It is normatively problematic because it does not come close to 'Habermasian' ideals. It may be unrealistic to expect policymakers, who often win power thanks to superior political judgment and who naturally trust their own abilities, to give up the position of strength they hold compared to other participants in public debate. But the Blair government worked especially hard to maximize its information advantage in a manner that demonstrated its lack of interest in an honest debate. When it subsequently transpired that Iraq did not in fact pose a threat to Britain, and that the legal grounds for action were in doubt, the resulting fallout undermined the invasion's fragile public support.

Openness

Securing legitimacy through communicative action, as Chapter 4 discusses, entails ensuring that every interested actor can participate in the relevant policy debate. Just as a government cannot credibly claim great normative legitimacy from a consensus based on incorrect information, so too it cannot really characterize the outcome of a restricted debate as a true consensus. At times the Blair government appeared reasonably willing to permit the widest possible discussion of its Iraq policy. Ministers regularly responded to public criticism by giving media interviews, holding press conferences, publishing dossiers and answering questions from MPs. Blair and Straw between them led no fewer than five set-piece House of Commons debates on Iraq in the pre-invasion period, including the ten-hour marathon on 18 March 2003. The picture looks less rosy, however, when we consider the government's refusal on several occasions to debate possible scenarios for the use of force before it took substantial decisions. Ministers' repeated refrain that 'no decisions have been taken' on the use of force raises two distinct difficulties in terms of their commitment to an open public debate. To begin with, the statement implicitly asserts the government's authority to make critical decisions and only then to permit their public debate. Every time Blair told MPs they did not need a debate on Iraq because he had not yet decided to invade, he effectively announced that they would not get a say until after he made up his mind. Given the impact that widespread media speculation had on the Iraq debate, this approach may have been a mistake. It played into a broader narrative about the government's unwillingness to engage with critics, and seemed to confirm suspicions that ministers were making irreversible commitments privately. A second difficulty then arises from the fact that ministers were actually making private commitments away from the public's gaze. Tony Blair laid the groundwork for co-operation with President Bush to bring about Iraqi regime change in December 2001 and offered Bush a partnership in confronting Saddam Hussein when they met at Crawford in April 2002. By July, Blair was pledging unstinting support to the US approach and instructing the Ministry of Defence to assume Britain would join any military move against Baghdad (Blair 2002). At the end of October, he approved a formal offer of British ground troops to inform the US military planning process (Wechsberg 2002), by the start of January he gave up on the UN inspection process and shortly afterwards he approved initial invasion plans (Hoon 2003). Even the Cabinet found itself excluded from several of these decisions – including the key 16 January troop commitment (Chilcot 2016d, 101). The wider public could only speculate.

Interestingly, the government's reticence partly reflected sincere concerns about the risks of premature public discussion, as Blair noted in his December 2001 note to Bush (Blair 2001). He later told Chilcot he felt he was "fighting a constant battle against people [in the media] utterly misrepresenting us, our motives, what we were trying to do" (Blair 2010, 214). He saw no hope of winning what he was well aware would be a difficult argument without first marshalling his case. Combined with the underlying concerns mentioned above, this attitude translated into heightened paranoia about the risk of information 'leaks', paranoia further fuelled by the propensity of some Cabinet ministers to leak everything they heard about Iraq. Gus O'Donnell, who succeeded Andrew Turnbull as Cabinet Secretary in 2005, told the Chilcot Inquiry that Blair "was reluctant at times to take as many Cabinet discussions as possible [on a range of issues, including Iraq], because he felt that they would become very public, very quickly" (O'Donnell 2011, 24). Jack Straw told Chilcot he expressed his own reservations about the prospect of war with Iraq in private for precisely this reason (Chilcot 2016c, 429). Straw later advised Goldsmith not to share the caveats surrounding his legal advice with the Cabinet owing to "the problem of leaks" (McDonald 2003).

Downing Street took unusual steps to minimize the spread of information through the government, and so to restrict the scope for policy debate. In early September 2002 Alastair Campbell told David Manning of Blair's concern that "parts of our thinking and planning on Iraq are seeping into the media in an uncoordinated and undisciplined way" (Campbell 2002). Only a handful of officials saw notes of Blair's subsequent meeting with Bush. A request by the MoD to offer the US substantial ground forces for military planning purposes towards the end of the month "was kept to a very tight group of people" amid "sensitivities about potential leaks" (Chilcot 2016d, 165–166, 218). Neither Straw nor Defence Secretary Hoon found out that Goldsmith had changed his mind about the need for a 'second' SCR until several days after the fact. Downing Street were worried Goldsmith's stance might "become public" while negotiations continued in New York (Chilcot 2016f, 82). Jonathan Powell ordered the FCO and MoD to destroy copies of earlier versions of Goldsmith's advice "to avoid further leaks" (Powell 2002). All this had concrete consequences. Though Chilcot concluded that the "Cabinet was not misled" over Goldsmith's legal advice, or the commitments Blair made to Bush without consulting colleagues, it clearly was not involved as closely in policy as it probably should have been (Chilcot 2016f, 168). Lord Wilson recalled his surprise that Cabinet members wound up asking questions about Iraq based on press reports, so unwilling was the Prime Minister to involve them actively in the debate (Chilcot 2016d, 26). Policymakers who were interested in legitimizing major decisions through communicative action needed to be much more willing than the inner circle of the Blair government was to permit participation in critical debates.

Flexibility

Flexibility is vital to securing legitimacy through communicative action. As Chapter 4 makes clear, policymakers can win an argument and elicit consensus around it without being willing to rethink their own attitudes, but they cannot credibly claim they seek the sort of mutual agreement among equals that Habermasian accounts describe. Tony Blair proved particularly inflexible in the face of public criticism. To some extent this attitude helped him survive the onslaught of opposition he faced. But its broader reflection throughout Whitehall caused practical, let alone theoretical, difficulties. Jack Straw still thought the UN process could work until well into March 2003. He pushed Blair to come up with a 'plan B' for what to do if Saddam Hussein in fact complied (Straw 2003). Blair decided at around the same time that there was little chance of a peaceful resolution (Blair 2003). It wasn't until 12 March that the two men got on the same page (Chilcot 2016f, 166). Most people resist dissonant information that challenges their established beliefs. But the Blair government proved particularly inflexible. Not only did that undermine its normative claim to legitimacy through public deliberation, it also contributed to practical shortcomings in the decision to go to war.

The first implication emerging from the analysis presented in this study, then, is that the way the Blair government sought to 'sell' the decision to go to war in Iraq made possible the legitimacy deficit that later surrounded it. Its failure to make clear and consistent claims, reliance on incorrect arguments, and visible unwillingness to engage in the widest possible debate provoked opposition and undermined consensus. That cast doubt over the political legitimacy of the decision to go to war. The government's stark failure to meet Habermasian standards of honesty, openness and flexibility then ensured whatever consensus did arise did not carry much normative weight. The lesson, perhaps, is that policymakers should take much greater care than the Blair government did in terms of how they make the case for military action abroad. Commitments ministers make in public become the criteria the public upholds.

A holistic approach

Adopting a holistic approach to understanding the relationship between public opinion and foreign policy works. By combining survey methods with indicators of active public debate it gets around the shortcomings of relying on either individually, while adding detail and nuance to our accounts. Chapter 3 used the holistic approach to track the basic balance between pro-war and anti-war attitudes across polls, parliament and press commentary during the pre-invasion period. Chapters 5 through 8 built upon this analysis to consider the substantive claims different actors made, their interaction with each other and how they collectively shaped the legitimacy deficit surrounding the decision to go to war in Iraq. Not much changed in terms of the balance between pro-war and anti-war attitudes between October 2001 and March 2003. Each of our three sources reported a fair plurality of actors opposed the use of force against Iraq. There were however three moments of progressively heightened intensity during the course of the debate, which were periods when the share of poll respondents, parliamentarians and press commentators who considered Iraq an important issue spiked upwards. Since these spikes broadly reflected rising opposition to the use of force, this created the impression amongst observers that Britain was rapidly turning against military action. The government responded accordingly, scrambling to step up its communication efforts in April 2002, rushing out the dossier in September and trying desperately to change the narrative by playing up the evils of Saddam and the perfidy of France during early 2003.

Salience and detail

The fact the Blair government responded to spikes in public attentiveness as if they reflected shifts in public opposition underlines a point that dates back to V.O. Key (1961, 17). What really concerns foreign policy decision-makers is not the active opposition they can see, but the prospect that hidden latent opposition might be activated. Bernard Cohen similarly highlighted the policymaker's true fear, not that they might themselves fail to understand the public, but that others would do so more effectively (Cohen 1995, 70). Downing Street knew it lacked public support for an invasion of Iraq throughout the pre-invasion period. For the most part faith that the public would ultimately rally round the flag and the Conservative Party's backing for military action insulated ministers from outside criticism. But when moments of particular tension arrived, they felt compelled to react. An approach based on surveys alone would struggle to explain why the government's engagement in public debate went through phases of intense activity, book-ended by relative quiet. This is significant in turn because the FPA literature, discussed in Chapter 2, identifies issue salience as a key factor shaping how powerful public opinion can be. Sometimes policymakers think the loudest voices represent the largest constituencies. Sometimes they rightly perceive that the quickest way to lower the tension in public debate is to quieten the loudest actors down. In any event, by placing issue salience at the heart of our analytical framework, the holistic approach can account for both types of policymaker response.

Crucially, for our purposes, the holistic approach allows us to understand in much greater detail what contributors to the British public debate over Iraq actually said. Reducing what very different actors think about complex foreign policy issues to single data points makes quantification easier, but at the cost of detail and nuance. Looking at public debate in the round allows us to contextualize our quantitative measures by talking about what each stance meant. This in turn allows us to break down pro-war and anti-war positions into their constituent attitudes towards the Iraqi threat, the nature of international law, the morality of military intervention and the locus of political and diplomatic authority. As Part II demonstrates, breaking down the British domestic debate over Iraq along these lines both reflects the actual pattern of Blair government communication efforts and links our discussion to the wider legitimacy discourse. It allows us to reframe the question of how public attitudes shape foreign policy by analysing how certain choices come to appear legitimate or otherwise through the course of public debate. We can redefine the public's role away from that of an actor in a simple, linear decision-making system to that of a context for, participant in and audience of much more iterative discursive practices of legitimation.

Substance and communication

By appreciating the iterative nature of public-policymaker relations, this step in turn allows us to see with much greater clarity the complexity of the pressures at work when leaders propose military interventions. Crucially, it highlights the close relationship between 'substantive' policy decisions, and supposedly more ephemeral 'communicative' actions. FPA traditionally treats communication as part of the 'implementation' phase (Hagan 1995, 133; Webber and Smith 2002, 88; Hill 2003, 277), frames rhetoric as a matter of style (Hermann 1980, 11), or dismisses talk as "cheap" (Baum and Groeling 2010b, 17). At both conceptual and empirical levels, however, this relative lack of interest in public debate looks problematic. The fact policymakers themselves take public communication seriously, a point evident in studying the Blair government, suggests that foreign policy analysts should do so too (Mitzen 2005, 402; Jacobsen 2008, 339).

It is conceptually important to recognize the close relationship between communication and substantive foreign policy decision-making because, as we have seen, communication can have substantive consequences, and substantive actions can be undertaken in pursuit of communicative goals. As Searle pointed out in his theory of "speech acts", under certain circumstances saying something means doing something (Searle 1995, 34). There are some things that foreign policy decision-makers do that are simultaneously communicative and substantive (Onuf 1989, 82). Kratochwil identified declaring war and appointing ambassadors as good general examples (Kratochwil 1993, 76; 2008, 457). In the context of British foreign policy, we might also highlight the role the discourse of 'special relationship' plays in both constituting the country's international role and shaping policymaker behaviour. Tony Blair's repeated declaration of British support for the Bush administration's confrontation with Iraq established effective diplomatic commitments that Blair later felt unable to break. At the same time, his rhetorical efforts to frame the invasion as a legitimate use of force sought to constitute it as a necessary response to a credible threat, carried out with proper political authority, in line with international law and in pursuit of high standards of international morality.

The fact Blair's framing attempts failed highlights the way substantive actions and material facts feed back into the discursive construction of social reality. It also highlights an important point Blair apparently failed adequately to heed. For public communication to work, it needs to be responsive to public attitudes (Ruggie 1998, 2; Risse 2000, 8). Official rhetoric needs to build on concepts and ideas that audiences already recognize (Breuning 1995, 236; Adler 1997, 322;

Hopf 2002, 20; Reus-Smit 2008, 409). This is a major reason why strategic persuasion looks more like communicative action over time (Doty 1993, 303; Cole 1996, 95; Risse 2000, 9). In the Blair government's situation, however, it also raises more practical implications. For public communication to 'work' it needs to influence media commentators and parliamentarians. That in turn means adapting to what journalists and MPs want.

Driven by both professional standards and commercial pressures, journalists typically seek to write stories that are "novel, conflictual, balanced and involve authoritative political actors" (Baum and Groeling 2010b, 20). Policymakers interested in influencing public debate, as the Blair government clearly was, accordingly try to present information favourable to their chosen policy course in such terms. As Habermas himself observed, that can involve "systematically creating news events or exploiting events that attract attention" (Habermas 1989, 193). This makes sense. 'News events' give journalists source material to report on while leaders retain control of the images created and issues raised (Gamson and Modigliani 1989, 6). This may not affect what the media writes, but it should influence what it writes *about*. Governments additionally hold privileged access to information about foreign policy (Hill 1981, 59–60; Jacobs 1992, 199). This allows them to shape news coverage through the inclusion or omission of specific facts (Hilsman 1987, 229). To the extent they understand public attitudes, and indeed possess sound political instincts, governments are expected to meet audience expectations (Hurwitz and Peffley 1987, 1115). Good news managers can do this, combining time and skill to give both journalists and their audiences what they want, in the format they want, and with consequences favourable to their policymaking masters (Entman 2004, 120). That was Alastair Campbell's role in Tony Blair's Downing Street, though both the JIC and the Attorney General showed some understanding of the processes at work.

The significance of this emerges in the way former Foreign Office press secretaries reflect upon their role. Donald Maitland, who held the job in the 1960s, described the "special relationship" he enjoyed with the Foreign Secretary (Maitland 1997, 10). As Christopher Meyer, who served as press secretary in the 1980s, put it, "you're effectively part of his private office" (Meyer 2004, 18). This "access", Meyer wrote, "inevitably takes the press officer into the realm of policy-making itself.... As important as his expertise on *presentation* is his advice on the *presentability* of a proposed course of action" (Meyer 1989, 38, emphasis in original). Media advisors, in other words, get involved well before leaders take substantive decisions. They help narrow down the options available to those that are 'presentable'. Under earlier governments most of the press advisors who became involved in foreign policy matters were drawn from the diplomatic service itself, and so were qualified to speak on both communication and substance (Leahy 2001, 14). By the time the Blair government came to power, however, its desire to professionalize public communications reduced the substantive experience expected of media advisors. Since ministers still needed advice on 'presentability', the result was that Alastair Campbell gained direct influence over supposedly substantive policy decisions (Daddow 2011, 226). At one point, Blair tried to shut Meyer, by then Ambassador to the US, out of a crucial White House meeting in order to include Campbell. Though the latter thought the resulting row "a bit silly" (Campbell and Stott 2007, 573), Meyer saw things rather differently. He later recalled that his response was "furious and expletive-laden". He threatened to resign on the spot (Meyer 2005, 202). As Campbell himself put it to the Chilcot Inquiry, "not just on issues to do with foreign affairs and security, but on any of the major issues and high profile issues, you have to have a communications element, if you like, embedded in those policy discussions" (Campbell 2010, 7–8). At times, as the Meyer incident suggested, that might mean excluding substantive advice.

Clearly the scope for substantive decisions to be tinged by communicative imperatives increases once communication advisers are brought in to policy-making discussions. It is a basic notion within FPA that the individuals involved in a process affect its nature and outcomes by shaping the information that reaches policymakers and the manner in which it is presented (Hermann and Hermann 1989, 362). If media advisers form part of a policymaker's inner circle, information and advice about the media will form part of the core set of materials policymakers have available as they make decisions. The introduction of communicability into substantive discussions establishes a "feedback loop" (Carlsnaes 1992, 261) between policymaking and public debate. Advice on public communication becomes inseparable from advice on policy substance, and so the agenda of public debate comes indirectly to shape policymaking (Cohen 1973, 178; Jacobs 1992, 212; Webber and Smith 2002, 101). The effect of these forces on the Blair government's approach to Iraq emerges most clearly in Chapters 5 and 6. Crucially, Chilcot concluded that Downing Street was still under-prepared for the post-invasion communication task it faced, despite the efforts undertaken in the build-up to war (Chilcot 2016b, 123).

By highlighting the importance of public communication and enabling us to trace its relationship to substantive policymaking over time, the holistic approach adds a dimension missing from traditional survey-based FPA work. It helps us get around the shortcomings of survey methods, and underlines the importance of issue salience. Above all, it better reflects our ultimate goal: to understand what policymakers actually do.

A two-level debate

The analysis presented in this book suggests, finally, that there is room to combine the insights of discursively-minded FPA scholars with more 'traditional' rationalist accounts. In particular, there appears to be a close link between the sort of public debate the Blair government engaged in and Robert Putnam's two-level game model of decision-making (Putnam 1988). Putnam talked about the challenge leaders face trying to negotiate with international bargaining partners without alienating support at home. He highlighted the difficulty of making credible commitments at one level without either establishing problematic expectations or prompting criticism at the other. That was exactly the Blair government's dilemma. Rather than the formal negotiating positions Putnam envisaged, British policymakers faced a more discursive problem. They had to engage in hostile domestic debate to constitute their chosen policy course as legitimate. At the same time, they had to assert rhetorically Britain's traditional international role of 'first ally' to the United States. Too often the requirements of these goals conflicted.

Putnam's great insight was that foreign policy decision-makers are simultaneously domestic politicians, and that any move they make internationally requires ratification at home. Our analysis points towards a slight reformulation of this model, while retaining its core logic. Rather than talking about 'ratification', which implies formal approval mechanisms, we might instead talk about legitimization. Significant international moves require domestic legitimization. Domestic legitimization takes place through public debate. At a political level it depends on policymakers making moves that public commentators will accept. At a normative level, it means engaging properly in deliberation, demonstrating honesty, openness and flexibility. Furthermore, just as rhetorical action can have substantive consequences (in part through its role in legitimization processes), substantive action can also affect public debate. Deploying troops sends a message, at both domestic and international levels, just as issuing an ultimatum or declaring war changes prevailing political and diplomatic circumstances.

At several points, the Chilcot Report identifies the difficulty the Blair government faced when balancing its need to send the right rhetorical signals to Washington, to Baghdad and to audiences at home. Nowhere was this more clear than with regard to the legality of military action. The Bush administration saw the Security Council as, at best, an inconvenience to be endured, and, at worst, an active threat to US national security. Meyer reported that Bush was "intensely suspicious of the UN" (Meyer 2002). Blair told Manning he feared "the Cheney temptation" to give the UN a "take it or leave it" ultimatum rather than trying to build consensus (Chilcot 2016d, 177). He remained unwilling, however, to use the domestic pressure he faced and the legal limits on the sort of action he could take as leverage to try to persuade President Bush to adopt a less confrontational approach. He believed doing so would alienate rather than influence Bush and that the US would turn away from the UN route if it did not offer good prospects of delivering regime change (Chilcot 2016e, 171; 2016d, 307). He also feared encouraging Chirac and Putin to push back against the US position, and suggesting to Saddam Hussein that international legal constraints might protect him from punishment should he simply stand his ground. Yet the domestic problems Blair faced were very real. He committed clearly and at an early stage in the Iraq debate to acting only in line with international law, and identified the Security Council as a key arbiter of what was and was not legal. His audiences understood these commitments, and sought to hold him to them. That raised difficulties as Blair tried to balance the domestic-level need to be seen obeying the law with the international-level need to avoid appearing beholden to it. It was a clash he proved unable to resolve.

Similar issues arose around the contentious issue of authority, and specifically whether the US, the UN or the UK would decide when and whether British troops went to war. Chilcot concluded there was a "clear divergence" between US and UK approaches in early 2003, with the US gearing up for an invasion while the UK tried to sustain coercive diplomacy (Chilcot 2016g, 589). There are signs this divergence took place even earlier, around the definition of Iraq as a threat and the role of the UN. In terms of the end result, the precise timing does not matter. What really mattered was the fact that the key decisions emerged from Washington. London's role was simply to endorse what the White House decided. Bush and Blair built a partnership of sorts, but it was never a partnership of equals. Straw was probably right to warn Blair that, in the end, his failure to use his domestic difficulties to influence Bush meant his support was taken for granted (Straw 2002). This failure also directly fuelled domestic demands for a parliamentary say in the final decision to use force, and so indirectly contributed to parliament's development of conventional war powers.

Conclusions

The Chilcot Report effectively concluded that Britain's involvement in the invasion of Iraq was not a "just war" (Walzer 1977). It was not a last resort (Chilcot 2016a). It was not proportionate to the threat that Iraq posed to British national interests, though it made more sense when set against the Blair government's exaggerated understanding of the danger WMD represented (Chilcot 2016d, 267). It was not supported by proper authority, with Britain and the US collectively "undermining the authority of the Security Council" by resorting to force when they did (Chilcot 2016e, 570). It was not likely to succeed, with ministers failing to accept or to understand evidence presented to them in the pre-invasion period showing that Iraq would fall apart in the event of war (Chilcot 2016b, 83).

Though these points are important, this book does not adopt a just war theory framework. Instead it analyses the British public debate over Iraq through categories the participants actually used. It considers the alleged Iraqi threat, the legal grounds for action, the morality of intervention and the multi-level politics of war. In the process, it looks to understand how public debate constituted the invasion of Iraq as a foreign policy action of questionable legitimacy. In particular, it tries to show how it was possible for Britain to wind up fighting an illegitimate war. The answer is simple, at one level. The Blair government faced no substantial political or constitutional impediments to using force without domestic approval. Its large parliamentary majority and Conservative Party support protected it from electoral punishment, while the Prime Minister retained the formal power to direct the armed forces through the ancient 'royal prerogative'. Tony Blair believed public backing was desirable but not necessary, and, in any event, that most people would rally 'round the flag if it actually came to war. He was right on that front. Chapter 3 shows a significant rally effect amongst poll respondents, press commentators and MPs in the final week before the invasion began. Whatever the quality of the arguments for action, the forces that allowed the Blair government to make the decision to join the coalition of the willing would likely have been the same. No wonder the Stop the War movement failed to stop the war.

The arguments ministers made, however, generated the legitimacy deficit that surrounded the invasion over the longer term. They lost support by making claims that were later proven incorrect. That made sustaining the sort of social consensus that underpins the political form of legitimacy impossible. They failed, at the same time, to present their arguments in a fair and balanced fashion. They were not always honest, especially about weaknesses in the evidence they held. They were often incorrect. They worked hard to limit the scope for public (and even private) debate over the decision to go to war. Blair excluded ministers he thought might disagree with him. He restricted information, prioritizing avoiding leaks over keeping colleagues informed. He delayed consulting the Attorney General and involved MPs only under extreme political pressure. Amongst policymakers, only Lord Goldsmith showed any real willingness to reconsider his position in the face of counter-arguments. Even the JIC resisted the impulse to revisit its assumptions, having received fresh information. Blair's moral fervour, his faith in his own abilities and his certainty that backing the US was right all reduced his flexibility. In communicative terms, the Blair government pursued a far more Foucauldian approach to public debate over Iraq by trying to persuade opponents rather than prioritizing achieving consensus as the Habermasian mindset requires. This made it difficult to claim that any domestic approval the government did achieve granted the invasion legitimacy in normative terms. It also, ultimately, undermined the search for consensus.

By adopting a holistic approach to understanding public opinion, linking it with the discursive construction of legitimacy and recognizing the difficult two-level game all foreign policy decision-makers play, this book has sought to contribute to the wider FPA literature on the relationship between domestic and international politics. It has offered along the way a detailed analysis of how the British public debate over the invasion of Iraq actually played out. Given Iraq's continued influence over how Britain approaches the use of force as a tool of foreign policy, and indeed over British politics more generally, it still seems important to understand how the country wound up fighting an illegitimate war. Understanding that question helps us understand the half-hearted Libyan operation, the 2013 Syria vote and the limitations of Britain's continued efforts against Da'esh. Downing Street still conducts foreign policy under the shadow of Tony Blair, thanks to Blair's approach to Iraq.

References

Adler, Emanuel. 'Seizing the middle ground: constructivism in world politics.' *European Journal of International Relations* 3, no. 3 (1997): 319–363.

Baum, Matthew, and Tim Groeling. 'Reality asserts itself: public opinion on Iraq and the elasticity of reality.' *International Organization* 64 (2010a): 443–479.

Baum, Matthew, and Tim Groeling. *War Stories: The Causes and Consequences of Public Views of War.* Oxford: Oxford University Press, 2010b.

Blair, Tony. 'Letter to President Bush.' 11 October 2001. www.iraqinquiry.org.uk/media/243721/2001-10-11-letter-blair-to-bush-untitled.pdf (accessed 15 July 2016).

Blair, Tony. 'Letter to President Bush.' 28 July 2002. www.iraqinquiry.org.uk/media/243761/2002-07-28-note-blair-to-bush-note-on-iraq.pdf (accessed 15 July 2016).

Blair, Tony. 'Memo to Downing Street staff.' 4 January 2003. www.iraqinquiry.org.uk/media/233490/2003-01-04-note-tb-blair-iraq-extract.pdf (accessed 18 July 2016).

Blair, Tony. 'Evidence to the Chilcot Inquiry.' 29 January 2010. www.iraqinquiry.org.uk/media/229766/2010-01-29-transcript-blair-s1.pdf (accessed 6 August 2016).

Blair, Tony. 'Evidence to the Leveson Inquiry.' 28 May 2012. http://webarchive.nationalarchives.gov.uk/20140122145147/www.levesoninquiry.org.uk/wp-content/uploads/2012/05/Witness-Statement-of-Tony-Blair1.pdf (accessed 12 August 2016).

Breuning, Marijke. 'Words and deeds: foreign assistance rhetoric and policy behavior in the Netherlands, Belgium and the United Kingdom.' *International Studies Quarterly* 39, no. 2 (1995): 235–254.

Campbell, Alastair. 'Memo to David Manning.' 2 September 2002. www.iraqinquiry.org.uk/media/224468/2002-09-02-minute-campbell-to-manning-untitled.pdf (accessed 15 July 2016).

Campbell, Alastair. 'Evidence to the Chilcot Inquiry, morning session.' 12 January 2010. www.iraqinquiry.org.uk/media/95142/2010-01-12-Transcript-Campbell-S1-am.pdf (accessed 6 August 2016).

Campbell, Alastair, and Richard Stott. *The Blair Years: Extracts from the Alastair Campbell Diaries.* London: Arrow Books, 2007.

Carlsnaes, Walter. 'The agency-structure problem in foreign policy analysis.' *International Studies Quarterly* 36, no. 3 (1992): 245–270.

Chandler, David. 'Rhetoric without responsibility: the attraction of "ethical" foreign policy.' *British Journal of Politics and International Relations* 5, no. 3 (2003): 295–316.

Chilcot, John. 'Statement by Sir John Chilcot.' 6 July 2016a. www.iraqinquiry.org.uk/media/247010/2016-09-06-sir-john-chilcots-public-statement.pdf (accessed 15 July 2016).

Chilcot, John. *Report of the Iraq Inquiry: Executive Summary.* London: HMSO, 2016b.

Chilcot, John. *Report of the Iraq Inquiry: Volume 1.* London: HMSO, 2016c.

Chilcot, John. *Report of the Iraq Inquiry: Volume 2.* London: HMSO, 2016d.

Chilcot, John. *Report of the Iraq Inquiry: Volume 3.* London: HMSO, 2016e.

Chilcot, John. *Report of the Iraq Inquiry: Volume 5.* London: HMSO, 2016f.

Chilcot, John. *Report of the Iraq Inquiry: Volume 6.* London: HMSO, 2016g.

Cohen, Bernard. *The Public's Impact on Foreign Policy.* Boston: Little, Brown and Co., 1973.

Cohen, Bernard. *Democracies and Foreign Policy: Public Participation in the United States and the Netherlands.* Madison, WI: University of Wisconsin Press, 1995.

Cole, Timothy. 'When intentions go awry: the Bush administration's foreign policy rhetoric.' *Political Communication* 13, no. 1 (1996): 93–113.

Daddow, Oliver. 'Conclusion.' In *British Foreign Policy: The New Labour Years*, by Oliver Daddow and Jamie Gaskarth, 221–235. Basingstoke: Palgrave Macmillan, 2011.

Doty, Roxanne. 'Foreign policy as social construction: a post-positivist analysis of US counterinsurgency policy in the Philippines.' *International Studies Quarterly* 37, no. 3 (1993): 297–320.

Entman, Robert. *Projections of Power: Framing News, Public Opinion, and US Foreign Policy.* Chicago: University of Chicago Press, 2004.

Gaber, Ivor. 'Too much of a good thing: the "problem" of political communications in a mass media democracy.' *Journal of Public Affairs* 7, no. 3 (2007): 219–234.

Gamson, William, and Andre Modigliani. 'Media discourse and public opinion on nuclear power: a constructionist approach.' *The American Journal of Sociology* 95, no. 1 (1989): 1–37.

Habermas, Jurgen. *The Structural Transformation of the Public Sphere.* Translated by Thomas Burger. Oxford: Polity Press, 1989.

Hagan, Joe. 'Domestic political explanations in the analysis of foreign policy.' In *Foreign Policy Analysis: Continuity and Change in its Second Generation*, by Laura Neack, Jeanne Hay and Patrick Haney, 117–144. Englewood Cliffs, NJ: Prentice Hall, 1995.

Hallin, Daniel. *The 'Uncensored War': The Media and Vietnam.* Oxford: Oxford University Press, 1986.

Heffernan, Richard. 'The Prime Minister and the news media: political communication as a leadership resource.' *Parliamentary Affairs* 59, no. 4 (2006): 582–598.

Hermann, Margaret. 'Explaining foreign policy behavior using the personal characteristics of political leaders.' *International Studies Quarterly* 24, no. 1 (1980): 7–46.

Hermann, Margaret, and Charles Hermann. 'Who makes foreign policy decisions and how: an empirical inquiry.' *International Studies Quarterly* 33, no. 4 (1989): 361–387.

Hill, Christopher. 'Public opinion and British foreign policy since 1945: research in Progress?' *Millennium: Journal of International Studies* 10, no. 1 (1981): 53–62.

Hill, Christopher. *The Changing Politics of Foreign Policy.* Basingstoke: Palgrave Macmillan, 2003.

Hilsman, Roger. *The Politics of Policymaking in Defense and Foreign Affairs: Conceptual Models and Bureaucratic Politics.* Englewood Cliffs, NJ: Prentice-Hall, 1987.

Hoon, Geoff. 'Iraq: UK land contribution: letter to Tony Blair.' 16 January 2003. www.iraqinquiry.org.uk/media/213663/2003-01-16-letter-hoon-to-prime-minister-iraq-uk-land-contribution-mo-6-17-15k-inc-manuscript-comments.pdf (accessed 12 August 2016).

Hopf, Ted. *Social Construction of International Politics: Identities and Foreign Policies, Moscow, 1955 and 1999.* Ithaca, NY: Cornell University Press, 2002.

Hurwitz, Jon, and Mark Peffley. 'How are foreign policy attitudes structured? A hierarchical model.' *American Political Science Review* 81, no. 4 (1987): 1099–1120.

Jacobs, Lawrence. 'The recoil effect: public opinion and policymaking in the US and Britain.' *Comparative Politics* 24, no. 2 (1992): 199–217.

Jacobsen, John. 'Why do states bother to decieve? Managing trust at home and abroad.' *Review of International Studies* 34, no. 2 (2008): 337–361.

Kaufmann, Chaim. 'Threat inflation and the failure of the marketplace of ideas: the selling of the Iraq War.' *International Security* 29, no. 1 (2004): 5–48.

Key, Vladimer. *Public Opinion and American Democracy.* New York: Alfred A. Knopf, 1961.

Knecht, Thomas, and Stephen Weatherford. 'Public opinion and foreign policy: the stages of presidential decision making.' *International Studies Quarterly* 50 (2006): 705–727.

Kratochwil, Friedrich. 'Sociological approaches.' In *The Oxford Handbook of International Relations*, by Christian Reus-Smit and Duncan Snidal. Oxford: Oxford University Press, 2008.

Kratochwil, Friedrich. 'The embarrassment of changes: neo-realism as the science of realpolitik without politics.' *Review of International Studies* 19, no. 1 (1993): 63–80.

Leahy, John. Interview by Charles Cullimore. *British Diplomatic Oral History Project* (21 August 2001). www.chu.cam.ac.uk/archives/collections/bdohp/ (accessed 8 January 2015).
Louw, Eric. *The Media and Political Process.* London: Sage, 2005.
Maitland, Donald. Interview by Malcolm McBain. *British Diplomatic Oral History Project.* (11 December 1997) www.chu.cam.ac.uk/archives/collections/bdohp/ (accessed 8 January 2015).
McDonald, Simon. 'File note: Foreign Secretary's meeting with the Attorney General, 13 March.' 17 March 2003. www.iraqinquiry.org.uk/media/76327/2003-03-17-Note-McDonald-Iraq-Meeting-With-The-Attorney-General.pdf (accessed 12 August 2016).
McNair, Brian. *Journalism and Democracy: An Evaluation of the Political Public Sphere.* London: Routledge, 2000.
Meyer, Christopher. 'Hacks and pin-striped appeasers: selling British foreign policy to the press.' *Fellowship Paper, Weatherhead Center for International Affairs, Harvard.* 1989.
Meyer, Christopher. 'Telegram to David Manning.' 11 October 2002. www.iraqinquiry.org.uk/media/210455/2002-10-11-telegram-1326-washington-to-fco-london-us-iraq-will-the-president-go-to-war.pdf (accessed 15 July 2016).
Meyer, Christopher. Interview by Malcolm McBain. *British Diplomatic Oral History Project,* (17 June 2004). www.chu.cam.ac.uk/archives/collections/bdohp/ (accessed 8 January 2015).
Meyer, Christopher. *DC Confidential.* London: Widenfield & Nicolson, 2005.
Mitzen, Jennifer. 'Reading Habermas in anarchy: multilateral diplomacy and global public spaces.' *American Political Science Review* 99, no. 3 (2005): 401–417.
Moloney, Kevin. 'The rise and fall of spin: changes of fashion in the presentation of UK politics.' *Journal of Public Affairs* 1, no. 2 (2000): 124–135.
Mueller, John. *War, Presidents and Public Opinion.* New York: Wiley, 1973.
Nincic, Miroslav. *Democracy and Foreign Policy: The Fallacy of Political Realism.* New York: Columbia University Press, 1992.
O'Donnell, Gus. 'Evidence to the Chilcot Inquiry.' 28 January 2011. www.iraqinquiry.org.uk/media/95458/2011-01-28-Transcript-ODonnell-S1.pdf (accessed 12 August 2016).
Onuf, Nicholas. *World of Our Making: Rules and Rule in Social Theory and International Relations.* Columbia, SC: University of South Carolina Press, 1989.
Page, Benjamin, and Robert Shapiro. *The Rational Public: Fifty Years of Trends in Americans' Policy Preferences.* Chicago: University of Chicago Press, 1992.
Powell, Jonathan. 'File note.' 31 July 2002. www.iraqinquiry.org.uk/media/210871/2002-07-31-note-for-no10-file-powell.pdf (accessed 15 July 2016).
Putnam, Robert. 'Diplomacy and domestic politics: the logic of two-level games.' *International Organization* 42, no. 3 (1988): 427–460.
Reus-Smit, Christian. 'Reading history through constructivist eyes.' *Millennium: Journal of International Studies* 37, no. 2 (2008): 395–414.
Risse, Thomas. 'Let's argue!: Communicative action in world politics.' *International Organization* 54, no. 1 (2000): 1–39.
Ruggie, John. *Constructing the World Polity: Essays on International Institutionalization.* London: Routledge, 1998.
Searle, John. *The Construction of Social Reality.* New York, NY: The Free Press, 1995.
Straw, Jack. 'Memo to Tony Blair.' 16 October 2002. www.iraqinquiry.org.uk/media/210187/2002-10-16-letter-straw-to-prime-minister-iraq-us.pdf (accessed 18 July 2016).

Straw, Jack. 'Memo to Tony Blair.' 3 January 2003. www.iraqinquiry.org.uk/media/242601/2003-01-03-minute-straw-to-prime-minister-iraq-plan-b.pdf (accessed 18 July 2016).

Taylor, Philip. *War and the Media: Propaganda and Persuasion in the Gulf War.* Manchester: Manchester University Press, 1992.

Walzer, Michael. *Just and Unjust Wars: A Moral Argument with Historical Illustrations.* New York, NY: Basic Books, 1977.

Webber, Mark, and Michael Smith. *Foreign Policy in a Transformed World.* Harlow: Prentice Hall, 2002.

Wechsberg, Anna. 'Letter to Peter Watkins.' 31 October 2002. www.iraqinquiry.org.uk/media/203284/2002-10-31-Letter-Wechsberg-to-Watkins-Iraq-Military-Options.pdf#search=wechsberg (accessed 12 August 2016).

Index

Page numbers in *italics* denote tables, those in **bold** denote figures.

45 minute claim *see* Weapons of Mass Destruction: '45 minute' claim
7/7 *see* London bombings 7 July 2005
9/11 *see* September 11 terrorist attacks

Afghanistan, 2001 invasion of 123, 125, 130, 132, 144, 146
Al Qaeda 72, 73, 82, 98, 189
Allen, Graham 49, 157
Attorney General *see* Goldsmith, Lord Peter
Axis of Evil *see* Bush, President George W.: first State of the Union
Aznar, Jose Maria: 2004 election 185

BBC 49; and David Kelly 8, 181; *Newsnight* 47
Blair, Tony: decision-making style 158, 198–200, 207; Doctrine of International Community 59, 88, 123; and international law 96, 100; and Iraqi WMD 73, 74, 83, 87; July 23, 2002 Downing Street meeting 132; letters to President Bush 34, 78, 103, 129, 147, 150, 153, 198–9; Liaison Committee appearance 48; and London bombings 190; and the media 180, 199; Messiah complex 121–3; press conference 48, 79; President Bush's 'poodle' 124, 146, 196; and public opinion 34, 122, 148; and regime change 119–20, 127, 131–3, 146; response to Chilcot Report 34, 176, 179; and 'second' UN Security Council Resolution 101–2; speech to the House of Commons 18 March 2003 162; speech to the Labour Party Conference, October 2001 123–4; speech to the Labour Party Conference, October 2002 99; speech to the Labour Party Spring Conference, February 2003 49, 122, 125–6, 133; speech to the TUC September 2002 37, 78; and 'special relationship' 143, 148, 150, 202, 205; and UNMOVIC 106, 109
Blix, Hans 75, 106, 108–10
Blumer, Herbert 20–3
Bourdieu, Pierre 20–3
Brenton, Tony 149, 162
Bush doctrine *see* Bush, President George W.: doctrine of pre-emption
Bush, President George W.: doctrine of pre-emption 77–9, 99; election 2004 185; first State of the Union 46–7; second State of the Union 104; speech to the UN General Assembly, September 2002 99; and Tony Blair 122, 140, 78
Butler Report 4, 72, 76, 81, 85, 184

Cameron, David 3
Campbell, Alastair 121, 124, 141, 143, 153, 160, 197, 199, 203–4; and David Kelly 182–3; and international law 187; and Iraqi WMD 76, 80; and 'second' UN Security Council resolution 104; and WMD 84, 86–7, 181
Campbell, Menzies 82
Cheney, Vice President Dick 46–7, 83
Chilcot Report 4, 8, 26–7, 51, 134, 142, 175–6; and British influence over US 145; criticism of individuals by 75, 86, 128, 130, 176, 206; criticism of systemic failings by 180, 204, 206; exoneration of

individuals by 84, 111, 199; and international law 94–5, 102–3, 191; and WMD 72, 73, 77, 81, 83, 85–7, 177, 183–4
Chirac, Jacques 50, 151–2
Clarke, Kenneth 148
communicative action 83, 85, 87, 111–12, 120–2, 124, 126, 130, 133–4, 141, 146–7, 149, 151, 155, 175, 191, 196, 198–9, 203; *see also* deliberative legitimacy; Habermas, Jürgen
confidence motion 163
constructivism: and legitimacy 60–1; and public opinion 25–6
Cook, Robin 39, 48, 122, 157, 179–80, 196; and international law 99–100, 109; and Iraqi WMD 79, 83, 85, 87; resignation 88, 158–60
Corbyn, Jeremy 3
Crawford, Texas 46–8, 130–2, 146, 148; and Blair's conditions for British support 148

Da'esh 2, 3, 24, 207
Dalyell, Tam 39, 46, 48, 157, 161
de Villepin, Dominique 105, 151–3
Dearlove, Richard 74–5, 109
Defence Intelligence Staff 183–4, 197
deliberative legitimacy 93, 127, 134, 140, 145, 155, 163, 205; *see also* communicative action; Habermas, Jürgen
doctrine of international community *see* Blair, Tony: Doctrine of International Community
dodgy dossier *see* Weapons of Mass Destruction: February 2003 'dodgy' dossier
domestic audience costs 141, 149
dossier *see* Weapons of Mass Destruction: September 2002 dossier
Downing Street memo *see* Blair, Tony: July 23, 2002 Downing Street meeting
Duncan Smith, Iain 81, 132–3, 144, 158, 186
Dyson, Stephen 122

elasticity of reality 175

Foucault, Michel 61–3, 197, 207
France: and failure of UN process 7, 50, 141, 151–7, 201

Galloway, George 39, 81, 145

general election 2005 112, 175–6, 185–90, 191
Gilligan, Andrew 8, 176, 181–5, 197
Goldsmith, Lord Peter 3, 119, 203, 207; evolution of legal opinion 102–4; exclusion from decision-making 102, 108, 111; 'full' version of legal advice 8, 176, 186–7; and international law 97–9, 111; and Iraqi WMD 74; and regime change 128; and second UN Security Council Resolution 95, 102; and 'unreasonable' veto 103
Gould, Philip 34, 50
Greenstock, Jeremy 94, 95, 101, 104–5, 108–9, 148–9, 154
groupthink 72
Guardian 38

Habermas, Jürgen 61–6, 141, 196, 198, 200, 203, 207
Hansard 27
Holmes, John 153–4
Hoon, Geoff: and international law 99; and Iraqi WMD 77–9
Howard, Michael 186
Hussein, Saddam: brutality of 133, 196; MPs' choice between Blair and 8
Hutton Report 4, 84–5, 176, 182, 184

inevitability of war 162
International Atomic Energy Agency 83, 88
International Institute of Strategic Studies: dossier on Iraqi WMD 80
international law 97–9, 132; Bush administration view 98–9, 147, 205; and morality 119, 127–9, 130, 133, 196; 'revival argument' 98
Iraq Survey Group 180–1
ISIL/ISIS *see* Da'esh

Joint Intelligence Committee 6, 72, 74–5, 83–8, 106–7, 110, 133, 177, 183, 189, 197, 203, 207
Just War Theory 6, 88, 134, 206

Kelly, David 4, 8, 175–6, 180–5, 191, 197
Kosovo 123, 130, 132

Labour Party: internal analysis of 2005 election 187; rebellion by MPs 157, 161
Lander, Stephen 73
leaks: from UK Cabinet 98, 111, 199

214   *Index*

legitimacy: as a communicative construct 59, 61–3; definition of 59–63; relationship to public opinion 15, 59
Leveson, Lord Brian: Report 2012 197
London bombings 7 July 2005 190

Madrid bombings 2004 189–90
Manning, David 73, 99–100, 104, 108, 123, 128–9, 141–2, 147–9
Manningham-Buller, Eliza 73
media: editorial position on invasion of Iraq of 39–41, *44*, **45**; hostility to Blair government 81, 147, 158, 179, 184; hostility to France 151–3; professional values of 203
messiah complex *see* Blair, Tony: messiah complex
methodology 26–8, 64–8
Meyer, Christopher 99–100, 108, 109, 130–1, 148–9, 203–5
MI6 *see* Secret Intelligence Service
Mirror 40
moral turn *see* Blair, Tony: and regime change
Morgan, Baroness Sally 187
Munich analogy 125
Murdoch, Rupert 5, 33, 39, 42, 156

news management 180, 197, 202–4

O'Donnell, Gus 199
Omand, David 77, 83–4, 108
Operation Desert Fox 98, 123
opinion poll *see* public opinion

parliament: March 18, 2003 vote 163, 175, 198; MPs' positions on invasion of Iraq 41–2, *44*, **45**; source of domestic legitimacy 160; war powers 2, 141, 156, 206
Pentagon *see* US Department of Defense
poll *see* public opinion
poodle problem *see* Blair, Tony: President Bush's 'poodle'
Powell, Colin 47, 110, 129
Powell, Jonathan: and David Kelly 181, 183–4; fear of leaks 98, 199; and international law 103; and Iraqi WMD 77, 85; and public opinion 34; and regime change 129; on Tony Blair 121
public opinion: and Da'esh 24; and David Kelly 182, 184; definition of 4–5, 15–20, 201; differences between US and UK 37, 177; and electoral politics 1, 186, 189;
and France 50, 156; and invasion of Afghanistan 34–6, 39; and invasion of Iraq **35–6**, 38, **43**, *44*, **45**, 47, 49, 177, **178**, 185, 188–9; and Iraqi WMD 74, 87; Labour Party internal polling data on 2, 8; and London bombings 190; methodology of studying 20–3, 27, 187, 195, 200, 204; and military casualties 178; rally 'round the flag effect 33, 35–6, 42, 50, 201, 206; in Spain 185; and Tony Blair 180; and United Nations 96, 111

rally 'round the flag *see* public opinion: rally 'round the flag effect
regime change 119–20, 128, 129–33; clash between US and UK attitudes toward 128; legality of 128; precedents for 130, 132
revival argument *see* international law: revival argument
Ricketts, Peter 154
Rumsfeld, Donald 140–1
Rycroft memo *see* Blair, Tony: July 23, 2002 Downing Street meeting
Rycroft, Matthew 153

Sawers, John 129
Scarlett, John 73, 75, 87
second resolution; *see* UN Security Council: 'second' resolution
Secret Intelligence Service 6, 72; errors of judgement by 75, 88, 183, 197; and lack of sources in Iraq 77
September 11 terrorist attacks 6, 37, 77, 82, 143–4
Short, Clare 158–9
Sierra Leone: as precedent for regime change 130, 132
SIS *see* Secret Intelligence Service
smoking gun *see* Taylor, AJP: theory of mobilization
special relationship 140–1, 142–50, 164, 202, 205–6
spin *see* news management
standard operating procedures 75
Stop the War Coalition 79, 207; 15 February 2003 protest and 49, 120, 125–6, 134, 158
Straw, Jack 47, 73, 77, 199; and domestic politics 126, 149; and France 152–5; and international law 95, 111, 128; and Iraqi WMD 74, 78, 80, 86; and regime change 130, 148; and UN Security Council 96, 101–3, 109, 200

Sun 39–40; *see also* Murdoch, Rupert
Syria 87, 176, 207

Taylor, A.J.P.: Theory of mobilization 107–10
Toynbee, Polly 41, 125–6, 149, 159
two-level game 7, 9, 103, 105, 140–1, 149, 195, 204–7

UN Security Council 3, 6; legal authority of 94–5, 96–7; resolution 1441 6, 100–5, 108; 'second' resolution 100, 105, 151; UNMOVIC 6–7, 74, 95, 105–10, 133, 152; 'unreasonable' veto 103, 151, 156; UNSCOM 71, 76, 98, 107
UNMOVIC *see* UN Security Council: UNMOVIC
unreasonable veto *see* UN Security Council: 'unreasonable' veto
UNSCOM *see* UN Security Council: UNSCOM

US Department of Defense: information leaks from 79; timetable for military action 140, 142

Vietnam War 197

war on terrorism 73
Weapons of Mass Destruction 6, 8, 119, 177, 179, 191; '45 minute' claim 76, 181, 183; February 2003 'dodgy' dossier 86, 110; Iraqi history of using 76, 82; September 2002 dossier 33, 38, 49, 71–88, 106, 157, 181–2, 184, 201
Webb, Simon 131–2
Whelan's law 181, 183
whitewash *see* Hutton Report
Wilmshurst, Elizabeth 111
WMD *see* Weapons of Mass Destruction
Wood, Sir Michael 102–3

Taylor & Francis eBooks

Helping you to choose the right eBooks for your Library

Add Routledge titles to your library's digital collection today. Taylor and Francis ebooks contains over 50,000 titles in the Humanities, Social Sciences, Behavioural Sciences, Built Environment and Law.

Choose from a range of subject packages or create your own!

Benefits for you
- Free MARC records
- COUNTER-compliant usage statistics
- Flexible purchase and pricing options
- All titles DRM-free.

Benefits for your user
- Off-site, anytime access via Athens or referring URL
- Print or copy pages or chapters
- Full content search
- Bookmark, highlight and annotate text
- Access to thousands of pages of quality research at the click of a button.

REQUEST YOUR FREE INSTITUTIONAL TRIAL TODAY — Free Trials Available
We offer free trials to qualifying academic, corporate and government customers.

eCollections – Choose from over 30 subject eCollections, including:

Archaeology	Language Learning
Architecture	Law
Asian Studies	Literature
Business & Management	Media & Communication
Classical Studies	Middle East Studies
Construction	Music
Creative & Media Arts	Philosophy
Criminology & Criminal Justice	Planning
Economics	Politics
Education	Psychology & Mental Health
Energy	Religion
Engineering	Security
English Language & Linguistics	Social Work
Environment & Sustainability	Sociology
Geography	Sport
Health Studies	Theatre & Performance
History	Tourism, Hospitality & Events

For more information, pricing enquiries or to order a free trial, please contact your local sales team:
www.tandfebooks.com/page/sales

 Routledge — Taylor & Francis Group | The home of Routledge books

www.tandfebooks.com